Religion in the Classroom

**Recent Titles in
Religion in Politics and Society Today**

Islam in America: Exploring the Issues
Craig Considine

Religion and Environmentalism: Exploring the Issues
Lora Stone

Antisemitism: Exploring the Issues
Steven Leonard Jacobs

Atheism and Agnosticism: Exploring the Issues
Peter A. Huff

Same-Sex Marriage: Exploring the Issues
Scott A. Merriman

Religion and War: Exploring the Issues
Timothy J. Demy and Gina Granados Palmer

Religion in the Classroom

Exploring the Issues

Jonathan M. Golden and Joseph J. McCallister

RELIGION IN POLITICS AND SOCIETY TODAY

BLOOMSBURY ACADEMIC
NEW YORK • LONDON • OXFORD • NEW DELHI • SYDNEY

BLOOMSBURY ACADEMIC

Bloomsbury Publishing Inc

1385 Broadway, New York, NY 10018, USA

50 Bedford Square, London, WC1B 3DP, UK

29 Earlsfort Terrace, Dublin 2, Ireland

BLOOMSBURY, BLOOMSBURY ACADEMIC and the Diana logo are trademarks of Bloomsbury Publishing Plc

First published in the United States of America 2023

Copyright © Bloomsbury Publishing Inc, 2023

Cover images © Ruslan Olinchuk/Dreamstime; artisteer/iStock

All rights reserved. No part of this publication may be reproduced or transmitted in any form or by any means, electronic or mechanical, including photocopying, recording, or any information storage or retrieval system, without prior permission in writing from the publishers.

Bloomsbury Publishing Inc does not have any control over, or responsibility for, any third-party websites referred to or in this book. All internet addresses given in this book were correct at the time of going to press. The author and publisher regret any inconvenience caused if addresses have changed or sites have ceased to exist, but can accept no responsibility for any such changes.

Library of Congress Cataloging in Publication Control Number: 2023008865

ISBN:	HB:	978-1-4408-7276-1
	ePDF:	978-1-4408-7277-8
	eBook:	979-8-216-17227-7

Series: Religion in Politics and Society Today

Typeset by Apex CoVantage, LLC

To find out more about our authors and books visit www.bloomsbury.com and sign up for our newsletters.

Contents

Alphabetical List of Entries, vii

Topical List of Entries, ix

Series Foreword, xi

Preface, xiii

Overview, xv

Chronology, xxix

A to Z, 1

Annotated Bibliography, 235

Index, 245

Alphabetical List of Entries

Abington School District v. Schempp (1963)
Accommodations
American Civil Liberties Union
American Council on Education
Americans United for Separation of Church and State
Bible Instruction, Teaching in Schools
Bible Riots
Bible Study
Christian Coalition of America
Comparative Religion and World Religion, Teaching in Schools
Creationism
Dawkins, Richard
Devotional/Doctrinal Curriculum
Edwards v. Aguillard (1987)
Equal Access Act (Title 20)
Everson v. Board of Education of the Township of Ewing (1947)
Evolution, Teaching
Faith-Based Initiative
Falwell, Jerry
First Amendment
Focus on the Family
Freedom from Religion Foundation
Indigenous Faiths
Intelligent Design
Lemon v. Kurtzman Supreme Court Decision
Moral Majority
National Council on Religion in Public Education
Nontraditional Religious Identities
People for the American Way
Pledge of Allegiance
Prayer in School
Religion and Pseudoscience
Religion and School Dress Code
Religion and Sexual Education, Teaching in Schools
Religion and Sports Competition
Religion in Performances
Religious Discrimination in Schools
Religious Diversity in the United States
Religious Pluralism Teaching
Religious Schools
Religious Symbols
Religious Texts as Literature and Research Sources
Robertson, M. G. "Pat"
School Calendar, Religious Holiday Observances

School Vouchers
Scopes Trial
Secularism and Secular
  Humanism
Student-Initiated Prayer, Clubs
Theistic Spectrum
Virginia Statute for Religious
  Freedom

Topical List of Entries

Controversies
Accommodations
Bible Riots
Creationism
Evolution, Teaching
Intelligent Design
Pledge of Allegiance
Prayer in School
Religion and Pseudoscience
Religion and School Dress Code
Religion and Sexual Education, Teaching in Schools
Religion and Sports Competition
Religion in Performances
Religious Discrimination in Schools
Religious Diversity in the United States
Religious Pluralism Teaching
Religious Schools
Religious Symbols
School Vouchers

Court Cases
Abington School District v. Schempp (1963)
Edwards v. Aguillard (1987)
Everson v. Board of Education of the Township of Ewing (1947)
Lemon v. Kurtzman Supreme Court Decision
Scopes Trials

Curriculum and Pedagogy
Bible Instruction, Teaching in Schools
Bible Study
Comparative Religion and World Religion, Teaching in Schools
Devotional/Doctrinal Curriculum
Religious Texts as Literature and Research Sources
School Calendar, Religious Holiday Observances
Student-Initiated Prayer, Clubs

Beliefs
Indigenous Faiths
Nontraditional Religious Identities
Secularism and Secular Humanism
Theistic Spectrum

Government and Laws
Equal Access Act (Title 20)
Faith-Based Initiative
First Amendment

Pledge of Allegiance
Virginia Statute for Religious
    Freedom

Organizations
American Civil Liberties Union
American Council on Education
Americans United for Separation
    of Church and State
Christian Coalition of America
Focus on the Family
Freedom from Religion
    Foundation
Moral Majority
National Council on Religion in
    Public Education
People for the American Way

People
Dawkins, Richard
Falwell, Jerry
Robertson, M. G. "Pat"

Series Foreword

Religion is a pervasive and powerful force in modern society, and its influence on political structures and social institutions is inescapable, whether in the United States or around the world. Wars have been fought in the name of faith; national boundaries have been shaped as a result; and social policies, legislation, and daily life have all been shaped by religious beliefs. Written with the reference needs of high school students and undergraduates in mind, the books in this series examine the role of religion in contemporary politics and society. While the focus of the series is on the United States, it also explores social and political issues of global significance.

Each book in the series is devoted to a particular issue, such as anti-Semitism, atheism and agnosticism, and women in Islam. An overview essay surveys the development of the religious dimensions of the subject and discusses how religion informs contemporary discourse related to that issue. A chronology then highlights the chief events related to the topic. This is followed by a section of alphabetically arranged reference entries providing objective information about people, legislation, ideas, movements, events, places, and other specific subjects. Each entry cites works for further reading and in many cases provides cross-references. At the end of each volume is an annotated bibliography of the most important print and electronic resources suitable for student research.

Authoritative and objective, the books in this series give readers a concise introduction to the dynamic interplay of religion and politics in modern society and provide a starting point for further research on social issues.

Preface

The authors of our nation's founding documents were intent on tackling a matter that had rarely, if ever, been addressed in human history: to create a system of governance guided by the principle of freedom of conscience, where all would feel free to practice their religion as they wish, or not at all, and where no one, including the government, could infringe upon the religious freedom of others. Concomitant with this idea, however, was a dilemma reflected in the opening portion of the First Amendment, specifically, the Establishment Clause and the Religious Freedom Clause, where one person's expression is another person's encroachment.

There are few places where the tension between freedom of religion and separation of church and state is more salient than in America's public schools. Students, teachers, administrators, school board members, public officials, and families with children in school are all in the front lines. But when we consider that schools are designed to educate the next generation of citizens, we come to recognize that this topic affects and thus *should* matter to everyone, including future educators and principals, who will, in turn, influence yet another generation and continue a cycle that charts a course for our nation.

This book serves as a point of reference for many of the most important instantiations of this tension, including the court cases, laws and legal documents, policies, and principles involved. Teachers, supervisors, and directors of curriculum may refer to cases that have gone to courts. School principals and district superintendents will benefit from the summaries included in this book. Students, parents, and Parent Teacher Association (PTA) members planning school activities related to their faith will also find this book useful. This book also provides a brief chronological overview of the most significant events and developments related to the subject, as well as an annotated bibliography that guides the reader through many of the most influential works in which these questions are addressed.

In this text, the authors discuss roughly 50 entries on a range of topics. Some entries focus on specific laws and legal documents, such as the First Amendment and Virginia Statute on Religious Freedom, while other entries look at specific subjects taught in schools that involve controversy because of religious implications, such as the teaching of evolution versus Creationism. We also cover individuals who have played a significant role in these controversies, as well as the myriad court cases, most of them reaching the Supreme Court of the United States, where school policies and practices have faced legal challenges, often involving the First Amendment. As it is impossible to cover every court case and school board decision that arises, we have elected to focus on a select set of topics and cases that best represent the broader, pervasive, and recurring questions.

The time frame covered in this book reaches back to the arrival of the first Europeans in North America to the present day, though the majority of material relates to the last 100 years. Questions are not limited to any particular state or region, though there are certain states where there is a greater diversity of views on religion that appear to be the sites of greater and more frequent controversy. We thank Drew University's Professor Patrick McGuinn and Philadelphia-based author/journalist Ron Avery for offering ideas and feedback on some of these controversies. Much of this book focuses on questions where school administrators, boards of education, teachers, students, families, and public officials could not come to a consensus. And although the resulting decisions become the law of the land, it is rare that all judges agree, let alone the hundreds of millions of people in this nation. Moreover, there is frequent change over time, as knowledge, views, and attitudes evolve. Work on this book commenced just prior to the COVID-19 pandemic, and even in the short period since alone, this relationship, how we interpret it and the impact this has on our schools, has changed dramatically.

Overview

The commitment to freedom of religious expression and to respect for religious pluralism are two core American values on which our democracy is built. In some cases, defending one of these principles may require compromising the other, thereby bringing these two ideals into direct conflict with one another. Schools are public institutions, funded and run by the government, are venues where this complex dynamic—balancing between an individual's right to express his or her religion and ensuring that the government does not exhibit favor for any one religion, or rather, for religion at all—often plays out.

The framers of the Constitution, and the Bill of Rights' First Amendment in particular, foresaw that a certain tension would likely always exist between protecting individual freedoms related to the exercise of religion and the idea of separation between church and state. As government institutions, public schools face decisions on a regular basis that must weigh the First Amendment's protection of free speech and religious exercise against the injunction, laid out in the Establishment Clause, prohibiting activities that appear to support the establishment of state religion. Indeed, most of the issues and topics addressed in this volume relate back to this core question. The "Establishment Clause" of the First Amendment reads, "Congress shall make no law respecting an establishment of religion." This seems to make clear that government institutions should avoid direct involvement in religious activity and that these restrictions apply to public schools where religious activity, speech, and imagery could give the impression of school, and thus government, favoring one religion over others.

At the same time, the second clause of that same First Amendment, known as the "Religious Freedom Clause," guarantees an individual's right to practice religion as they like or not at all. Accordingly, a school should, on the one hand, seek to protect a student's right to engage in religious activity such as prayer or Bible study in school while on the other hand must refrain from certain religious activities that could give the impression that it has the school's endorsement. And so there exists a conundrum. Read on just a few words in the First Amendment, and we learn that freedom of speech is another protected right. But what happens when one preaches one particular faith's message under the auspices of a state-sponsored institution such as a school, or when a school tells a student that his or her attire is too "religious" for school? Yet another constitutional dilemma. Envisioning an endless number of scenarios where these questions would arise, the Bill of Rights was worded in such a way as to juxtapose the First Amendment's two "religion clauses," leaving it to schools, citizens, and the courts, to navigate.

In this volume, we tackle a number of different topics, focusing on roughly 50 specific examples that represent the types of questions that most frequently arise when religion and state, vis-à-vis the public schools, come into conflict. Broadly speaking, these matters fall into four broad categories: (1) teaching and talking about religion in the classroom and on campus, (2) religious expression and ritual practice in the classroom and on campus, (3) religion as the basis for curricular decisions about what subjects are included/excluded, and (4) religious schools as an alternative to public schools.

The first category involves drawing a distinction between teaching religion and teaching about religion; put in simplistic terms, the general rule for a public school should be "teach, don't preach." In the landmark 1961 Supreme Court case, *Abington v. Schempp*, the Court made clear that certain activities, specifically prayer, are prohibited but hastened to add that teaching *about* religion is imperative for our citizens to have at least a basic level of religious literacy. The second category relates to a wide range of activities that are either allowed or disallowed when striking a balance between the principle of separation of church and state, on the one hand, and freedom of expression, on the other. So, for instance, is any form of prayer permissible in a school setting? Can religious images be posted on school property? Can religious garb be worn in school, or is the school within its right to prohibit it?

The third category opens a number of questions where religion may loom largely in the background but is not always immediately apparent on the surface. A salient example pertains to teaching about sexual and reproductive health. Some people believe that sexual relations should be restricted to marriage and should be represented as such in the classroom, basing this belief on their religious convictions. Should schools be permitted to teach abstinence only, effectively censoring relevant scientific information about human reproductive biology, because of someone's religious beliefs? Evolution and other forms of science that seem to contradict the literal veracity of scripture have also been the source of controversy, where such subjects have either been banned altogether or taught alongside Creationism and forms of pseudoscience that are allotted equal time.

The fourth category pertains to questions about religious schools and whether they are eligible to receive public funds, the same as public schools do. This can take multiple forms, thus complicating the picture. For instance, when public funds are used to underwrite secular activity (e.g., a playground) at religious schools, does this constitute a First Amendment violation? If a student opts to attend a private religious school, is it a violation of their First Amendment rights to free exercise to deny them reimbursement for transportation costs?

To this day, there are disagreements about what the framers of the Constitution intended with the religious clauses of the First Amendment. But one thing is clear: this new nation was built on the idea that no person would be compelled to follow any particular religion, or religion at all for that matter. The significance of these groundbreaking ideas regarding religious pluralism is demonstrated not only by their inclusion in the Bill of Rights but is enshrined in the Constitution itself, under Article VI: "[N]o religious Test shall ever be required as a Qualification to any Office or public Trust under the United States." It is important to note that not all delegates to the Constitutional Convention of 1787 agreed on this point about separation of church and state and equal treatment of all faiths. Ultimately, however, those principles would be approved by the majority and enshrined in our founding documents.

One hundred and eighty years later, the Supreme Court affirmed the idea of separation of church and state as it applies to schools with its landmark decision *Everson v. Board of Education*, underscoring the Establishment Clause's prohibition against laws or policies that prefer one religion over another; aid one, any, or all religions; or favor religion generally over nonreligion. One major concern has always been that religion could be used to alienate students not of the majority religion in this country. Conservative Justice Sandra Day O'Connor understood religion's potential for marginalization, especially when it comes to schoolchildren, and in a 1984 case involving nativity scenes, expressed misgivings about the risks of government endorsement or disapproval of religion, writing,

"Endorsement sends a message to nonadherents that they are outsiders, not full members of the political community, and an accompanying message to adherents that they are insiders, favored members of the political community." It is not difficult to envision the scenario Justice O'Connor describes, where certain students, either atheists or students of religions other than Christianity, would feel marginalized in an environment where the Christian faith is clearly favored.

Still, another dilemma arises when it comes to teaching *about* religion in the school. In this book we cite multiple instances when curricula designed to teach *about* religion got teachers and schools into hot water because they crossed the line with either too much religion in general or, in the view of some families, too much of one particular religion. This was the case in 2015 when a world geography teacher at Riverheads High School in Augusta County, Virginia, gave an assignment on Arabic calligraphy as part of a lesson about Islam. For this task, the teacher selected a passage known as the *Shahada*, the Muslim declaration of faith, roughly translated to mean "there is no God but God and Muhammed is his messenger." The angry backlash from parents caused schools to close with some calling for the teacher's dismissal. In Chatham, New Jersey, a unit on world religions led to limited but loud complaints when the class covered Islam but not Christianity.

Living up to the promise of pluralism requires religious literacy. Citizens of a nation that respects and embraces religious diversity must have at least a fundamental understanding of religious traditions (e.g., sacred doctrines) other than their own. In Modesto, California, school district, a required course dedicated entirely to world religions had a positive impact, increasing students' knowledge about other religions, their respect for the rights of people of other faiths, their willingness to act in support of vulnerable religious minorities, and their esteem for First Amendment and political rights in general (Lester and Roberts 2011: 55). In fact, cultural awareness, in general, can have a positive impact on schools overall. A 2016 Stanford study found that in three high schools in San Francisco that piloted ethnic studies programs, students saw improvement in academic performance, attendance, and course credits earned (Donald 2016).

Still, this requires thoughtfulness and nuance. Schools should always be sure to provide adequate context in terms of what they are presenting and why. Schools should also strive to allot roughly equal time to their coverage of various faiths, though determining what to include/exclude is a complicated task in itself. This is one of the principles conveyed in the

Supreme Court's *Washegesic v. Bloomingdale* 1995 decision, where it was determined that a portrait of Jesus, in the absence of any other religious figures, violated the Establishment Clause in promoting Christianity above all other faiths. This also raises a question that has perplexed public schools since their inception: how can we increase understanding about our nation's many different religions while stopping short of pushing religion onto students, that is, teaching without preaching? The First Amendment Center, a useful resource for understanding the dynamic between religion and state, recommends that schools "may educate about all religions, but may not promote or denigrate any religion" and "may inform the student about various beliefs, but should not seek to conform him or her to any particular belief" (Haynes and Thomas 2007: 98). Others disagree, believing that protecting the right to freedom of religious expression takes precedence and that the strict separationist approach is overly stringent. Some argue that dogmatic adherence to secularism itself amounts to a violation of the Establishment Clause, in effect making secular humanism the favored "religion" (see "Secularism and Secular Humanism").

The Significance of Religion in Shaping the Debate

It is important to recognize the ways in which religion has shaped the debates over public schools and how this has shifted dramatically over time, often as the political pendulum swings back and forth from right to left. Of course, a pivotal development was advent of the public school itself. Around the mid-nineteenth century, public school systems began to take form, and by turn of the century, a majority of states required children to attend school though up to what age varied from state to state. But it was not until the twentieth century that the Supreme Court began to play a larger role in interpreting how the First Amendment applies to school cases.

The very first public schools in America, in fact, were often led by religious leaders and regularly included Bible study. Questions about whether or not this violated the Establishment Clause were not raised on a conspicuous level until in the early twentieth century. One of the most renowned court cases in American history, the "Scopes Trial," took place in a hot Tennessee courthouse in the summer of 1925, when arguments centered on the teaching of Darwin's theory of human evolution as opposed to religiously rooted creationism. Beginning in the 1920s and growing in the 1940s and 1950s, the Supreme Court began to take on an increasing number of cases involving questions about the separation of church and state. As noted earlier, in *Everson v. Board of Education* (1947), the Supreme Court ruled that in cases involving rights guaranteed by the First Amendment, including religious freedom, those rights apply to local as well as federal decisions, as per the Fourteenth Amendment. The *Everson* decision was complicated and messy, with justices shifting opinions as they went. "[Government] cannot make public business of religious worship or instruction, or of attendance at religious institutions of any character," wrote Justice Robert H. Jackson in his dissenting opinion. "This freedom was first in the Bill of Rights because it was first in the forefathers' minds; it was set forth in absolute terms, and its strength is its rigidity. It was intended not only to keep the states' hands out of religion, but to keep religion's hands off the state, and, above all, to keep bitter religious controversy out of public life by denying to every denomination any advantage from getting control of public policy or the public purse." While Everson did not easily resolve these questions, it succeeded in setting off an ongoing debate about what is meant by "establishment" (Ward 2009). Was the idea of non-establishment meant to refer narrowly to something like the Church of England, or was it intended as much broader prohibition against any state involvement with religion? Crucial decisions in 1962 and 1963 on questions of school prayer (*Abington v. Schempp*) and Bible study appeared to add more bricks in the wall of separation.

Through the end of the twentieth century, the Supreme Court continued to maintain a strong separation of church and state. In *Lee v. Weisman* (1992), a slim Supreme Court majority decided that subjecting students to a graduation prayer in a Rhode Island school amounted to a form of coercion. And in *Washegesic v. Bloomingdale* (1995), the Supreme Court again landed on the side of the Establishment Clause and principle of separation, rejecting the school's assertion that the First Amendment's protection of religious exercise and free speech, in this case, a portrait of Jesus, takes precedent. The Court concluded that the portrait's location immediately outside the entrance to the principal's office bears the imprimatur of the school.

The current Supreme Court, with a 6–3 conservative super majority, has taken a sharp turn, questioning just how high the wall of separation should stand and opening the way for increased expression of religion in schools. In the 2017 decision, *Trinity Lutheran Church of Columbia v. Comer*, the Court determined that states cannot deny religious people or religious institutions the same public benefits available to others on grounds that they are religious. And in the 2020 *Espinoza v. Montana*

Department of Revenue decision, the Court ruled that the state's tuition tax credit program cannot exclude private, faith-based schools from public benefits "solely because of the religious character of the schools." In June 2022, *Carson v. Makin*, the Court examined Maine's tuition assistance program, which stipulated that tuition dollars could only be spent at "nonsectarian" schools. The Court overruled the state's decision, with Chief Justice Roberts writing that "a neutral benefit program in which public funds flow to religious organizations through the independent choices of private benefit recipients does not offend the Establishment Clause." Rather, he argued, the Maine program, in excluding students wishing to attend private religious schools, "effectively penalizes the free exercise of religion."

Today, the Court's swing toward the free exercise of religion and de-emphasis on separation are most evident in *Kennedy v. Bremerton School District*, a case involving a Washington State high school coach who led prayers after football games at his school. Coach Kennedy began his ritual with a silent, individual prayer immediately following the conclusion of a game, win or loss. Initially, there was nothing particularly controversial about this ritual as public school employees are not prohibited from engaging in prayer at work, even in full view of students, so long as it is a quiet, individual prayer. But according to Richard B. Katskee, a lawyer for Americans United for Separation of Church and State, Kennedy crossed the line when he "insisted on [conducting] audible prayers at the 50-yard line with students" (as quoted by de Vogue, Sneed, and Cole 2022). By 2016, as his silent devotion morphed into a public spectacle with an audible group prayer joined by many students in front of a sizable audience, the school became concerned about Establishment Clause violations. Still, they offered the coach accommodations and asked Kennedy to move his prayer to an off-field site.

When Kennedy refused to cease his actions, he was placed on administrative leave and was suspended from the football program. After receiving a poor performance evaluation with a recommendation not to rehire, Kennedy, in 2017, filed a lawsuit claiming that the board had violated his First Amendment rights to freedom of speech and freedom of religious expression. A lower court rejected Kennedy's claim as did the Ninth Circuit Court, concluding that his prayer could be viewed as bearing the school board's approval given the context and that the district had a compelling interest in avoiding violation of the Establishment Clause.

Kennedy v. Bremerton School District reached the Supreme Court in 2021–2022, and in June 2022, a 6–3 majority ruled that the coach was within his First Amendment rights when he led prayer on the 50-yard line of the football field after the game. The Court ruled that the school board had violated a coach's rights by demanding that he cease his practice of on-field prayer and refusing to renew Kennedy's contract after he ignored repeated directives to cease. It remains to be seen how this decision may change decades of precedent limiting the prayer in schools more generally.

Beyond the particularities of *Kennedy v. Bremerton*, as a case where both the plaintiff and the defendant claim the same First Amendment, it represents the much broader tensions between the Establishment and Religious Exercise Clauses. These two views, for instance, are also reflected in the dissenting voices within the Supreme Court. In the majority opinion, Justice Neil Gorsuch wrote, "The Constitution and the best of our traditions counsel mutual respect and tolerance, not censorship and suppression, for religious and nonreligious views alike," thereby making clear his view that individual religious freedom ought to be given priority. In the dissenting opinion, on the other hand, Justice Sonia Sotomayor argued that it is the Establishment Clause that creates a "backstop" protecting religious freedom and that the *Kennedy* decision "elevates one individual's interest in personal religious exercise, in the exact time and place of that individual's choosing, over society's interest in protecting the separation between church and state, eroding the protections for religious liberty for all."

Conflict surrounding religion in schools often involves questions about "original intent"; in other words, do we truly understand what the framers intended with the language they chose, and are we faithfully following their intentions? This is especially interesting with regard to relevant material coming from outside court cases, laws, and official government policies. For example, the aforementioned letter written by Thomas Jefferson in 1802 to the Danbury Baptist Association in which he stated that the First Amendment had the effect of "building a wall of separation between Church & State." In *Lynch v. Donnelly* (1984), a case involving a Rhode Island town's inclusion of a creche in its public Christmas display, the Supreme Court revisited the concept of a "wall of separation," diminishing this phrase as a "useful metaphor" that does not accurately reflect the "practical aspects of the relationship that in fact exists." The Court argued that the Constitution does not actually require complete separation of church and state, but rather, it "affirmatively mandates accommodation, not merely tolerance, of all religions, and forbids hostility toward any." This interpretation of the Establishment Clause, asserted the Court, "comports with the contemporaneous understanding of the Framers' intent" and clearly departs from the strict separationist view.

Those who prioritize the Free Exercise Clause and call for a weakening of the wall of separation often argue that neither the framers of the Constitution nor any members of the First Congress vocalized objections to the offering by chaplains of daily prayers in the Congress. In the *Lynch v. Donnelly* decision, the Supreme Court referred to this a "striking example of the accommodation of religious beliefs intended by the Framers" (673–74). It is also true that the late-eighteenth-century America they refer to was quite homogenous, composed almost entirely of white Anglo-Saxon Protestants; in fact, the First Congress had only two non-Protestant members, both from Maryland. Today, by comparison, the U.S. Congress includes members of the Catholic, Jewish, Muslim, Hindu, and Buddhist faiths and at least one avowing no faith at all. According to a Pew Research study of the 117th Congress, just over half (55.4%) identify as Protestant, while nearly 30% are Catholic and roughly 8% are of faiths other than Christianity (Pew Research Center 2021). The current Congress, in other words, is much more reflective of the religious diversity characteristic of the United States today. In any event, the relevance of prayer offered in an elected body of adults, virtually all of the same faith, to the matter of prayer pushed onto a captive audience of religiously diverse children, is questionable.

This also raises questions about the seemingly growing role of religion in school practice and policy today. There appear to be countervailing trends in the United States right now. Pew Research's most recent survey, for instance, found the American people overall to be shifting steadily toward greater secularism and away from structured religious affiliation. In 2021, self-identified Christians constituted roughly 63% of U.S. population, a significant decline from the 75% of just a decade prior. This trend is true of Protestants in particular, whose numbers have declined 10 percentage points since a decade ago, with both evangelical and nonevangelical Protestants declining overall to 40% of U.S. adults. In a separate study, where respondents were asked how important religion is in their lives, 53% of Americans said "very important." While that number is down slightly from 56% in a previous survey, it reflects a strong core in which religion continues to maintain a firm hold. Overall, these data seem to be reflective of an America where many are becoming more secular, while at the same time, believers are remaining or becoming more religious.

By definition, the various types of nonreligious and unaffiliated people—atheists, agnostics, spiritual but not religious, "nones"—are not nearly as well organized or connected politically as are people associated with religious institutions. This translates to a lack of power, influence, and representation for the unaffiliated in decision-making processes, meaning there is often little to no organized nonreligious block pushing against the influence of religion in schools. It is also true that school administration and school boards are not always responsive to the demands of their communities, and the courts are not always in step with public opinion.

As demographics in the United States have changed over time, so have institutions such as the public school system and religious organizations. Demographic shifts can be accompanied by shifts in attitudes. Certain policies of the early- to mid-twentieth century, for example, emerged not so much from deep theorizing about what our public education system should look like but, rather, out of concerns about the growing influence of Catholicism in American public life and anti-immigrant sentiment. In 1891, the National Council of Education launched an attempt to eradicate "non-American" influence from the curriculum (Tyack and Hansot 1992), and as immigration continued to grow, so did the pressure on public schools to "Americanize" immigrant children (Glenn 2019). In other cases, laws requiring only English as the language of instruction for major subjects were enacted as a way to constrain religious schools.

A critical turning point in the relationship between religion and public schools came with the ratification of the Fourteenth Amendment in 1868. Prior to the amendment and even well into the twentieth century, virtually no cases involving religion and schools came before the Supreme Court. To that point, the Court had played very little part in determining the application of the First Amendment in matter of school policy. By mid-century, this changed as the Court's reach into cases of this nature expanded, and by the 1960s, multiple critical decisions regarding devotional prayer and Bible reading in schools were handed down.

While values, views, and attitudes change over time, they also vary at any given time *within* the United States. Public opinion and political leanings tend to vary considerably from state to state. People in rural states, for example, often have libertarian impulses and therefore may tend to be anti-regulation, while states with large metropolitan populations tend to be more progressive and secular. Some states have older or younger populations, which is also an important factor. These regional differences contribute to a complex national dynamic. Still, many of the most important and controversial cases make their way to the Supreme Court where decisions become the law of the land, applied evenly across the states.

An important question that arises, especially today, is whether religion is qualitatively different from nonreligious matters and should thereby be singled out for special treatment. Those more concerned with freedom of exercise find many of the laws designed to keep religion out of the schools to be overly restrictive. In the recent case, *Kennedy v. Bremerton*, Justice Gorsuch writes, "We are aware of no historically sound understanding of the Establishment Clause that begins to '[make] it necessary for government to be hostile to religion' in this way." Still, one concern has always been whether non-Christian students are made to feel marginalized by activities, be it prayer or religious symbols, that do not acknowledge religious difference. It is true that some are hostile toward religion and any form of religious expression, but those professing to defend religious freedom must also take measures to ensure that religious freedom means freedom to express any religion or no religion at all.

On another level, the problem of religion and schools in America involves essential questions related to the original and ongoing debate in the United States over centralized federal governance versus states' rights and localized governance. In theory, public schools are localized institutions organized into districts usually defined along the lines of townships. A 2020 survey counts 13,452 regular school districts across the United States (National Center for Education Statistics [NCES] 2020). While each district has broad decision-making power, schools must often comply with certain state standards, such as highly debated standardized testing and core curriculum, subjects, and materials that all schools are required to teach. For example, six states mandate Holocaust education, and in 2020, the New Jersey Board of Education approved a state curriculum titled "New Jersey Student Learning Standards—Comprehensive Health and Physical Education."

Accordingly, there are examples of students, and their families, resisting state-mandated education standards. Responding to New Jersey State's revised sex education standards, the Morris County Board of Commissioners unanimously passed a resolution requesting that the state ban the curricula and create a "Parents Bill of Rights." The proposed legislation would prohibit the state and local school districts from interfering with a parent or guardian's ability to engage in and direct a student's education while granting individual families greater say in what and when their children learn; families, for example, would be allowed to opt out of school district curricula. Many teachers and parents, it should be noted, support the new curriculum, which aims to be more inclusive and sensitive to diversity. We also saw the assertion of state power over school districts with the COVID-19 pandemic as decisions about masking and vaccination requirements throughout the country were often made at the state level.

The federal government also has influence over public schools. In the aforementioned *Kennedy v. Bremerton* case, the Supreme Court overturned a school district's decision on school prayer, which has been supported by the circuit court. It should be noted that the Supreme Court, whose composition may be subject to multiple factors—the electoral college, the timing of justice's retirement or death, and the whims of Senate majority leaders—can be out of touch with the will of the people. The *Dobbs* ruling, where the Supreme Court overturned *Roe v. Wade*, a decision that provided more than 50 years of federal protection for reproductive choice, is a case in point. Voters across the United States, including in normally "purple" or even "red" states such as Kansas, Michigan, and Kentucky, voted in favor of ballot measures to either protect abortion rights or at least to allow for challenges to state bans, suggesting that the Supreme Court may not represent the will of the people on the issue, which is often construed as a religious question.

Ultimately, there looms the underlying question about whether schools should be teaching values in any form, religious or not, and on this point too opinions have vacillated over time. In 1985, the *New York Times* reported that "many educators in the New York area say they deliberately avoid trying to tell students what is ethically right and wrong," adding that "values are much less discussed in public schools now than they were in the late 1960s." Families want the best education possible for their children, and they entrust the schools to teach them. It is understood that certain basic values and skills such as self-regulation may be taught. But there can be gray area between secular social values and religious values and, thus, potential questions about where the church-state line of separation lies. In the 1987 Supreme Court case, *Edwards v. Aguillard*, the Court argued, "families entrust public schools with the education of their children, but condition their trust on the understanding that the classroom will not purposely be used to advance religious views that may conflict with the private beliefs of the student and his or her family" (*Edwards v. Aguillard* 584, 107 S. Ct. at 2577).

Conflicts involving First Amendment rights are numerous and varied, and cases involving religion and schools can be especially sensitive and charged. Indeed, many families value their religious commitments as highly as anything. And with both religion and education so near and dear to people's hearts, it is no surprise that questions involving religion and school can be volatile. Schools need to recognize the myriad ways that students and their families live their religious and cultural lives in an increasingly diverse America. As such, school districts must take into account the needs of all their constituents as they design curricula and formulate school policy (Bigelow 2010). Religious Studies scholar Fraser put it well when he wrote, "The toleration of beliefs that one considers deeply misguided is one of the most difficult challenges for any true believer in both democracy and religious freedom. Yet, without such toleration, a pluralistic, multicultural school, indeed a free society, is impossible. Unfortunately, this toleration does not come easily" (Fraser 2016: 137).

Each year brings new questions where the Establishment Clause and Religious Freedom Clause come into direct conflict with each other, and we are no closer to a "one-size-fits-all" solution today than we were at the time the First Amendment was created. At present, the pendulum has swung back in the direction of prioritizing religious expression over concerns about establishment, with a Supreme Court decision that has ruled in support of school prayer and the allocation of tax dollars in support for religious schools. The following book does not offer any easy answers either. Rather, it is our goal to inform the reader about the issues through a select sample of specific topics representing the wide range of questions that have arisen and continue to arise.

Further Reading

Bigelow, M. *Mogadishu on the Mississippi: Language, Racialized Identity, and Education in a New Land*. Malden, MA: Wiley-Blackwell, 2010.

de Vogue, Ariane, Tierney Sneed, and Devan Cole. "Supreme Court Further Erodes Separation between Church and State in Case of Praying Football Coach." CNN.com. June 27, 2022. https://www.cnn.com/2022/06/27/politics/football-coach-prayer-high-school-supreme-court-kennedy/index.html.

Donald, Brooke. "Stanford Study Suggests Academic Benefits to Ethnic Studies Courses." Stanford News Service. January 12, 2016. https://news.stanford.edu/2016/01/12/ethnic-studies-benefits-011216/.

Fraser, James W. *Between Church and State: Religion and Public Education in a Multicultural America*. Second edition. Baltimore, MD: Johns Hopkins University Press, 2016.

Glenn, Charles L. "Does Catholic Distinctiveness Matter in Catholic Schools?" *Review of Faith & International Affairs* 17, no. 4 (October 2, 2019): 63–71. https://doi.org/10.1080/15570274.2019.1681757.

Haynes, Charles C., and Oliver Thomas. *Finding Common Ground: A First Amendment Guide to Religion and Public Schools*. Nashville, TN: First Amendment Center, 2007.

National Center for Education Statistics. "The Condition of Education—Preprimary, Elementary, and Secondary Education—Elementary and Secondary Enrollment—Private School Enrollment—Indicator." May 2020. https://nces.ed.gov/programs/coe/indicator_cgc.asp.

Pew Research Center. "Faith on the Hill: The Religious Composition of the 117th Congress." January 4, 2021. https://www.pewresearch.org/religion/2021/01/04/faith-on-the-hill-2021/.

Smith, Gregory A. "About Three-in-Ten U.S. Adults Are Now Religiously Unaffiliated." Pew Research Center. December 14, 2021. https://www.pewresearch.org/religion/2021/12/14/about-three-in-ten-u-s-adults-are-now-religiously-unaffiliated/.

Tyack, David, and Elizabeth Hansot. *Learning Together: A History of Coeducation in American Public Schools*. Revised edition. New York: Russell Sage Foundation, 1992.

Ward, Artemus. "Everson v. Board of Education (1947)." The First Amendment Encyclopedia. 2009. https://mtsu.edu/first-amendment/article/435/everson-v-board-of-education.

Chronology

1786—*Virginia Statute for Religious Freedom*: Virginia General Assembly passes the Virginia Statute for Religious Freedom, written by Thomas Jefferson, anticipating religious freedoms that would soon be guaranteed in the Constitution and the First Amendment.

1788—U.S. Constitution ratified: Article VI, which states "no religious Test shall ever be required as a Qualification to any Office or public Trust under the United States," signals the new nation's commitment to religious pluralism.

1791—Bill of Rights/First Amendment is passed, protecting an individual's right to practice his or her religion while prohibiting the establishment of a state religion.

1844—Bible Riots: As Catholics gain a greater foothold in America and exercise their rights to religious freedom, including the establishment of independent private schools, "nativists" and Catholics clash in cities across the Northeast.

1925—Scopes Trial: This famous court case centers on the question of religion and science in schools, prompted by the fining of a Tennessee school teacher for allegedly teaching evolution in violation of state prohibitions against it.

1933—The Humanist Manifesto is drafted. This document outlined the beliefs and positions of humanism, proposing a new form of religion, grounded in the natural world and the human experience within it, and which rejects "supernatural or cosmic guarantees of human values." Humanism, and secular humanism in particular, would go on to draw criticism from conservative and religious figures and organizations.

1947—*Everson v. Board of Education*: The Supreme Court rules that the Fourteenth Amendment extends First Amendment protections to local as well as federal decisions in cases involving religious freedom.

Everson also serves to establish the "child benefit test," based on the idea that as long as children who attend faith-based schools are the primary beneficiaries of state aid, the government is not directly involved in supporting religious schools.

1954—**The Pledge of Allegiance**, originally written by Francis Bellamy in 1892, and revised in 1923 to include the phrase "the Flag of the United States," was revised a final time to include the full phrase "one nation under God." This revision came in response to the perceived threat of Communism to the American way of life and the belief that the Soviet Union sought to eliminate religion.

1963—*Abington v. Schempp*: The Supreme Court case involving Pennsylvania state law requiring Bible study in the public schools. In an 8–1 decision, the Supreme Court rules that school-sponsored prayer is unconstitutional.

1965—**Immigration Act**, aka the Hart–Celler Act, signed into law by President Lindon B. Johnson, abolishes the National Origins Formula of the earlier twentieth century, opening the door for mass immigration from non-Western countries, resulting in religious diversification in the United States.

1971—*Lemon v. Kurtzman*: This Supreme Court decision centers on statutes in Pennsylvania and Rhode Island involving state aid to church-related schools. The Court looks to cumulative decisions to establish the "Lemon Test," three criteria for determining whether an act violates the First Amendment: (1) the statute must have a secular legislative purpose, (2) its principal or primary effect must be one that neither advances nor inhibits religion, and (3) the statute must not foster an excessive government entanglement with religion.

1971—**National Council on Religion in Public Education** is founded to promote the objective study of religion in schools.

1978—**American Indian Religious Freedom Act** is passed, which required that the United States "protect and preserve for American Indians their inherent right of freedom to believe, express, and exercise" their religious traditions, including "access to sites, use and possession of sacred objects, and the freedom to worship through ceremonial and traditional rites." The act also serves as official recognition of the U.S. government's role in stifling Native American religion, including in the Native American boarding schools of the nineteenth and twentieth centuries.

1979—The Moral Majority is formed to mobilize conservative Christian voters and promote legislative agendas that worked to minimize the perceived influence of secularism on American society, including in public schools. Among issues for which the Moral Majority lobbied were "prayer and the teaching of creationism in public schools." The organization was dissolved in 1989, when one of its founders, Rev. Jerry Falwell stated that with the religious right "solidly in place," the organization was no longer needed.

1984—Equal Access Act is passed, requiring that any secondary school that receives federal funding and that has a "limited public forum" must not "deny equal access or a fair opportunity to, or discriminate against, any students who wish to conduct a meeting." The law effectively opens the door for the creation of student-led clubs pertaining to religion and religious views, as well as clubs sometimes opposed by religious groups, such as LGBTQ clubs.

2004—*Bannon v. School District of Palm Beach*: The 11th Circuit Court of Appeals upholds a Florida high school's decision to remove the religious content in murals painted by students and displayed in prominent locations in the school, some including religious Christian messages and symbols.

2017—*Trinity Lutheran Church of Columbia v. Comer*: The Supreme Court rules that states cannot deny religious people or institutions public benefits generally available to all schools solely on ground that they are religious.

2020—*Espinoza v. Montana Department of Revenue*: The Supreme Court decides that the state's tuition tax credit program cannot bar private, faith-based schools from receiving public benefits solely on the basis of the religious character of those schools.

2022—*Carson v. Makin*: The Supreme Court rules that Maine's tuition assistance program violates the First Amendment because its requires that payments be used exclusively at "nonsectarian" schools and removes parents' choice in school selection. The decision states that families eligible to receive state aid for private school tuition are permitted to use that money for schools with faith-based curricula.

Abington School District v. Schempp (1963)

School District of Abington Township, PA v. Schempp (374 U.S. 203) is a Supreme Court case involving the question of Bible reading and school prayer in public schools. The case originated when 16-year-old Ellery Schempp refused to take part in school-sponsored Bible reading at his high school in the Abington School District, outside of Philadelphia. The school's practice of Bible reading was sanctioned by a Pennsylvania State Law (24 Pa. Stat. 15–1516, as amended, Pub. Law 1928) requiring that "at least ten verses from the Holy Bible [be] read, without comment, at the opening of each public school on each school day." The school also conducted collective recitations of the Lord's Prayer. When student Ellery Schempp refused to participate, he was singled out and disciplined. Edward Schempp, Ellery's father, filed a suit with the Philadelphia District Court of Eastern Pennsylvania, challenging the statute contending that it violated his and his family's rights under the First and Fourteenth Amendments. The complaint sought:

> to enjoin enforcement of the statute, contending that their rights under the Fourteenth Amendment to the Constitution of the United States are, have been, and will continue to be, violated unless this statute be declared unconstitutional as violative of these provisions of the First Amendment. They sought to enjoin the appellant school district, wherein the Schempp children attend school, and its officers and the [206] Superintendent of Public Instruction of the Commonwealth from continuing to conduct such readings and recitation of the Lord's Prayer in the public schools of the district pursuant to the statute.

In a letter appealing to the American Civil Liberties Union (ACLU) for help, the Schempps wrote, "I thank you for any help you might offer in freeing American youth in Pennsylvania from this gross violation of their religious rights as guaranteed in the first and foremost Amendment in our United States' Constitution."

The District Court held that the statute violated the First Amendment's Establishment Clause as applied to the states by the Due Process Clause of the Fourteenth Amendment. The school district, together with the Superintendent of Public Instruction of the Commonwealth of Pennsylvania, appealed the decision; in the meantime, the state legislature had amended the law to allow students to opt out of the religious activities with a written request. Based on this amendment, the original District Court decision was vacated and remanded back to the court, which still ruled in Schempp's favor. Upon ultimately reaching the Supreme Court, Abington was merged with another suit, *Murray v. Curlett*, which involved atheists Madalyn Murray and her son, William, challenging a similar practice of school prayer and Bible reading in Maryland. It is important to note that one year prior, the Court had ruled against public prayer in schools in *Engel v. Vitale* (1962).

Abington v. Schempp was argued before the Supreme Court in February 1963 and was decided on June 17, 1963. Justice Thomas Clark was joined by Justices Warren, Black, White, Douglas, Goldberg, Harlan, and Brennan as the Supreme Court handed down an 8–1 majority affirming the District Court's decision; the sole dissenter was Justice Potter Stewart. The majority held that these activities were religious in purpose, rejecting the argument that the Bible was being used "as an instrument for nonreligious moral inspiration" and that sanctioned and organized Bible reading in public schools is unconstitutional. The Court also reversed and remanded the Maryland decision.

A concurrent opinion was offered by Justice Brennan, who made a point to recognize religious diversity as a key consideration in the case. He wrote:

> There are persons in every community—often deeply devout—to whom any version of the Judaeo-Christian Bible is offensive. There are others whose reverence for the Holy Scriptures demands private study or reflection and to whom public reading or recitation is sacrilegious. . . . To such persons it is not the fact of using the Bible in the public schools, nor the content of any particular version, that is offensive, but the manner in which it is used.

Justice Brennan also noted that the America of his time was way more religiously diverse than that of our forefathers and viewed pluralism in public schools as a guiding principle in "the American experiment in free public education available to all children."

In a dissenting opinion, Justice Stewart argued that both cases involved a substantial free exercise claim on the part of those who support school prayer, asserting:

> if religious exercises are held to be an impermissible activity in schools, religion is placed at an artificial and state-created disadvantage. Viewed in this light, permission of such exercises for those who want them is necessary if the schools are truly to be neutral in the matter of religion. And a refusal to permit religious exercises thus is seen not as the realization of state neutrality, but rather as the establishment of a religion of secularism. ("Abington Township, School District of, Pennsylvania, et al. v. Schempp et al. 374 U.S. 203 (1963)," n.d.)

It its noteworthy that in *Abington v. Schempp*, the Court reaffirmed religion's place in school. Justice Clark wrote, "It might well be said that one's education is not complete without a study of comparative religion or the history of religion and its relationship to the advancement of civilization. . . . It certainly may be said that the Bible is worthy of study for its literary and historic qualities." Clark also made a point to clarify that the Court was not attempting to establish a "religion of secularism," entirely devoid of religion, nor did it intend to throw religion out of the schools entirely.

As part of the decision, the Court established a test, asking, "[W]hat are the purpose and the primary effect of the enactment? If either is the advancement or inhibition of religion, then the enactment exceeds the scope of legislative power as circumscribed by the Constitution. That is to say that, to withstand the strictures of the Establishment Clause, there must be a secular legislative purpose and a primary effect that neither advances nor inhibits religion." This test, advanced in the *Abington v. Schempp* decision, presaged the "Lemon test" put forth in 1971 in *Lemon v. Kurtzman*.

See also: First Amendment; *Lemon v. Kurtzman* Supreme Court Decision; Secularism and Secular Humanism

Further Reading

Abington Township, School District of, Pennsylvania, et al. v. Schempp et al. 374 U.S. 203 (1963). Appeal from the United States District Court for the Eastern District of Pennsylvania. No. 142. n.d. https://www.law.cornell.edu/supremecourt/text/374/203.

French, Kimberly. "Ellery Schempp Stood Up for Religious Minorities." February 2003. https://www.uuworld.org/articles/ellery-schempp-stood-religious-mi.

Murray et al. v. Curlett et al. 228 Md. 239, 179 A.2d 698 (1962).

Solomon, Stephen D. *Ellery's Protest: How One Young Man Defied Tradition and Sparked the Battle over School Prayer*. Ann Arbor: University of Michigan Press, 2007.

UUA.org. Civil Liberties. Statement of Conscience by the Unitarian Universalist Association of Congregations. 2004.

Vile, John. "Abington District v. Schempp." The First Amendment Encyclopedia. n.d. https://www.mtsu.edu/first-amendment/article/1/abington-school-district-v-schempp.

Accommodations

Public schools should accommodate the religious beliefs and practices of students of all different faiths while avoiding the advancement of or discrimination against any one particular religion; that is, tension that exists between the Free Exercise and Establishment Clauses. This question has been addressed by Congress and the courts, and professional organizations have offered guidance.

Students and their families make a range of requests for accommodations pertaining to religious practices. One common request is for excusal from activities or programs that either inhibit the student's religious observance or require them to take part in activities deemed inappropriate in the view of the student's faith tradition. The National Parent Teacher Association (PTA)/First Amendment Center along with the National Education Association (NEA) offer direction concerning excusal requests, recommending that schools make efforts whenever possible to accommodate requests for excusal from classroom discussions, lessons, or activities for religious reasons. It is also suggested that schools generally try to avoid lessons and activities that significantly burden a student's free exercise of religion, lest they prove a compelling interest in requiring participation. For example, Jehovah's Witnesses refrain from birthday celebrations, an activity that is not curricular and should not be compulsory.

Students also request to be excused from school in order to attend religious instruction at religious institutions during times that conflict with public school hours. According to the NEA, "[S]ubject to state law, districts may allow students to be released for such religious instruction off school property. School officials should neither encourage nor discourage participation" (National Education Association, n.d.). The No Child Left Behind (NCLB) guidance states, "[I]t would be lawful for schools to excuse Muslim students briefly from class to enable them to fulfill their religious obligations to pray during Ramadan." This question came before the courts in *Zorach v. Clauson*, when New York Education Law (§ 3210), which permitted students to leave school during the school day for the purpose of attending religious educational or devotional activities, was challenged as unconstitutional. The Supreme Court upheld the law concluding that the program didn't involve religious education in public school classrooms, the expenditure of public funds, or any coercion of students.

Similarly, schools should aim to be flexible and creative, where possible, to accommodate schedules and duties that involve religious observance, permitting students and school employees to take time off for religious holidays not covered by the official school calendar. School districts may sometimes be required to modify the work schedule of religiously observant faculty and other employees. There are also cases where students may be expected to take exams, complete labs, or perform other intensive tasks while fasting, and schools should consider reasonable accommodations in these instances as well.

Requests for accommodations often involve the provision of appropriate space for prayer and reflection during the school day. Such requests may be granted without raising constitutional concerns, so long as the prayer is not school sponsored or organized and no students feel compelled to participate. A typical example would be Muslim or Jewish students requiring a quiet space for prayer during lunch or in between classes.

Requests may sometimes concern dietary needs, but because children usually have the option to bring their own lunch, schools are typically not required to provide special meals. School districts with large numbers of such students do sometimes attempt to accommodate dietary needs with kosher, halal, or vegetarian options; a notable example being the school district in Dearborn, Michigan, which provides halal meals for its predominantly Muslim schools. Certain school districts may eliminate meat on Fridays during Catholic Lent or offer matzoh to Jewish students during Passover. Schools must be careful, however, to avoid situations where they fall into violation for not offering special meals equally to students of all faiths.

Dress codes and the display of religious apparel are often the reason for accommodation requests. In *Cheema v. Thompson*, a 1994 9th Circuit case, a group of Sikh students sued their school district when they were suspended for wearing religious ceremonial knives ("kirpans") to school. The suit argued that the school failed to accommodate their religious beliefs under the Religious Freedom Restoration Act (RFRA). Schools typically have discretion with regard to policies concerning student dress codes and school uniforms. The NEA urges schools to maintain neutrality and avoid policies that single out certain religious attire. Schools should accommodate students and employees who wear certain items of clothing such as a hijab or yarmulke. The U.S. Equal Employment Opportunity Commission, in their "Best Practices for Eradicating Religious Discrimination in the Workplace" (U.S. Equal Employment Opportunity Commission, n.d.), recommends that employers (i.e., schools) make efforts to accommodate employees who need to wear religious garb and offer creative solutions, suggesting, for instance, that hijabs or yarmulkes could be worn in school colors. They also suggest that managers and employees be trained to avoid stereotyping based on religious garb and appearance.

RFRA (1993) provided clear protections for religious accommodations in school settings. RFRA established that schools must demonstrate both a compelling interest and use of the least restrictive means possible before placing a burden on a student's religious exercise. Another congressional law, the Equal Access Act, guarantees that schools honor requests by religious student clubs to use school facilities the same way as they do for nonreligious student groups.

In 1995, President Bill Clinton issued a Memorandum on Religious Expression in Public Schools outlining schools' obligations; while not legally binding, this represented a strong statement on the issue. The NCLB Act of 2003 included Guidance on Constitutionally Protected Prayer in Public Elementary and Secondary Schools, asserting that school districts should treat parent requests for accommodation of religious needs in the same manner that they treat parents' nonreligious requests. The

National PTA and the First Amendment Center have collaborated to prepare "A Parent's Guide to Religion in the Public Schools," and the NEA has also issued a document titled "Backgrounder: Religion and Public Schools: Promoting Mutual Respect and Understanding" (National Education Association, n.d.).

Court cases have also tested the limits of religious accommodations. In 1993–1994, a New York State statute, allowing a distinct group, the Satmar Hasidic Jewish sect, to carve out a separate school district based on their religious identity and needs, was challenged. The constitutionality of the statute was questioned by taxpayers and the local school board in *Board of Education v. Grumet* (512 U.S. 687), with lower courts all concluding that the statute had the primary effect of advancing religion. When the case reached the Supreme Court, Justice David H. Souter delivered the majority opinion that the statute violated the Establishment Clause because it failed the test of neutrality toward religion and risked showing religious favoritism.

McCollum v. Board of Education (333 U.S. 203) is a 1948 Supreme Court case exploring the limits of states' powers to use tax dollars to aid religious instruction. The case tested the principle of "released time," when a Champaign, Illinois, public school program set aside class time for religious instruction. Though the classes were not mandatory, an atheist family complained that the student was ostracized for not attending the classes and sued the school board on grounds of First and Fourteenth Amendment violations. Justice Black wrote the majority opinion determining that the program violated the Establishment Clause because it involved the public school system's administration as well as the use of tax-supported property. The Court ruled that the program was "beyond question a utilization of the tax-established and tax-supported public-school system to aid religious groups and to spread the faith." At the time, the Court noted, some 2,000 districts across the United States offered similar released time programs.

Law professor Scott Idleman (2001) advises school administrators to keep apprised of religious freedom laws within their region since this area of law is rather dynamic and protections afforded to religious practices are subject to change. It is also important to note that while students have rights to engage in certain religious practices, students should never be compelled to take part in a religious activity.

See also: Equal Access Act (Title 20); Religion and School Dress Code

Further Reading

Board of Education of Kiryas Joel Village School District v. Grumet, 512 U.S. 687 (1994).

Cheema v. Thompson, 194 U.S. App. Lexus, 24 160 (9th Cir.) (1995). https://www.casemine.com/judgement/us/5914bd53add7b049347a1b64.

Dipanwita, Deb. "Of Kirpans, Schools, and the Free Exercise Clause: Cheema v. Thompson Cuts through RFRA's Inadequacies." *Hastings Constitutional Law Quarterly* 23, no. 3 (1996): 877–919.

Idleman, Scott C. "Religious Freedom and the Interscholastic Athlete." *Marquette Sports Law Review* 12 (2001): 295–345.

McCollum, Illinois ex rel. v. Board of Ed. of School Dist. No. 71, Champaign County. 333 U.S. 203 (1948). https://www.law.cornell.edu/supremecourt/text/333/203.

National Education Association. "Backgrounder: Religion and Public Schools: Promoting Mutual Respect and Understanding." n.d. http://www.nea.org/assets/docs/19228_Religion%20in%20the%20public%20schools3-BGH.pdf.

Orange County Department of Education. "Public Schools and Religion." n.d. https://ocde.us/LegalServices/Documents/Public-Schools-and-Religion-Workbook-2016.pdf.

"Religious Accommodation for Students." Last updated June 20, 2016. https://education.findlaw.com/student-rights/religious-accommodation-for-students.html.

U.S. Equal Employment Opportunity Commission. "Best Practices for Eradicating Religious Discrimination in the Workplace." n.d. Accessed June 21, 2020. https://www.eeoc.gov/laws/guidance/best-practices-eradicating-religious-discrimination-workplace.

American Civil Liberties Union

The American Civil Liberties Union (ACLU) is an organization of more than 1.5 million members, including thousands of attorneys, both staff and volunteers, that "vigorously defend[s] individual freedoms including speech and religion, a woman's right to choose, the right to due process, citizens' rights to privacy" and more ("ACLU History," n.d.). According to the organization's About Us section on the website, the ACLU stands up for these rights, "even when the cause is unpopular, and sometimes when nobody else will" ("ACLU History," n.d.).

FOUNDING AND BACKGROUND

The ACLU was founded in the years following World War I, in response to American reaction to the Communist Revolution in Russia.

During 1919 and 1920, American law enforcement authorities conducted a series of raids meant to round up suspected leftist radicals and anarchists ("Palmer Raids," n.d.). These raids, known as "Palmer Raids," named for Attorney General A. Mitchell Palmer, resulted in arrests and deportations that "proved disastrous and sparked vigorous debate [in America] about constitutional rights" ("Palmer Raids," n.d.). In 1920, the ACLU was created to "take a stand" against what its members saw as "egregious civil liberties abuses" that took place during the Palmer Raids ("ACLU History," n.d.).

Since its founding, the ACLU has "evolved from [a] small group of idealists into the nation's premier defended of the rights enshrined in the U.S. Constitution" ("ACLU History," n.d.).

PAST ACTIVITIES

One of the earliest legal cases in which the ACLU played a pivotal role was the 1925 Scopes Trial, also referred to as the "Scopes Monkey Trial." In this trial, science teacher John Scopes was prosecuted for teaching evolution in a Tennessee public school, which, at the time, was illegal (see "Scopes Trial"). Scopes had been recruited by civic leaders and the ACLU, specifically to teach about evolution "as a way to challenge [the] Tennessee law that forbade it in public schools" (mtsu.edu/first-amendment). Attorney for the defense, Clarence Darrow, was a leading member of the ACLU ("Palmer Raids," n.d.).

In 1981, the ACLU would once again play a role in a case regarding the instruction of evolution in the classroom. Specifically, the ACLU "challenged an Arkansas statute requiring that the biblical story of creation be taught as a 'scientific alternative' to the theory of evolution" ("ACLU History," n.d.). The plaintiffs in the case included a dozen clergy "representing Methodist, Episcopal, African Methodist Episcopal, Catholic, Southern Baptist, Reform Jewish, and Presbyterian groups," "to counter the rhetoric of the Moral Majority and other fundamentalist groups" who hoped the case (*McLean v. Arkansas*) would serve as an example of a larger "national struggle between atheism and Christianity" ("McLean v. Arkansas Board of Education," n.d.).

CURRENT ACTIVITIES

Among other contemporary issues, such as cases involving Internet free speech, equal treatment for lesbian and gay couples, and protecting people's right to privacy, the ACLU continues to work toward keeping religious instruction separate from public education. In 2005, in the case of *Kitzmiller v. Dover Area School District*, the ACLU represented a group of parents who objected to a school district requirement that "intelligent design" be taught as an "alternative to evolution in high school biology classes" ("ACLU History," n.d.). Federal judge John E. Jones III ruled that the district requirement was unconstitutional because intelligent design "is a religious viewpoint that advances 'a particular version of Christianity'" (Goodstein 2005).

See also: Creationism; First Amendment; Intelligent Design; Religion and Pseudoscience; Scopes Trial

Further Reading

"ACLU History." American Civil Liberties Union. n.d. Accessed July 9, 2020. https://www.aclu.org/about/aclu-history.

Goodstein, Laurie. "Judge Rejects Teaching Intelligent Design." *New York Times*, December 21, 2005.

"McLean v. Arkansas Board of Education." Encyclopedia of Arkansas. n.d. Accessed July 9, 2020. https://encyclopediaofarkansas.net/entries/mclean-v-arkansas-board-of-education-2243/.

"Palmer Raids." History.Com. n.d. Accessed July 9, 2020. https://www.history.com/topics/red-scare/palmer-raids.

"Scopes Trial." History.Com. n.d. Accessed June 10, 2019. https://www.history.com/topics/roaring-twenties/scopes-trial.

American Council on Education

The American Council on Education (ACE) is an organization that advocates for various policies and initiatives in higher education in the United States, to "shape public policy and foster innovative, high-quality practice" ("About the American Council on Education," n.d.) among institutions of higher learning. To this end, the ACE "convenes, organizes, mobilizes, and leads advocacy efforts that shape effective public policy and help colleges and universities best serve their students, their communities, and the wider public good" ("About the American Council on Education," n.d.).

FOUNDING AND BACKGROUND

The ACE was founded in 1918, during the final months of World War I. As former ACE president George Zook writes, the council was created "as a direct result of the obvious need to coordinate the services which educational institutions and organizations could contribute to the government in the national crisis" of the Great War (Zook 1950). At the first major meeting of the organization, on January 1918, in Washington, D.C., it was named the "Emergency Council on Education," but in July, the name was changed to the "American Council on Education," to reflect the need for a more permanent status, and in "recognition of the continuing needs of cooperation in education" in peacetime (Zook 1950).

During the time between the First and the Second World Wars, the council's work began to shift to projects "designed to promote better international understanding and relations" (Zook 1950).

ROLE IN MODERN EDUCATION AND RELIGION IN PUBLIC SCHOOLS

The role the ACE has played in the discussion of religion in public schools over the past several decades has been, perhaps, indirect but significant, nonetheless. The ACE describes its vision as "a vibrant democratic society that relies on postsecondary education to expand knowledge, equity, and social progress" ("About the American Council on Education," n.d.). To this end, it has encouraged educational policies that encourage diversity and inclusion in higher education, seeking academic leadership that is representative of the American population, as a whole, and that is "increasingly diverse." The ACE's goal, by way of promoting more diverse academic communities, is to expose learners to diversity and, by extension, to teach them to be more inclusive of diversity in their lives beyond the classroom.

One such case, in which the ACE took a stance on inclusion in America, and religious inclusion, specifically, was in 2018 when the U.S. Supreme Court upheld an executive order by President Donald Trump that "among other things, suspended entry for 90 days of foreign nationals from seven countries identified" as presenting a terrorism-related risk ("Trump v. Hawaii," n.d.). Five of the seven countries were Muslim majority. The ACE filed an amicus brief in the case and issued a statement expressing concern about the implied message that the travel ban might send to the global academic world. ACE president Ted Mitchell said in that statement, "While we strongly support the government's efforts to keep our nation secure, we fear this broadly written prohibition will have a long-term impact on our standing as a global leader and hamper our education and research enterprise and the overall U.S. economy" ("Supreme Court Upholds Trump Travel Ban" 2018). Mitchell went on to warn that "the harsh rhetoric around immigration issues nonetheless can fuel a perception of exclusion," which "makes it far more difficult to maintain the United States as the destination of choice for the world's best students, faculty, and scholars, regardless of their nationality" ("Supreme Court Upholds Trump Travel Ban" 2018).

More generally, the ACE has stood as an advocate for greater emphasis on broader liberal arts education at all academic levels, as opposed to a narrower focus on only science, technology, engineering, and mathematics (STEM) fields, which are distinctly less focused on subjects such as history, philosophy, and religion. In a column for the ACE, Carol Geary Schneider, president of the Association of American Colleges and Universities, expressed concern that elected officials "blithely dismiss[ed] history, philosophy, religion, languages and literatures, cross-cultural studies, political science, and political theory, as though a nation could forget its history and political foundations, ignore its cultural legacies and neighbors, give up on understanding alternative world views, and still somehow perpetuate itself as a global power" (Schneider 2015). Schneider further defended liberal arts, writing that "degree holders in the humanities and social sciences contribute disproportionately to a family of social services and education professions that may pay less well than some other fields, but which are absolutely necessary to the health of our communities and to our educational system." Without liberal arts, she wrote, "the institutions that support democracy and the social safety net would be left dangerously weakened" (Schneider 2015).

The ACE also has advocated for increased multicultural and global education, arguing that such education "reveals more when it consciously includes the consideration of racial, ethnic, religious, linguistic, and other kinds of diversity as critical elements of the global experience" ("At Home in the World Toolkit," n.d.).

Ada Meloy, general counsel for the ACE, wrote in 2011 that it was increasingly important that American colleges and universities "foster interaction among students in diverse extracurricular student organizations," for doing so provides students with opportunities for "growth and development, while simultaneously teaching students about civility, social tolerance, and mutual respect for others who harbor conflicting viewpoints" (Meloy 2011). At the same time, Meloy argued, institutions need to be diligent in ensuring that such extracurricular activities are respectful of First Amendment protections of free speech and free exercise of religious beliefs.

See also: Religious Diversity in the United States; Religious Pluralism Teaching; Theistic Spectrum

Further Reading

"About the American Council on Education." American Council on Education. n.d. Accessed July 9, 2020. https://www.acenet.edu/About/Pages/default.aspx.

"At Home in the World Toolkit." American Council on Education. n.d. Accessed August 22, 2020. https://www.iastatedigitalpress.com/jctp/article/591/galley/471/view/.

Meloy, Ada. "The Latest Debate Over Church and State." *Presidency* 14, no. 2 (2011): 10–12.

Schneider, Carol Geary. "How to Explode a Myth: Reshaping the Conversation about the Liberal Arts." *Higher Education Today*, April 8, 2015. https://www.higheredtoday.org/2015/04/08/how-to-explode-a-myth-reshaping-the-conversation-about-the-liberal-arts/.

"Supreme Court Upholds Trump Travel Ban." June 28, 2018. Accessed August 22, 2020. https://www.acenet.edu/News-Room/Pages/Supreme-Court-Upholds-Trump-Travel-Ban.aspx.

"Trump v. Hawaii." Oyez. n.d. Accessed July 9, 2020. https://www.oyez.org/cases/2017/17-965.

Zook, George F. 1950. "The American Council on Education." *The Phi Delta Kappan* 31, no. 7 (1950): 312–18.

Americans United for Separation of Church and State

Americans United for Separation of Church and State (Americans United) is a nonprofit organization composed of "lawyers and lobbyists, students and activists, religious leaders and impassioned Americans," who seek to advance the "separation and government as the only way to ensure freedom of religion" in the United States ("Who We Are | Americans United," n.d.). According to the organization's mission statement, Americans United defends "church-state separation in Congress, and the state legislatures" and "in courtrooms" and invites activism among students through its Youth Advisory Council and among religious leaders through its Faith Leaders United initiative ("Who We Are | Americans United," n.d.).

FOUNDING AND BACKGROUND

Americans United was founded in 1947 as Protestants and Other Americans United for Separation of Church and State (POAU), with the intention of countering the perceived growing influence of the Catholic Church on American politics (Jeffries and Ryan 2001). Over the next three decades, the group increasingly found most of its support coming from non-Protestants, "including atheists, Jews, and humanists," which led to the shortening of its name to "Americans United for Separation of Church and State" (Jeffries and Ryan 2001), to reflect its broader coalition.

It was established shortly after the U.S. Supreme Court case *Everson v. Board of Education*, which ruled that a New Jersey law that allocated taxpayer funds to bus children to religious schools was constitutional because "it did not breach 'the wall of separation' between church and state" (Ward, n.d.). Justice Hugo L. Black reasoned that "the law did not pay money to parochial schools, nor did it support them directly in anyway [sic]. It was rather enacted to assist parents of all religions with getting their children to school" ("Everson v. Board of Education of the Township of Ewing," n.d.). Leaders of Americans United feared that "the case represented a harbinger of greater state support for Catholic schools" (den Dulk and Vile 2017). In keeping with this concern, the organization's earliest work was focused on the constitutionality of parochial schools receiving state aid.

PAST ACTIVITIES

In the 1960s, Americans United expanded its mission to address other issues involving the relationship between church and state, including the matter of prayer in school; in the decades since, it has taken positions on several other high-profile church-state issues, such as "religion in public schools, government subsidies of religion, including through school vouchers, and religious-based objections to marriage or restrictions on women's healthcare" (den Dulk and Vile 2017).

RECENT ACTIVITIES

Since the 1970s, Americans United has become distinctly less Protestant in its positions and instead "operates as a liberal interest group, a junior cousin to the American Civil Liberties Union" (Jeffries and Ryan 2001). The organization continues to advocate for strict separation of church and state, but instead of teaming with Protestant organizations, it now "usually appears alone or with liberal Jewish groups" (Jeffries and Ryan 2001).

Among the school-related issues Americans United currently concerns itself with are private school vouchers, religion in classroom instruction, school-sponsored prayer, religion in school-sponsored events and clubs, and public charter schools ("Public Charter Schools," n.d.). The organization's stated position is that public schools "are a unifying force in our society" and that "no student should feel excluded in their own school because of their beliefs, and no parent should have to worry that their children are being given religious instruction in a public school" ("Schools," n.d.).

See also: Abington School District v. Schempp (1963); American Civil Liberties Union; Bible Study; Equal Access Act (Title 20); First Amendment; Intelligent Design; School Vouchers; Scopes Trial; Student-Initiated Prayer, Clubs

Further Reading

den Dulk, Kevin R., and John R. Vile. "Americans United for Separation of Church and State." The First Amendment Encyclopedia. May 2017. https://www.mtsu.edu/first-amendment/article/1174/americans-united-for-separation-of-church-and-state.

"Everson v. Board of Education of the Township of Ewing." Oyez. n.d. Accessed July 9, 2020. https://www.oyez.org/cases/1940-1955/330us1.

Jeffries, John C., Jr., and James E. Ryan. "A Political History of the Establishment Clause." *Michigan Law Review* 100, no.2 (2001): 93.

"Public Charter Schools." Americans United for Separation of Church and State. n.d. Accessed July 9, 2020. https://www.au.org/issues/public-charter-schools (URL no longer active).

"Schools." Americans United for Separation of Church and State. n.d. Accessed July 9, 2020. https://www.au.org/issues/schools.

Ward, Artemus. "Everson v. Board of Education (1947)." The First Amendment Encyclopedia. n.d. Accessed July 9, 2020. https://www.mtsu.edu/first-amendment/article/435/everson-v-board-of-education.

"Who We Are | Americans United." Americans United for Separation of Church and State. n.d. Accessed July 9, 2020. https://www.au.org/who-we-are.

B

Bible Instruction, Teaching in Schools

The Bible, the foundational text of the Christian world, is a book that is as ubiquitous in America as it is often misunderstood.

Recent figures indicate that 87% of American households have at least one copy of the Bible in the home and that about half of Americans use the Bible during prayer. Of Americans who have increased their engagement with the Bible in the past decade, more than half say that it has been central to their "faith journey," and more than half of Americans report that they "wished they could use the Bible more" (Lesley 2017).

But what is meant by "the Bible" is not always clear or consistent from one reader to another. For example, referring to the Bible as a single, unified text is, to some extent, inaccurate, as it is actually a compilation of many religious texts, compiled over the course of centuries. The first section of the Bible, commonly referred to as the "Old Testament," includes scriptures that predate the birth of Jesus and are most commonly associated with the Hebrew Bible, the writings that have been preserved as the sacred texts of Judaism, with some scriptures being written as early as the eighth century BCE ("Amos," "First Isaiah," and others) ("When Was Each Book of the Bible Written?"). The "New Testament," in contrast, is a collection of writings that date from as early as the mid-first century CE (several of the letters said to be written by the Apostle Paul) to as late as the second century CE (possibly the second letter of Peter).

And while the canonical list of texts that are included in the Bible, and the order in which they appear, is largely consistent throughout Christendom, there are some significant differences between Bible versions, such as the Bible used by Protestants and the one used by Roman Catholics: the Catholic Bible includes books of the Old Testament that the

Protestant Bible omits. Furthermore, even for each denomination's preferred form of the Bible, there are multiple translations, some of which are considered more faithful to the original language of the scriptures, while others are less true to the original diction but purport to be more representative of the authors' intent ("Bible Versions and Translations Online," n.d.).

Despite a lack of consensus among Christians on what constitutes an accurate and authoritative version of the Bible, for nearly all of American history, Christians and Christian groups have found some commonality by advocating for teaching the Bible in public schools.

HISTORY OF BIBLE INSTRUCTION IN SCHOOLS

In the earliest years of American history, Bible instruction in the classroom would have been considered not only acceptable but also as the norm. Formal education in the 1600s, and through most of the 1700s, usually took place in private schools, which often were founded and operated by religious groups. These schools, as one might expect, had curricula that were "rooted in the Bible and denominational doctrines" (Kniker 1985). As schools moved away from being primarily parochial institutions to more secular ones, one might expect that they would become less reliant on the Bible as a source for instruction. Indeed, Horace Mann, one of the earliest proponents of American public education, believed that while the Bible could be used to teach "moral character, Judeo-Christian values, and responsible, virtuous citizenship," it should not be used in a sectarian way or to teach any particular theology ("Horace Mann: The Bible in Public Schools," n.d.). Nonetheless, sectarian Bible instruction in public schools has persisted throughout the centuries, to varying degrees, often leading to legal challenges that have risen to the level of the Supreme Court. These cases have roundly affirmed that public schools may not sponsor or require Bible readings in any way that is not demonstrably secular (see *Abington School District v. Schempp* (1963)").

ARGUMENTS FOR TEACHING THE BIBLE IN SCHOOL

Advocates of Bible instruction in public schools often turn to a few key arguments when making their case, recognizing, of course, that the courts have determined sectarian study of the Bible in public schools to be a violation of the First Amendment's Establishment Clause.

One argument is that knowledge of the Bible is essential to a comprehensive education. Chuck Stetson, the CEO of Essentials in Education, the parent company of the Bible Literacy Project, wrote in 2019 that "without knowledge of the Bible, students can't fully understand the English language, English literature, history, art, music or culture" (Stetson 2019). He cites, as evidence, texts such as Herman Melville's *Moby Dick*, which starts with the sentence, "Call me Ishmael," an allusion to a prominent figure in the Old Testament, and the works of Shakespeare, which employ more than 1,200 biblical references across his 36 plays.

Robert L. Simonds, the founder and president of the National Association of Christian Educators and Citizens for Excellence in Education, similarly defended Bible instruction as essential when he wrote in 1996 that the Bible is "not only 'appropriate,' but necessary for students to have a complete historical picture of mankind" (Simonds 1996), indicating that it is both "a great documented history book of man's beginnings" and the "only documented ancient history account" to cover the 4,000 years prior to the birth of Jesus. Further bolstering his argument, Simonds cited the ruling of the Supreme Court case *Abington v. Schempp*, in which Justice Tom C. Clark, writing for the majority opinion, asserted that "it might well be said that one's education is not complete without a study of comparative religion or the history of religion and its relationship to the advancement of civilization" ("School Dist. of Abington Tp. v. Schempp, 374 U.S. 203 (1963)," n.d.).

As Stetson and Simonds' credentials suggest, defense for Bible instruction in public schools often comes from people who profess religious faith, particularly Christianity; however, there are some prominent advocates among the secular and even atheist communities as well. Educator and outspoken atheist Richard Dawkins, for example, is a vocal opponent of what he considers "religious indoctrination" in classrooms, yet he has gone on the record as supporting Bible instruction for many of the same reasons indicated by both Stetson and Simonds. In 2017, for instance, Dawkins acknowledged the importance of Bible instruction in understanding many allusions in English literature. He also recognized knowing the Bible as an essential part of understanding much of Western civilization, saying that "[s]o much of European history is dominated by disputes against rival religions" that one "can't understand history unless [one knows] about the history of the Christian religion and the Crusades and so on" (O'Neil 2017).

Another argument that is frequently invoked when defending Bible instruction in public schools is the role that the Bible plays in developing children's moral character. The Public School Bible Study Committee cites a study by the National Council on Crime and Delinquency that concludes that students who study the Bible "perform better than their classmates as a whole in almost every category with reinforced moral and character development that is antithetical to engaging in criminal or delinquent behavior" ("Why Teach the Bible," n.d.). This argument does meet some resistance, though, from those who believe that the Bible is not or should not be the basis of human morality.

ARGUMENTS AGAINST TEACHING THE BIBLE IN SCHOOL

For all the arguments advocating for Bible instruction in public schools, there are ample arguments opposing the practice, as well, again, coming from a fairly diverse set of voices and positions.

One of the most common objections to Bible instruction in public schools is that such courses might (intentionally or inadvertently) serve to promote a religion, specifically Christianity, in violation of the First Amendment's Establishment Clause. In Odessa, Texas, in 2005, the community found itself divided about the inclusion of a Bible course in the Ector County Independent School District. An Odessa College English professor, David Newman, emerged as one of the most notable opponents to the course. Newman worried that "the course might promote Christianity" and expressed particular concern about the potential effect on his Jewish daughter, a high school student in the district (Chancey 2009). Newman worried that his daughter's classmates might "ask her why 'your people' killed Jesus. Or if she knows that Jesus is her savior" (Chancey 2009).

Another concern, expressed by groups such as the American Civil Liberties Union, is that when a school decides to offer Bible instruction, it might show "favoritism for one version or religious interpretation of the Bible over another, whether Jewish, Catholic, Protestant, Orthodox, or other" ("Statement on the Bible in Public Schools: A First Amendment Guide" 2007). Further, teachers who conduct the courses might not have the proper training to teach the Bible in a purely academic way. In both of these scenarios, the school potentially will have violated the First Amendment's Establishment Clause.

Ironically, for some opponents of public school Bible instruction, the concern is not that schools will *not* teach the Bible in an objective or secular way but that they *will*—or at least that they will attempt to.

Chuck Queen, a Baptist pastor in Kentucky, argued in 2014 that the Bible should not be taught in public schools, not because of its content or because it runs afoul of constitutional limitations but because to teach the Bible in accordance with the Constitution potentially dilutes the spiritual importance of the text. In response to the notion that the Bible could be taught "from a purely academic viewpoint," Queen wrote, "How is it possible not to treat the Bible as a holy book?" (Queen 2014). The Bible, he continued, "is a collection of religious documents written from particular theological viewpoints" (Queen 2014). "No part of the Bible is 'secular' or 'objective,'" he concluded. "It is impossible not to teach the Bible as a 'holy' book" (Queen 2014). Jonathan Merritt, an award-winning writer on the subjects of religion, culture, and politics, expressed this same view in 2013, when he argued that while "the strongest support for implementing [a curriculum that teaches the Bible] comes presumably from conservative evangelicals who mostly claim to read the Scriptures literally," these supporters incorrectly assume "the Bible would be taught accordingly" (Merritt 2013). "By advocating for teaching the bible in schools," Merritt wrote, "Christians are unwittingly lobbying for something they could never accept. They think they want it, but they really don't" (Merritt 2013).

TEACHING OTHER RELIGIOUS TEXTS

Potentially lost in the discussion about whether the Bible should be taught in public schools is whether *other* religious texts should be taught or whether *any* should be taught at all. The Quran, for instance, is the holy text for nearly 2 billion Muslims worldwide and an estimated 3.45 million in America. For Hindus, which make up about 15% of the world population at about 1 billion adherents, and about 0.7% of the U.S. population at an estimated 2.2 million followers, scripture is contained in the Vedas. In the interest of taking a neutral and inclusive stance toward religion, a school might opt to teach about these texts, and others, alongside the Bible (see "Comparative Religion and World Religion, Teaching in Schools"); as long as the instruction is grounded in objective and secular purpose, the Constitution would very likely support such a curriculum.

On the other hand, a school might avoid introducing non-Judeo-Christian texts out of concern for backlash from a largely Judeo-Christian population. Such concerns are not unfounded. The evangelical group Proclaiming Justice to the Nations, for instance, has objected to several programs in American public school systems that require students to learn about Islamic principles and to read from the Quran on the grounds that such programs are "being used to indoctrinate [American] children with unconstitutional pro-Islamic content" ("More Unconstitutional Pro-Islamic Content in U.S. Schools?" 2019).

A final option that schools might opt to pursue would be to refrain from teaching about any religious texts at all. Doing so would almost certainly be constitutionally sound but, as with all of the options addressed previously, would very likely face some degree of opposition.

See also: *Abington School District v. Schempp* (1963); Bible Riots; Bible Study; Comparative Religion and World Religion, Teaching in Schools; First Amendment; Religious Pluralism Teaching; Religious Schools

Further Reading

"Bible Versions and Translations Online." Bible Study Tools. n.d. Accessed July 9, 2020. https://www.biblestudytools.com/bible-versions/.

Chancey, Mark A. "The Bible, the First Amendment, and the Public Schools in Odessa, Texas." *Religion and American Culture: A Journal of Interpretation* 19, no.2 (2009): 169–205.

"Horace Mann: The Bible in Public Schools." Museum of the Bible. n.d. Accessed July 9, 2020. http://www.museumofthebible.org/book/minutes/620.

Kniker, Charles R. *Teaching about Religion in the Public Schools. Fastback 224.* Bloomington, IN: Phi Delta Kappa Educational Foundation, 1985.

Lesley, Alison. "The Bible Is in 87% of American Households." World Religion News, April 5, 2017. https://www.worldreligionnews.com/religion-news/bible-87-american-households.

Merritt, Jonathan. "Why Conservative Christians Should Oppose Teaching the Bible in Public Schools." Religion News Service, March 4, 2013. https://religionnews.com/2013/03/04/why-conservative-christians-should-oppose-teaching-the-bible-in-public-school/.

"More Unconstitutional Pro-Islamic Content in U.S. Schools?" Proclaiming Justice to The Nations. September 4, 2019. https://www.pjtn.org/more_unconstitutional_pro_islamic_ content_in_u_s_schools.

O'Neil, Tyler. "Richard Dawkins: Kids Should Read the Bible in Public Schools." Pjmedia.Com. June 14, 2017. Accessed August 22, 2020. https://pjmedia.com/faith/tyler-o-neil/2017/06/14/richard-dawkins-kids-should-read-the-bible-in-public-schools-n98711.

Queen, Chuck. "Teaching Bible in Public Schools: Not a Good Idea." Baptist News Global. May 6, 2014. https://baptistnews.com/article/teaching-bible-in-public-schools-not-a-good-idea/.

"School Dist. of Abington Tp. v. Schempp, 374 U.S. 203 (1963)." Justia Law. n.d. Accessed July 9, 2020. https://supreme.justia.com/cases/federal/us/374/203/.

Simonds, Bob. "Teaching the Bible in Public Schools?" Institute for Creation Research. September 1, 1996. https://www.icr.org/article/teaching-bible-public-schools/.

"Statement on the Bible in Public Schools: A First Amendment Guide." American Civil Liberties Union. April 2007. https://www.aclu.org/other/statement-bible-public-schools-first-amendment-guide.

Stetson, Chuck. "Teach the Bible in Public Schools So That Students Can Learn to Better Understand the World around Them." Fox News. March 13, 2019. https://www.foxnews.com/opinion/the-compelling-case-for-teaching-the-bible-in-public-schools.

"When Was Each Book of the Bible Written?" *Bible Gateway Blog* (blog). February 1, 2016. https://www.biblegateway.com/blog/2016/02/when-was-each-book-of-the-bible-written/.

"Why Teach the Bible." Bible in the Schools. n.d. Accessed July 9, 2020. https://www.bibleintheschools.com/5.21/why-teach-the-bible-.

Bible Riots

The "Bible Riots" were a series of incidents involving anti-Catholic and anti-immigrant mob violence in and around the city of Philadelphia in the early-mid-1840s. The proximate causes of the conflict began when Catholics, forced to read from the King James Bible during public school prayer, requested permission to substitute an alternative Catholic version of the Bible. The root causes of the Bible Riots represent a much broader conflict involving anti-Catholic nativism in Protestant American society at the time. One outcome of the Bible Riots, intended or not, was the creation of the first Catholic (aka, parochial) school system in the United States.

In the span of two decades (1830–1850), the Catholic population in the United States had increased from 35,000 to 170,000, and some 70 new Catholic churches were built. Some American Protestants, by far the largest religious group, felt threatened by this, and anti-Catholic and anti-immigrant sentiment was beginning to reach a fever pitch. Publicly, Protestants aired a fear of losing their jobs to immigrants willing to work for lower pay as well as loss of political power as newcomers gained the right to vote. It was around this same time that Philadelphia had created a free public school system, established by Protestants and, in the view of many nativists, *for* Protestants.

Catholics, wary of their secondary status at the time, generally avoided direct confrontation over matters of religion in schools. But tensions increased with the creation of public schools that required prayer and Bible reading. In 1834, Catholics in Boston raised concerns about required readings from the King James Bible in public schools. An angry anti-Catholic mob responded by burning down a convent. The following year, this conflict escalated as Roman Catholics in New York raised similar objections to enforced reading of the King James Bible in their schools. This fueled the growing anti-immigrant movement and the rise of the nativist "Know Nothing" party.

Catholic-Protestant tensions had been flaring up around the country when the conflict seemed to peak in Philadelphia in 1844 (Beyer-Purvis 2016). Francis Patrick Kenrick, Irish Catholic Bishop of the rapidly growing Philadelphia diocese, sought a compromise for the Bible conflict, requesting that the school's Board of Controllers allow Catholic children to use the Douay Bible, the only Catholic Bible widely available in English at the time. The board agreed to allow the use of alternative versions of the Bible but insisted that these substitutes contain scripture only with no commentary, a caveat that effectively excluded the Douay Bible. Meanwhile, rumors had begun to spread that the Catholics sought to have the Protestant Bible banned from schools. Some even believed Catholics were attempting to take over the schools and stockpiling weapons inside churches. In March 1842, attempting to dispel the anti-Catholic rumors, Bishop Kenrick issued a public statement: "Catholics have not asked that the Bible be excluded from public schools. They have merely desired for their children the liberty of using the Catholic version in case the reading of the Bible be prescribed by the controller or directors of the schools."

Nativist leaders, however, were not dissuaded and only increased their efforts to demonize Catholics. Protestant clergymen founded the American Protestant Association with the goal of warning the public about the growing threat of "popery." And the following year, Lewis Levin, a newspaper editor and soon to be congressman, helped found the American Republican Association, later renamed the Native American Party. On May 3, 1844, the latter organized a rally in Kensington, a working-class, industrial neighborhood just north of Philadelphia populated by many Irish immigrants, both Catholic and Protestant. The rally appears to have ended peacefully, but on May 6, thousands of nativist demonstrators returned to

Kensington, leading to an outbreak of violence, and ultimately, the death of several nativists, including a young man named George Schiffler. Schiffler would be made into a martyr by nativists, with hundreds attending his funeral and circulating images and accounts of his death while defending their cause. The following days saw rounds of reprisal attacks and spiraling violence between the two groups, including the burning of Catholic homes, schools, and churches—most infamously, Saint Michael's and Saint Augustine's. Local police were overwhelmed, and ultimately, it took a combination of state and local militia to end the violence. An estimated 15–20 people, including militia and civilians, Catholics, and Protestants, were killed, and as many 100 people were injured, and many were forced from their homes. Protestants suffered the greater share of deaths, while both groups claimed they were acting in self-defense.

An important contemporary of Kenrick's was of New York bishop John Hughes (later archbishop), who was equally involved with the struggle for religious freedom and equal rights for Catholics. Hughes was especially interested in the way this played out in the schools. At a meeting of the Friends of Freedom of Education in Carroll Hall in 1841, Hughes made an appeal to Protestants and Catholics, saying:

> In the public schools, which were established according to the system now in force, our children had to study books which we could not approve. Religious exercises were used which we did not recognize, and our children were compelled to take part in them. Then we withdrew them from the schools and taught them with our own means. . . . Now, the Public School Society has introduced just so much of religious and sectarian teaching as it pleased them, in the plenitude of their irresponsible character, to impart. They professed to exclude religion, and yet they introduced so much in quantity as they thought proper, and as much a quality as violated our religious rights. If our children cannot receive education without having their religious faith and feelings modeled by the Public School Society . . . it is tyranny to tax them for its support. We do not ask the introduction of religious teaching in any public school, but we contend that if such religious influences be brought to bear as the business of education, it shall be, so far as our children as concerned, in accordance with the religious beliefs of their parents and families. (Kehoe 2012)

In retrospect, the conflict can be attributed to multiple factors. The riots most certainly involved anxiety over Catholic immigration and its economic implications as well as the inter-Irish ethno-religious dimensions of the conflict, an Old World fight that had been imported to America (Clark 1973; Feldberg 1975; Oxx 2013). Some scholars have focused on broader questions concerning the place of religion in the fledgling public school system and the separation of church and state (Dorsey 2008).

As Catholics increasingly pushed for rights to freedom of conscience, and to decide the form of education in public schools for their own children, the Protestant majority pushed back against those demands. According to historian Beyer-Purvis (2016: 366), the question of citizenship played central role in the riots, as an issue that encompasses religion, economics, rights, and race. "The concerns expressed by the nativists that framed Catholics as incompatible with American religiosity, capitalism, and democratic voluntarism made who could have access to citizenship the central issue driving their actions." The Philadelphia Bible riots, argues Beyer-Purvis (2016), represented an attempt by the nativists to regulate citizenship in the United States at the expense of Catholic rights.

It is noteworthy that the Bible Riots also contributed to the founding of the parochial school system. Ultimately, Bishop Kenrick came to view his efforts to influence the public schools as futile and would shift strategies altogether, instead focusing on founding the United States' first Catholic school system in Philadelphia. In 1851, Kenrick became archbishop of Baltimore where the parochial school system continued to expand.

See also: Religious Diversity in the United States; Religious Pluralism Teaching

Further Reading

Beyer-Purvis, Amanda. "The Philadelphia Bible Riots of 1844: Contest over the Rights of Citizens." *Pennsylvania History* 83, no. 3 (2016): 366. https://doi.org/10.5325/pennhistory.83.3.0366.

Clark, Dennis. *The Irish in Philadelphia : Ten Generations of Urban Experience.* Philadelphia: Temple University Press, 1973.

Dorsey, Bruce. "Freedom of Religion: Bibles, Public Schools, and Philadelphia's Bloody Riots of 1844." *Pennsylvania Legacies* 8, no. 1 (2008): 12–17.

Feldberg, Michael. *The Philadelphia Riots of 1844 : A Study of Ethnic Conflict.* Contributions in American History: No. 43. Westport, CT: Greenwood Press, 1975.

Kehoe, Lawrence (ed.). *Complete Works of the Most Rev. John Hughes, Archbishop of New York: Comprising His Sermons, Letters, Lectures, Speeches, etc.* Vol. 1.

New York: Catholic Publication House, 2012. https://archive.org/stream/completeworksofm01hugh/completeworksofm01hugh_djvu.txt.

Oxx, Katie. *The Nativist Movement in America: Religious Conflict in the Nineteenth Century*. Critical Moments in American History. New York: Routledge, 2013.

Bible Study

The teaching of Bible study as part of public school curricula has long been a contentious issue in the United States. Advocates for Bible study emphasize the secular motives for teaching the Bible and assert that scripture forms the basis of Western legal, moral, and cultural traditions and thus has a place in any American classroom. They point, for example, to innumerable references to biblical stories and characters in Western art and literature, and as the Bible represents one of the most widely read books in the world, biblical literacy is a part of global literacy. Opponents argue that teaching the Bible in public schools, especially when presented in a devotional context, violates the Establishment Clause. Central to this debate is the question of intent and context, that is, whether the Bible is being taught as an object of study or as an article of faith.

The Supreme Court has grappled with this question on multiple occasions. In *Abington v. Schempp*, a case that examined state laws in Pennsylvania and Maryland requiring Bible study, the Court decided that devotional teaching in state-sponsored school was unconstitutional. The Court was clear to state, however, that this did not rule out secular teaching of the Bible, writing,

> It certainly may be said that the Bible is worthy of study for its literary and historic qualities. Nothing we have said here indicates that such study of the Bible or of religion, when presented objectively as a part of a secular (public school) program of education, may not be effected consistently with the First Amendment.

Justice Thomas Clark added, "[O]ne's education is not complete without a study of comparative religion or the history of religion and its relationship to the advancement of civilization." In fact, the Supreme Court has consistently supported the teaching of the Bible in public schools. In the 1962 case, *Engel v. Vitale* (370 U.S. 421), the Court stated that "[t]he history of man is inseparable from the history of religion" (434). And in *Stone v. Graham* (449 U.S. 39, 1980), it concluded, "the Bible may constitutionally be used in an appropriate study of history, civilization, ethics, comparative religion, or the like."

The American Academy of Religion (AAR 2010) has contributed to this discussion by publishing a guide outlining three ways in which religion can be taught without violating the First Amendment: the historical approach, the literary approach, and the cultural studies or tradition-based approach. The first approach acknowledges the historical value of the Bible. Miracles aside, the text contains descriptions of people, places, and even some events that can be corroborated by historical and archaeological evidence. Extra biblical texts from Egypt and Mesopotamia name many of the cities mentioned in the Bible. Pontius Pilate is both a biblical and a historical figure, known from scripture as well as archaeological evidence (Notley 2017). At the same time, anachronisms, such as Genesis' account of Abraham's encounter with the Philistines, demonstrate that the Bible is not reliable as a historical source (Golden 2009).

The second approach recognizes the frequency of allusions to the Bible appearing in Western literature and art. For example, widely read literary works, like Hemingway's *Old Man and the Sea*, contain biblical allegories that may be more fully appreciated when the reader is familiar with the New Testament. Similarly, the third approach, cultural studies and tradition-based approach, also acknowledges the pervasive nature of the Bible in the American cultural canon: from St. Patrick's Cathedral and the history of church architecture to classic paintings like DaVinci's *The Last Supper* to traditional popular songs like "Go Down Moses" and the musical *Joseph and the Techni-color Dreamcoat* and *Jesus Christ, Superstar*.

In recent years, there has been a renewed push to reinsert Bible Studies into public school curricula. Multiple states, including Florida, Kentucky, Indiana, Missouri, North Dakota, Virginia, and West Virginia, have considered legislation not only allowing but also requiring Bible Studies as part of the curriculum. North Dakota's Senate Bill 2136, for instance, required that students complete half a unit on Bible Study, along with one unit each of Algebra II, Biology, and World History, and of three required units of Social Studies, one half unit could be replaced with Bible Studies. In 2019, Bill 373 was introduced to the Indiana State Senate, proposing that secondary public school students may receive elective academic credits for released time religious instruction classes if certain conditions are met (http://iga.in.gov/legislative/2019/bills/senate/373#digest-heading).

This movement is supported by public officials and lawmakers such as Aaron McWilliams, Republican state representative of North Dakota and co-sponsor of Bill 2136, who said, "The Bible is an integral part of our society and deserves a place in the classroom" (quoted in *USA Today*). Religious groups, particularly Evangelicals, point to what they perceive as an environment that is hostile toward religion and justify their efforts to inject Christianity into the public schools as a response to unfair prohibitions against religion in the curricula. See, for instance, the *Christian Observer* 2019 article denouncing "the exclusion of Christianity in politically correct education" (Renfro 2019).

Opponents, such as Americans United for the Separation of Church and State, on the other hand, see these bills as part of a coordinated effort to insert Christian beliefs and values into the schools (e.g., see Clarkson 2018). The American Civil Liberties Union (ACLU) has pointed to a document called the "Report and Analysis on Religious Freedom Measures Affecting Prayer and Faith in America" as evidence in support of this assertion. This report, produced jointly by the National Prayer Caucus Foundation and National Legal Foundation, among other groups, also calls for the posting of signs saying "In God We Trust" in schools. Critics of pro-Bible Studies legislation argue that by this same logic regarding the need for basic religious literacy, American students should be conversant in a range of world religions. This is especially true as the U.S. population becomes increasingly diverse in its religious composition. It is noteworthy that most public schools offer students little to no exposure to non-Western sacred books, such as the Bhagavad Gita and Quran, in fact, there is often strong opposition to the teaching of Islam. Including lessons on other faiths in the curriculum is one way of navigating First Amendment concerns by avoiding preferentialism and thus violations of the Establishment Clause.

In some cases, organizations dedicated to promoting Bible classes have attempted to create their own curriculum. The National Council on Bible Curriculum in Public Schools (NCBCPS), for example, was created with the aim of bringing a "state certified Bible course (elective) into the public high schools nationwide" and to ensure that "reliable information" is available (National Council on Bible Curriculum in Public Schools, n.d.). According to NCBCPS, the curriculum has been endorsed by prominent national Christian leaders such as D. James Kennedy, Joyce Meyer, Jerry Falwell (see "Falwell, Jerry"), and John Hagee (Ridenour 2001). The curriculum, however, has faced serious criticism and multiple legal challenges. Law professor Amanda Colleen Brown reviewed NCBCPS' "Bible in History and Literature" curricula (Brown 2007: 193) using three different legal tests applied by the Supreme Court to determine the legality of Bible courses, concluding that the NCBCPS curriculum is unfit for use in the classrooms of public schools. "Given that the curriculum has a sectarian nature and promotes religious viewpoints," she argues, "the fact that the Bible serves as the only text makes the effect of the advancement of religion even more likely." An alternative curriculum called "The Bible and Its Influence," offered by the Bible Literacy Project, has been vetted by numerous scholars and education officials and is widely accepted and praised (Essentials in Education.org, n.d.).

See also: *Abington School District v. Schempp* (1963); Religious Diversity in the United States

Further Reading

AAR Guidelines for Teaching about Religion in K-12 Schools in the United States. Produced by the AAR Religion in the Schools Task Force; Diane L. Moore, Chair. Copyright © 2010 American Academy of Religion. https://aarweb.org/common/Uploaded%20files/Publications%20and%20News/Guides%20and%20Best%20Practices/AARK-12CurriculumGuidelinesPDF.pdf.

Brown, Amanda Colleen. "Losing My Religion: The Controversy over Bible Classes in Public Schools." *Baylor Law Review* 59(2007): 194–240.

Clarkson, Frederick. "'Project Blitz' Seeks to Do for Christian Nationalism What ALEC Does for Big Business Religion Dispatches." 2018. https://religiondispatches.org/project-blitz-seeks-to-do-for-christian-nationalism-what-alec-does-for-big-business/.

Essentials in Education.org. "Teach the Bible in a First Amendment Safe Course." n.d. https://www.essentialsineducation.org/.

Golden, Jonathan Michael. *Ancient Canaan and Israel : An Introduction*. Oxford: Oxford University Press, 2009.

Haynes, Charles. *Finding Common Ground: A First Amendment Guide to Religion & Public Education*. Darby, PA: Diane Publishing, 1997.

Indiana State Senate Bill 373 Authored by Sen. Dennis Kruse, Sen. Jeff Raatz. Sponsored by Rep. Timothy Wesco, Rep. Jack Jordan, Rep. John Bartlett, Rep. Christy Stutzman. 2019.

National Council on Bible Curriculum in Public Schools. n.d. https://www.bibleinschools.net/index.php.

Notley, R. Steven. "Pontius Pilate: Sadist or Saint?" *Biblical Archaeology Review* 43, no. 4 (August 7, 2017): 40–60.

Renfro, Joe. "The Exclusion of Christianity In Politically Correct Education." 2019. Accessed June 18, 2020. http://christianobserver.org/the-exclusion-of-christianity-in-politically-correct-education/.

Ridenour, Elizabeth. "Courts Pave Way for Bible Curriculum in America's Public Schools." *AFA Journal*, February 2001. https://afajournal.org/past-issues/2001/february/courts-pave-way-for-bible-curriculum-in-america-s-public-schools/.

Simonds, Robert, "Teaching the Bible in Public Schools?" Institute for Creation Research. 1996. https://www.icr.org/article/teaching-bible-public-schools/.

Christian Coalition of America

The Christian Coalition of America is an organization designed to advocate for Christian positions and values in politics. The Coalition describes as its goal identifying, educating, and mobilizing Christians for effective political action ("About Us | Christian Coalition," n.d.). To this end, the Coalition distributes voter guides throughout the United States, lobbies Congress and the White House on issues of concern, and conducts training seminars and other events to draw supporters and organize activists.

The central mission of the Coalition is advocating for legislation and political action that it believes is more "pro-family." These actions include ending what is commonly referred to as "partial birth abortion," improving American education, and lowering taxes ("About Us | Christian Coalition," n.d.).

FOUNDING AND BACKGROUND

The Christian Coalition of America is one of several evangelical Christian organizations that arose during the 1970s and 1980s as part of a broader social movement to restore conservative values, which the founders often characterized as being threatened or under direct assault by increasingly liberal and secular beliefs and practices within society.

The Coalition was founded in 1989 by religious broadcaster Pat Robertson, a year after his brief foray into national politics. Robertson had sought to be the Grand Old Party (GOP) nominee for president in 1988 but lost to the eventual nominee, George H. W. Bush, who went on to defeat Democrat Michael Dukakis in the general election ("1988 Presidential General Election Results," n.d.). In the years that followed, the Coalition grew to have great sway in Republican politics and, by the end of the 1990s, had played major roles in the elections of numerous candidates by way of information and grassroots organizational efforts ("Christian Coalition," n.d.).

The Coalition's distribution of voter guides has been one of its most effective strategies in shaping the outcome of elections. In 2000, the organization distributed nearly 70 million guides, which included information designed to "give voters a clear understanding of where candidates stand on important pro-family issues" before casting their ballots ("About Us | Christian Coalition," n.d.). By some measures, the Coalition's voter information campaign may have helped the GOP gain control of Congress in the 2002 elections ("Christian Coalition," n.d.).

PAST ACTIVITIES

While much of the Christian Coalition's work centers on elections and ensuring strong voter turnout for candidates aligned with its goals and mission, the organization has also dedicated efforts to influencing legislation. In 1997, for example, the group rallied in Washington, D.C., to push for the passage of a proposed "religious freedom" amendment to the Constitution. The amendment, introduced by Representative Ernest Istook, a Republican from Oklahoma, would have explicitly allowed prayer in public school, religious symbols on government property, and tax dollars for private religious schools (Seelye 1997). Ralph Reed, then executive director of the Christian Coalition, said the group's goal was to "deluge Capitol Hill with over a million petitions, telegrams and phone calls" to move the proposed amendment to vote before the 1998 election. Reed added that there was "no issue that will take a back seat to seeing a day when every child in America can bow their head and begin their day in a public school with prayer" ("Christian Coalition Kicks Off National School Prayer Campaign" 1997).

The organization has also taken aim at public education more broadly, advocating for school voucher programs and offering workshops aimed at teaching voters and elected leaders how to promote such programs. School voucher programs allow parents to send their children to private schools, including religiously affiliated schools, using funding that would ordinarily be set aside for the students' public education (see "School Vouchers").

In addition to lobbying for legislation, the Coalition has offered "candidate-training seminars" intended for individuals wishing to run for elected office, including on local school boards. These seminars instructed potential candidates on how to fundraise, canvass, recruit volunteers, and get voters to the polls to secure board seats (Deckman 2004).

RECENT ACTIVITIES

While the Christian Coalition is still an active voice in American politics, it has seen a decline in the strength of its organization since its peak in the 1990s. In the early 2000s, several state chapters of the coalition began to break ties with the national organization, owing in part to what chapter leaders saw as the organization "drifting to the left" and broadening its mission to include nontraditional causes, such as Internet neutrality and the environment (Jarvie 2006).

See also: *Abington School District v. Schempp* (1963); Bible Study; Evolution, Teaching; First Amendment; Prayer in School; School Vouchers

Further Reading

"1988 Presidential General Election Results." n.d. Accessed August 22, 2020. https://uselectionatlas.org/RESULTS/national.php?year=1988.

"About Us | Christian Coalition." Christian Coalition. n.d. Accessed July 9, 2020. https://uncaccoalition.org/about-us.

"Christian Coalition." Law Library: American Law and Legal Information. n.d. Accessed July 9, 2020. https://law.jrank.org/pages/5212/Christian-Coalition.html.

"Christian Coalition Kicks Off National School Prayer Campaign." *Jewish News of Northern California*, May 30, 1997. https://www.jweekly.com/1997/05/30/christian-coalition-kicks-off-national-school-prayer-campaign/.

Deckman, Melissa M. *School Board Battles: The Christian Right in Local Politics*. Washington, DC: Georgetown University Press, 2004.

Jarvie, Jenny. "Christian Coalition Is Splintering." *Los Angeles Times*, September 5, 2006. https://www.latimes.com/archives/la-xpm-2006-sep-05-na-coalition5-story.html.

Seelye, Katharine Q. "Religion Amendment Is Introduced." *New York Times*, May 9, 1997, sec. A.

Comparative Religion and World Religion, Teaching in Schools

In numerous Supreme Court cases over the past 60 years, the Court has clearly ruled that it is unconstitutional to teach religion in public schools. These rulings were in response to growing challenges against schools that required mandatory devotional Bible reading, that started the school day with prayer, and other overtly religious practices.

At issue in these cases were both the Establishment Clause and the Free Exercise Clause of the First Amendment. The courts held that a public school could not partake in any activity that gave the impression of endorsing or encouraging a specific religion ("Establishment"), nor could the school penalize a student who declined to participate in such activities ("Free Exercise") (see "First Amendment").

Since the first rulings in the 1960s, many people have understood them, and similar rulings have followed, to mean that the very subject of religion could not be mentioned in schools. But, in fact, even the justices who handed down these landmark rulings recognized the value of students learning about religion.

In *Abington v. Schempp*, the 1963 case that ruled mandatory Bible reading as unconstitutional, Justice Tom Clark wrote for the majority that "it might well be said that one's education is not complete without a study of comparative religion or the history of religion and its relationship to the advancement of civilization" ("School Dist. of Abington Tp. v. Schempp, 374 U.S. 203 (1963)," n.d.; "School District of Abington Township, Pennsylvania v. Schempp," n.d.). In other words, while a school may not teach religion in a devotional or doctrinal way, it is appropriate (and legal) to teach *about* religion (see "*Abington School District v. Schempp* (1963)").

Such instruction may occur in a variety of contexts, from a discussion of Puritanism in early American history to a reading of Anglo-Saxon religious poetry as a prelude to a study of *Beowulf*. In the view of the Supreme Court, as long as the instruction is secular, objective, and neutral in nature and not intended to indoctrinate students into a particular religion or to proselytize, it falls within constitutional limits.

WORLD RELIGION/COMPARATIVE RELIGION CURRICULUM

One way in which a school might teach about religion in a more formal but still constitutional manner is by offering classes in world religions or comparative religion as part of its curriculum.

In such a course, students would learn about multiple religious traditions and would use this knowledge to develop a greater understanding of subjects spanning the disciplines, such as art, literature, history, sociology, philosophy, politics, and even science and math. The course would, ideally, expose students to traditions beyond the most popular world religions, such as the Abrahamic faiths, and give them an opportunity to better understand, and perhaps even sympathize with, other people's experiences.

In its publication, *A Teacher's Guide to Religion in the Public Schools*, the First Amendment Center cites guidelines issued by a coalition of 17 major religious and educational organizations that indicate why religion instruction ought to be included in public school curricula:

> Because religion plays a significant role in history and society, study about religion is essential to understanding both the nation and the world. Omission of facts about religion can give students the false impression that the religious life of humankind is insignificant or unimportant. Failure to understand even the basic symbols, practices, and concepts of the various religions makes much of history, literature, art, and contemporary life unintelligible.
>
> Study about religion is also important if students are to value religious liberty, the first freedom guaranteed in the Bill of Rights. Moreover, knowledge of the roles of religion in the past and present promotes cross-cultural understanding essential to democracy and world peace. (quoted in Haynes 2004)

Worth noting is that the coalition that authored this statement includes a wide variety of religious and secular voices, such as the American Academy of Religion (AAR), the American Association of School Administrators, the American Federation of Teachers, the American Jewish Congress, the Baptist Joint Committee on Public Affairs, the Christian Legal Society, the Church of Jesus Christ of Latter-day Saints, the National Association of Evangelicals, and the National Conference of Christians and Jews, among others. In other words, there is broad support among both religious and nonreligious Americans for at least some level of education about religion in public schools.

So the question many schools and teachers might have when considering a course or unit in world religions or comparative religion is not *whether* they should teach such material but *how*.

RECOGNIZING THE VALUE AND PURPOSE OF TEACHING ABOUT RELIGION

First, schools and teachers must understand the point of offering instruction about religion. Noted scholar and educator Philip H. Phenix once wrote that "[e]very scholarly endeavor serves some human purpose," and therefore, one must fully consider the purpose of teaching comparative religion. He identified five purposes that could be said to have "sparked" comparative study of religion: (1) to propagate a faith, (2) to undermine the claims of all religions, (3) to gain an understanding of religion, (4) to find a more adequate personal faith, and (5) to satisfy a social or political concern (Phenix 1957).

Of the reasons Phenix proposed, three are unconstitutional on their faces. The Supreme Court has stated, in no uncertain terms, that a school may not endorse a particular faith, disparage a particular faith, or guide students in any sort of doctrinal or devotional study of faith. The reasons that remain (to further understanding of religion, as a whole, and to address the needs of an increasingly diverse and pluralistic society) are the only ones that would be appropriate in an American public school.

The AAR, in its publication, *Guidelines for Teaching about Religion*, proposed that education about religion would improve religious literacy, which could, in turn, improve communication and relationships among people of differing traditions. While the AAR acknowledges that religious illiteracy is not the only cause of bigotry and violence in society, it argues that it is still a significant contributor and can be linked to anti-Semitism, Islamophobia, and even inter-denominational disputes, such as those between Protestant and Roman Catholic Christians or Sunni and Shia Muslims (*Guidelines for Teaching about Religion in K-12 Public Schools in the United States* 2010).

TEACHER TRAINING AND EDUCATION

Before any school embarks on a journey of developing a curriculum that includes teaching about religion, its teachers must be thoroughly and appropriately trained. The Association for Supervision and Curriculum Development noted in 2002 that while the discussion of teaching about religion was not new, "teacher training [lagged] far behind" (Douglass 2002). The association urged preservice and in-service training to increase teachers' knowledge and comfort level with the material.

To this end, the association added, teachers need to have access to high-quality curriculum and instructional resources, which must come as a product of collaboration among multiple parties, including scholars of religion, educators, and members of diverse faith communities.

In response to this need for better teacher training, colleges and universities have developed programs to teach educators how to effectively and sensitively teach about religion in their classrooms. Harvard Divinity School, for instance, trained educators in this field through its Program in Religion and Secondary Education (PRSE) for nearly 40 years. Diane L. Moore, a lecturer at Harvard Divinity School, and onetime director of the PRSE, suggested that one of the hurdles to effectively teaching about religion is that many people are "deeply and broadly religiously illiterate" and often know little about their own faith traditions, let alone the faith traditions of others (Brustman 2006). In the program, educators learned how to impart information about religion to students in a way that is legal, constitutional, and educationally sound. The program also encouraged educators to recognize religious diversity and to focus on "the intersection of religion, history, and culture" (Brustman 2006).

Moore has been involved in other similar programs, such as the Hartford Teacher Education Project, a four-year program (2013–2016) that worked with middle and secondary school teachers in the greater Hartford area to provide teachers with a better grasp of and comfort with teaching about religion ("Diane L. Moore," n.d.). She now heads the Religious Literacy Project at Harvard Divinity School, where she has continued her work in training people from diverse professions to be more knowledgeable about religion and led the AAR's Task Force on Religion in the Schools, which published guidelines for teaching about religion in public K–12 schools ("Diane L. Moore," n.d.).

EDUCATION ABOUT RELIGION IN PRACTICE

Once a school recognizes the value of teaching about religion, and its teachers have been appropriately trained in the subject, the final step is putting it all into practice, a step that requires careful and precise consideration of both what is being taught and who is expected to learn from it.

The AAR suggests four approaches to teaching about religion: (1) the historical approach, which is commonly used in social studies classes; (2) the literary approach, which is most common in English language arts classes; (3) the traditions-based approach, which is often used in electives or stand-alone courses, such as comparative religion studies; and (4) the cultural approach, which is suited for classes that apply a multicultural lens of analysis (*Guidelines for Teaching about Religion in K–12 Public*

Schools in the United States 2010). All these approaches come with caveats and potential pitfalls, though, from oversimplifying the complexities of a faith tradition and selecting texts from a very narrow religious viewpoint to overlooking the evolution of a given tradition and allowing one's own religious experience to influence how a given source is interpreted or discussed.

In the context of a world religions or comparative religion course in a high school, a teacher might opt to use a combination of these approaches, so the teacher should be aware of all of their potential strengths and weaknesses. A teacher would need to be cautious, for example, to not limit the instruction to only the most widely observed traditions, to not use language that disparaged or praised the beliefs of a particular religion (intentionally or inadvertently), and to respond to student questions in an objective and neutral manner.

OBJECTIONS

Despite whatever evidence might exist to justify instruction about religion in public schools, there are some people and groups that have and continue to object to its inclusion in curriculum.

One objection to such courses is that they put all religions on the same level, so to speak, which some religious adherents see as inappropriate and offensive. Peter Kreeft, for example, a professor of philosophy and a convert to Roman Catholicism, wrote in 1988 that the field of comparative religion is the source of the "most popular of all objections against the claims of Christianity" (Kreeft 1988).

Kreeft ranked the world's religions by "how much truth they teach," listing Roman Catholicism as the most truthful, with Protestantism, traditional Judaism, Islam, Hinduism, Buddhism, several ethical positions, idolatry, and finally Satanism following. "To collapse these nine levels, he wrote, "is like thinking the earth is flat" (Kreeft 1988). To treat all religions as objectively "the same" would, according to Kreeft's argument, deny the uniqueness of any one religion—specifically, in Kreeft's case, Roman Catholic Christianity.

Another concern about classes in comparative religion is how they might classify given faiths. The Church of Jesus Christ of Latter-day Saints, for example, professes to be Christian, but a sizable segment of the American population denies this claim. According to the church, its adherents "worship God the Eternal Father in the name of Jesus Christ," and the church's founder, Joseph Smith, emphasized the importance of Jesus to the faith, asserting that "[t]he fundamental principles of [the] religion is the testimony of the apostles and prophets concerning Jesus Christ, 'that he died, was buried, and rose again the third day, and ascended up into heaven'" ("Are Mormons Christian?" n.d.). However, according to the Pew Research Center, nearly a third of Americans believe that Mormonism is not a Christian religion. Many Americans, in fact, consider the church to be less of a religion and more of a cult (Heimlich 2007). If a course on comparative religion were to include Mormonism in a unit on Christianity, or to identify it as a religion at all, chances are that at least some of the students and/or their parents may take it as an affront to their own understanding of their faith.

There might also be opposition to a course in world religions or comparative religion on the grounds that students might not be able to distinguish between doctrinal or devotional instruction and objective, secular instruction. The organization American Atheists, for instance, not only agrees that a "comparative religion class or a unit on the Bible as a literary work as part of a high school curriculum could very well be constitutionally sound" but also recognizes that the age of the students "is highly relevant to determining whether a discussion of religious matters is constitutional," adding that "[e]lementary school students will be less able to disentangle the teacher's role as an authority figure from the substance of the discussion than high school students" ("Schools: FAQ," n.d.).

Regardless of any objections that might arise, teaching about religion in public schools is protected by the Constitution and, as many experts suggest, might be essential to educating future generations in an increasingly diverse world.

See also: Abington School District v. Schempp *(1963); First Amendment; Religious Diversity in the United States; Religious Pluralism Teaching*

Further Reading

"Are Mormons Christian?" The Church of Jesus Christ of Latter-Day Saints. n.d. Accessed July 9, 2020. https://www.churchofjesuschrist.org/study/manual/gospel-topics-essays/christians?lang=eng.

Brustman, Bob. "Training Teachers to Teach about Religion." *Harvard Gazette*, February 16, 2006. https://news.harvard.edu/gazette/story/2006/02/training-teachers-to-teach-about-religion/.

"Diane L. Moore." Harvard Divinity School. n.d. Accessed July 9, 2020. https://hds.harvard.edu/people/diane-l-moore.

Douglass, Susan L. "Teaching about Religion." *Educational Leadership* 60, no.2 (2002): 32–36.

Guidelines for Teaching about Religion in K-12 Public Schools in the United States. Atlanta: American Academy of Religion, 2010.

Haynes, Charles C. *A Teacher's Guide to Religion in the Public Schools*. Nashville: The First Amendment Center, 2004.

Heimlich, Russell. "Mormonism Not a Christian Religion." Pew Research Center. November 2, 2007. https://www.pewresearch.org/fact-tank/2007/11/02/mormonism-not-a-christian-religion/.

Kreeft, Peter. "Answering Common Objections to the Uniqueness of Christianity." Catholic Education Resource Center. 1988. https://integratedcatholiclife.org/2013/06/dr-peter-kreeft-answering-common-objections-to-the-uniqueness-of-christianity/.

Phenix, Philip H. "Comparative Study in Religion and Education." *Comparative Education Review* 1, no.2 (1957): 7–10.

"School Dist. of Abington Tp. v. Schempp, 374 U.S. 203 (1963)." Justia Law. n.d. Accessed July 9, 2020. https://supreme.justia.com/cases/federal/us/374/203/.

"School District of Abington Township, Pennsylvania v. Schempp." Oyez. n.d. Accessed July 9, 2020. https://www.oyez.org/cases/1962/142.

"Schools: FAQ." American Atheists. n.d. Accessed July 9, 2020. https://www.atheists.org/legal/faq/schools/.

Creationism

Ever since Darwin first published *The Origin of Species*, his seminal work on evolution, in 1859, there has been resistance, largely from people of faith who see evolution as a contradiction of biblical views on the creation of humanity. This anti-evolution movement, known as "Creationism" because it holds to the biblical story of creation, gained momentum in the 1920s with the sensational trial *State of Tennessee v. John T. Scopes*, aka "the Scopes Trial" (see this volume).

Although the Scopes Trial ruled in favor of teaching evolution, practically speaking, the strong backlash to the decision may have had the adverse effect. Publishers were pressured to omit evolution from their textbooks, and once it was out of the textbooks, evolution fell out of the classroom. By 1930, five years after the trial, roughly 70% of classrooms omitted evolution (Larson 1999: 85).

Creationism begins with the basic belief that the universe, Earth, and all living things were created in their present form by God in six days as outlined in the Book of Genesis in the Hebrew Bible. Creationists attempt to refute Darwin's theory of evolution by arguing that there is insufficient evidence to support the model. Henry Morris, one of the founders of so-called creation science, in *The Biblical Basis for Modern Science* (2002, defends the literal truth of the Bible and, writing with John Whitcomb in *The Genesis Flood*, presents Noah's flood as a real event that can explain most geological formations seen today. Young Earth Creationism is another core concept of Creationism, positing that Earth is no more than 10,000 years old.

Creationism also involves science denial. For example, creationists assert that there is a dearth of transitional fossils in the material record, "proving" that life forms are static. However, this overlooks important discoveries that do indeed represent transitions, or links, in evolutionary history. For example, the *Tiktaalik roseae* is a creature that developed a skull, neck, ribs, and pectoral fin roughly 375mya, representing a transitional species between fish and land-dwelling mammals (tetrapods) (Daeschler, Shubin, and Jenkins 2006; Dalton 2006). Important discoveries of the past two decades, such as *Orrorin tugenensis* and *Sahelanthropus tchadensis*, represent a transition between chimps and humans (Brunet et al. 2002; Pickford and Senut 2001). Creationists also argue that evolution is unobservable, an assertion that has also proven false. Scientists, for instance, see antibiotic-resistant bacteria or mosquitoes that are immune to some insecticides. Some creationists deny the reality of the fossil record altogether, arguing that fossils have been planted on Earth by Satan to tempt men from God.

Creationists have pushed not only to keep evolution out of the school curriculum but also to put Creationism in. The push to insert Creationism into school curriculum, however, has suffered a series of setbacks from the courts. In the 1968 case, *Epperson v. Arkansas*, the U.S. Supreme Court invalidated an Arkansas statute that prohibited the teaching of evolution and, in 1981, in *Segraves v. State of California*, the Court denied a claim that teaching evolution infringed on another's free exercise of religion. The following year, in *McLean v. Arkansas Board of Education*, a federal court held that an Arkansas statute requiring "balanced treatment" be given to "creation-science" and "evolution-science" in public schools violated the Establishment Clause. The decision involved a detailed definition of the term "science," which excluded "creation science," and ruled that the statute did not have a secular purpose, citing its use of language peculiar to creationist literature. In the 1987 landmark case, *Edwards v. Aguillard*, the Supreme Court ruled Louisiana's "Creationism Act" unconstitutional. This statute had required that unless accompanied by instruction in "creation science," the teaching of evolution was otherwise prohibited in public schools (see "*Edwards v. Aguillard*"). The Court determined this to be an endorsement of religion in its advancement of the belief that a supernatural being created humankind. At the time, the decision was widely hailed as a ban on the teaching of Creationism, soon reinforced by a set of district court decisions prohibiting Creationism, namely *Webster v. New Lenox School District* (1990) and *Peloza v. Capistrano School District* (1994). Traditional creationism lost steam after these decisions only to reemerge as so-called Intelligent Design shortly thereafter (see this volume).

Resistance to evolution in the United States is relatively high compared to other Western nations (Coyne 2012). When Gallup in 1982 first asked Americans questions about their beliefs in these terms, over three-quarters of Americans said they believe God was involved in man's creation, with 44% taking a strict literalist view of creation and 38% believing in "theistic evolution," that is, God has guided the evolutionary process, and only 9% believing in biological evolution. According to a 2012 Gallup poll (Newport 2012), these views have changed little in the ensuing decades with 46% of Americans the creationist view, 3% theistic view, with a slight increase, to 15% of people believing in evolution.

There are several reasons behind the resistance to Darwin's theory of evolution, all related in one way or another to religious beliefs. For one, it challenges the divine word of the Bible and obviates the role of God as sole creator. It also promotes the semblance of a morally indifferent world with forces like random genetic mutation and deterministic laws of natural selection. Stephen J. Gould, in a series of books, articles, and popular media, argued that evolution has no direction with human consciousness being little more than an evolutionary, albeit glorious accident (Gould 1977, 2007). Because the scientific theory of evolution has been used to legitimize atheism, it has been called "Darwin's dangerous idea." Daniel Dennett, in his book by this title (1995), asserts that creationists find unsettling the idea of a meaningless process and impersonal laws because this implies a subjective moral code and a universe with no inherent meaning.

(See also Harrold and Eve [1986] or Toumey [1994] for sociological explanations of the anti-evolution movement.)

Another problem for Creationism concerns its exclusive reference to the biblical account of creation as a singular alternative to evolution. As such, it ignores the ideas and beliefs about cosmology and the origins of the universe and humanity espoused by other faith traditions, thus favoring certain religions over others, thereby risking violation of the Establishment Clause.

See also: First Amendment; Intelligent Design

Further Reading

Begley, Sharon. "Two New Discoveries Answer Big Questions in Evolution Theory." *Wall Street Journal*—Eastern Edition 247, no. 81 (April 7, 2006): B1, 1/5p, 1c.

Behe, Michael J. *The Edge of Evolution: The Search for the Limits of Darwinism.* Reprint edition. New York: Free Press, 2007.

Brunet, M., F. Guy, D. Pilbeam, et al. "A New Hominid from the Upper Miocene of Chad, Central Africa." *Nature* 418 (2002): 145–151. https://doi.org/10.1038/nature00879.

Campbell, John Angus, and Stephen C. Meyer (Eds.). *Darwinism, Design, and Public Education.* East Lansing: Michigan State University Press, 2004.

Coyne, George V. "Evolution and Intelligent Design. What Is Science and What Is Not." *Revista Portuguesa de Filosofia* 66, no. 4 (2010): 717–20.

Coyne, G. "Science, Religion and Society: The Problem of Evolution in America." *Evolution* 66, no. 8 (2012): 2654–63.

Coyne, Jerry. "When Science Meets Religion in the Classroom." *Nature* 435, no. 7040 (2005): 275. https://doi.org/10.1038/435275a.

Daeschler, Edward B., Neil H. Shubin, and Farish A. Jenkins Jr. "A Devonian Tetrapod-like Fish and the Evolution of the Tetrapod Body Plan." *Nature* 440, no. 7085 (2006): 757–763.

Dalton, Rex. "The Fish That Crawled Out of the Water." *Nature* (2006). https://doi.org/10.1038/news060403-7.

Discovery Institute. "Discovery Institute | Public Policy Think Tank Advancing a Culture of Purpose, Creativity, and Innovation." n.d. Accessed June 19, 2020. https://www.discovery.org/.

Discovery Institute: Center for the Renewal of Science and Culture. "The Wedge." 1999. http://www.antievolution.org/features/wedge.pdf.

Epperson v. Arkansas 393 U.S. 97, 37 U.S. Law Week 4017, 89 S. Ct. 266, 21 L. Ed 228 (1968). n.d. https://www.law.cornell.edu/supremecourt/text/393/97.

Eve, Raymond A., and Francis B. Harrold. "Creationism, Cult Archaeology, and Other Pseudoscientific Beliefs: A Study of College Students." *Youth & Society* 17, no. 4 (1986): 396–421.

Gould, Stephen Jay. "Evolution's Erratic Pace." *Natural History* 86.5 (1977): 12–16.

Gould, Stephen Jay. *The Richness of Life: The Essential Stephen Jay Gould.* New York: WW Norton & Company, 2007.

Larson, Edward J. "Summer for the Gods: The Scopes Trial and America's Continuing Debate over Science and Religion." *Journal of the History of Biology* 32, no. 1 (1999): 220–222.

Matsumura, Molleen, and Louise Mead. "Ten Major Court Cases about Evolutionism and Creationism." National Center for Science Education. 2007. http://ncse.com/taking-action/ten-major-court-cases-evolution-creationism.

McLean v. Arkansas Board of Education 529 F. Supp. 1255, 50 U.S. Law Week 2412 (1982). n.d. https://law.justia.com/cases/federal/district-courts/FSupp/529/1255/2354824/.

Morris, Henry. *The Biblical Basis for Modern Science: The Revised and Updated Classic.* Green Forest, AR: New Leaf Publishing Group, 2002.

National Academy of Sciences Institute of Medicine. *Science, Evolution, and Creationism.* Washington, D.C.: Academic Press, 2008.

Nature. "Dealing with Design." 434 (2005): 1053.

Newport, Frank. "In U.S., 46% Hold Creationist View of Human Origins." Gallup.com. June 1, 2012. https://news.gallup.com/poll/155003/Hold-Creationist-View-Human-Origins.aspx.

Newton, Steven. "Creationism in the New Texas Standards for Earth and Space Science." *The Earth Scientist* 25, no. 2 (2009): 30–33.

Peloza, John E. v. Capistrano Unified School District 37 F. 3rd 517 (1994). n.d. https://law.justia.com/cases/federal/district-courts/FSupp/782/1412/2185854/.

Pickford, M., and B. Senut. "'Millennium Ancestor,' a 6-Million-Year-Old Bipedal Hominid from Kenya: News & Views." *South African Journal of Science* 97, no. 1–2 (January 1, 2001): 22.

Scott, Eugenie C. *Evolution vs. Creationism: An Introduction.* Foreword by Niles Eldredge. 2nd Edition. Berkeley/Los Angeles: University of California Press, 2009.

Shanks, Niall. *God, the Devil, and Darwin: A Critique of Intelligent Design Theory.* New York: Oxford University Press, 2004.

Toumey, Christopher P. *God's Own Scientists: Creationists in a Secular World.* New Brunswick, NJ: Rutgers University Press, 1994.

Webster v. New Lenox School District #122, 917 F. 2d 1004 (1990). n.d. https://law.justia.com/cases/federal/appellate-courts/F2/917/1004/350874/.

Wilgoren, Jodi. "Politicized Scholars Put Evolution on the Defensive." *New York Times,* August 21, 2005. http://www.nytimes.com/2005/08/21/national/21evolve.html.

D

Dawkins, Richard

In the discussion about religion in public schools, Professor Richard Dawkins has become somewhat of a de facto spokesperson for the cause of secularism and atheism. Raised in a community of religious faith, having attended an Anglican boarding school as a child, and being confirmed at 13 into the Church of England, Dawkins walked away from the church when he was 17 and has since spent a lifetime as an avowed atheist and vocal critic of religion, particularly in matters of public policy and scientific education.

Richard Dawkins was born March 26, 1941, in Nairobi, Kenya, the son of Clinton John Dawkins, a civil servant in the British Colonial Service, and Jean Mary Vyvyan née Ladner. Dawkins immigrated to England in 1949, where he has lived for most of his life, apart from a brief stint as an assistant professor of zoology at the University of California, Berkeley, from 1967 to 1969 ("Dawkins, Richard 1941–" n.d.).

By profession, Dawkins is an educator. With degrees from Oxford University, he has taught at Berkeley and has spent the majority of his academic career at Oxford as a lecturer in zoology and fellow of New College (1970–1990), reader in zoology (1990–1995), and Charles Simonyi Professor in the Public Understanding of Science (1995–2008). However, he is probably more well known in the United States as a fierce opponent of what he considers a threat to the "enlightenment," specifically in the form of "religious indoctrination" of young people in public school classrooms. ("NOW with Bill Moyers. Science & Health. Battle Over Evolution: Richard Dawkins Biography" 2010; "Richard Dawkins," n.d.).

Dawkins takes exception to the notion that America's founders intended for the nation to be anything other than secular. In his book *The God Delusion*, Dawkins is pointed in his criticism, writing, "The genie of religious fanaticism is rampant in present-day America, and the Founding Fathers would have been horrified. . . . [T]he founders most certainly were secularists who believed in keeping religion out of politics, and that is enough to place them firmly on the side of those who object, for example, to ostentatious displays of the Ten Commandments in government-owned public places" (Dawkins 2007).

In an effort to push back against the increasing presence of religion in the science classroom, Dawkins founded the Richard Dawkins Foundation in 2006, with the mission of "promot[ing] scientific literacy and a secular worldview" ("Richard Dawkins Foundation," n.d.). Through the foundation, Dawkins hopes to completely "remove the influence of religion in science education and public policy, and eliminate the stigma that surrounds atheism and non-belief" ("Richard Dawkins Foundation," n.d.).

Of particular concern to Dawkins is how science classes approach the issue of evolution. For example, Dawkins cites the 2005 case of Dover, Pennsylvania, where members of an elected school board had attempted to enforce the teaching of intelligent design in the schools. The effort was subsequently quashed by voters, drawing the ire of conservative pundit Pat Robertson, who warned that the people of Dover had "just voted God out" of their city. Dawkins worries that science is "under attack from a well-organized, politically well-connected and, above all, well-financed opposition" and believes that the teaching of evolution is in, as he puts it, "the front-line trench" (Dawkins 2008).

Dawkins also has taken aim at court cases that have relied too heavily on religion to support individual expression in public schools. In 2004, in Ohio, for instance, a 12-year-old boy won the right to wear a T-shirt that bore the words, "Homosexuality is a sin, Islam is a lie, abortion is murder. Some issues are just black and white" (Dawkins 2008). The court upheld the boy's right on the grounds that his wearing the shirt was an expression of his freedom of religion. Dawkins took the position that the boy's parents would have had a more "conscionable" case if they had based their complaint on the First Amendment's guarantee of free speech rather than turning to the Free Expression clause.

While Dawkins has garnered a great deal of support over the years from those who agree with his positions on science education, he has also attracted significant criticism from those who object to his stance as an atheist and those who challenge his rhetorical strategy. Douglas Todd, a writer for the *Vancouver Sun* in Vancouver, British Columbia, wrote in 2007 that Dawkins focuses "almost exclusively on the bad aspects of religion, creating a caricature of it." In 2008, Todd followed up on his original article, writing, "I have no trouble with someone being an atheist. It's quite a defensible position. It's just that Dawkins' brand of atheism is particularly prone to skapegoating [*sic*]. I don't agree with religious fundamentalists either. But can you be an atheist fundamentalist? I definitely think so. Fundamentalists of any sort are the problem, not religion" (Todd 2008).

Perhaps paradoxically, Dawkins might agree. While Dawkins has taken a hard-line position against the teaching of religion in the sciences, he has also been vocal in his support of education in comparative religion.

Dawkins has said that "understanding religion can help students get a better grasp of the world's history and culture" (Geggel 2017). He has gone so far as to say that "ignorance of the Bible is bound to impoverish one's appreciation of English literature" (Dawkins 2008). Dawkins does not view the presentation of religious history and doctrine as inherently detrimental to a well-rounded education. In fact, he's argued, it was comparative religion that led him to his own rejection of faith. He found that in learning about other religions when he was a young boy, he began to recognize that the Christian faith in which he was raised was "mutually incompatible" with other faiths (Dawkins 2008). This conclusion, he explains, was not a negative one. He writes, "Let children learn about different faiths, let them notice their incompatibility, and let them draw their own conclusions about the consequences of that incompatibility. As for whether any are 'valid,' let them make up their own minds when they are old enough to do so" (Dawkins 2008).

See also: Bible Instruction, Teaching in Schools; Creationism; Evolution, Teaching; Intelligent Design; Religion and Pseudoscience

Further Reading

"The Barbary Treaties 1786–1816: Treaty of Peace and Amity, Signed at Algiers September 5, 1795." September 5, 1795. http://avalon.law.yale.edu/18th_century/bar1795t.asp#1.

Carter, Claire. "Richard Dawkins Admits He Is a 'Cultural Anglican.'" *Telegraph*, September 12, 2013. https://www.telegraph.co.uk/news/religion/10303223/Richard-Dawkins-admits-he-is-a-cultural-Anglican.html.

Dawkins, Richard. *The God Delusion*. London: Black Swan, 2007.

"Dawkins, Richard 1941–." n.d. Accessed August 22, 2020. https://www.encyclopedia.com/arts/educational-magazines/dawkins-richard-1941.

Farndale, Nigel. "Is the Church of England Still in God's Own Country?" *Telegraph*, March 6, 2010. https://www.telegraph.co.uk/comment/columnists/nigelfarndale/7386930/Is-the-Church-of-England-still-in-Gods-own-country.html.

Geggel, Laura. "Why Atheist Richard Dawkins Supports Religious Education in Schools." June 12, 2017. Accessed August 22, 2020. https://www.livescience.com/59455-richard-dawkins-on-school-religious-education.html.

Muscato, David. "An Interview with Richard Dawkins." *American Atheist Magazine* 52, no. 1 (Winter/Spring 2014): 8.

"NOW with Bill Moyers. Science & Health. Battle over Evolution: Richard Dawkins Biography." April 2010. Accessed August 22, 2020. http://www.pbs.org/now/science/dawkins.html.

"Richard Dawkins." n.d. Accessed August 22, 2020. https://www.richarddawkins.net/richarddawkins/.

"Richard Dawkins Foundation." n.d. Accessed August 22, 2020. https://www.richarddawkins.net/.

Smith, Alexandra. "Dawkins Campaigns to Keep God Out of Classroom." *Guardian*. Last modified November 27, 2006. https://www.theguardian.com/education/2006/nov/27/schools.religion.

Todd, Douglas. "Controversy over Richard Dawkins Interview." *Vancouver Times*, April 29, 2008. Accessed August 22, 2020. https://vancouversun.com/news/staff-blogs/controversy-over-richard-dawkins-interview.

Whittell, Giles. "The World according to Richard Dawkins." *Times*, September 7, 2013. https://www.thetimes.co.uk/article/the-world-according-to-richard-dawkins-rnldds8vk2q.

Yester, Katherine. "Epiphanies: Richard Dawkins." *Foreign Policy*. Last modified October 7, 2009. https://foreignpolicy.com/2009/10/07/epiphanies-richard-dawkins/.

Devotional/Doctrinal Curriculum

Under the First Amendment of the Constitution, and affirmed by multiple Supreme Court rulings, public schools are expressly permitted and, to some extent, encouraged to teach about religion in their curricula.

In the Supreme Court case, *Abington v. Schempp* (1963), Justice Tom Clark famously wrote that "one's education is not complete without a study of comparative religions or the history of religion and its relationship to the advancement of civilization" ("School Dist. of Abington Tp. v.

Schempp, 374 U.S. 203 (1963)," n.d.; "School District of Abington Township, Pennsylvania v. Schempp," n.d.).

That said, in order to comply with the protections outlined in the First Amendment, any public school instruction regarding religion must be presented in a strictly neutral, secular, and academic way and may not be doctrinal or devotional in nature.

WHAT IS MEANT BY "DOCTRINAL"?

The origins of the word "doctrine" would seem to make it a natural fit for a public school setting. It derives from Latin and Old French words meaning "teach" or "teaching." In fact, the word "doctor" shares similar origins, with it coming to mean "learned person" by the middle ages. Taken at its strictest modern definition, "doctrine" means a belief or set of beliefs held and taught by a particular group.

Under this definition, one might argue that modern public schools do engage, to some extent, in doctrinal instruction, such as in a social studies class, in which students learn about shared American values, or when students recite the Pledge of Allegiance. On their face, both these examples can be defended as purely academic exercises, but depending on how they are presented by teachers, the ages of the students, and social climate of a given school, they could also be seen as means by which to "indoctrinate" students into a particular view of America (Meyrat 2018).

Doctrinal instruction, in a religious sense, would therefore be any instruction that could be used to teach students to accept or embrace a particular religious view.

One such form of instruction that has been denounced by civil liberties groups is the teaching of Creationism, creation science, or intelligent design in science classes (see "Creationism"). The Anti-Defamation League (ADL), for instance, has argued that because these three subjects are grounded in belief, and not in empirical fact, they should "not be taught as science under any circumstances" ("Religious Doctrine in the Science Classroom," n.d.). The ADL cites the National Academy of Sciences' definition of science as being limited to explanations "that can only be inferred from confirmable data—the results obtained through observations and experiments that can be substantiated by other scientists" (quoted in "Religious Doctrine in the Science Classroom," n.d.). With this definition in mind, they add, the only scientific explanation for the history of life on earth and, therefore, the only explanation that should be taught in a science class, is evolution.

The common argument against subjects such as Creationism and creation science is not that they may *never* be discussed in a public school setting but that they may not be presented as fact, as such a presentation might indoctrinate students to a particular religious worldview. In a course on religion, philosophy, or myth, for example, "[c]reationism and intelligent design fit squarely within this category of study" ("Religious Doctrine in the Science Classroom," n.d.).

Similar concerns of indoctrination sometimes arise when schools attempt to offer instruction in the history of a particular religion. A recent example of this situation occurred in 2017, in Chatham, New Jersey, when two parents complained that their children were being "indoctrinated in Islam," by way of instruction and homework assignments in their 8th-grade class. During one of the class lessons, students watched a brief animated video that taught the five pillars of Islam. In a homework assignment that followed, students were expected to fill in the blanks of a sentence about Islamic belief, which, when complete, would read, "There is no god but Allah and Mohammed is his messenger" (Katz 2017).

School officials defended the instruction as being required by state educational standards, but the parents enlisted the assistance of the Thomas More Law Center, a conservative law firm, to bring suit against the district (Zuckerman 2017). One of the parents involved in the suit claimed that the school had "'assailed' her child's First Amendment rights by forcing children to endure the promotion of Islam in their public schools, including an explicit and direct call to the children for conversion to the religion of Islam" (Hochron 2018), a claim which the district dismissed as "baseless" (Alexander 2018).

In 2018, U.S. District Court judge Kevin McNulty denied a motion by the defendants to dismiss the case ("Hilsenrath v. School District of the Chathams et al Court Docket Sheet," n.d.; "Hilsenrath v. SCHOOL DISTRICT OF THE CHATHAMS et al, No. 2:2018cv00966—Document 22 (D.N.J. 2018)," n.d.). As of June 2020, the case was still ongoing.

In November 2020, a New Jersey District Court Judge issued a summary judgment in favor of the school district. Hilsenrath appealed the decision, and in June 2022, the U.S. Court of Appeals for the Third District vacated the federal court ruling, with Chief Judge Michael Chagares and Justices Thomas Hardiman and Paul Matey writing that, in light of a 2022 Supreme Court ruling (*Kennedy v. Bremerton*), they were "remand[ing] this case to the District Court for further consideration" (Barmakian 2022).

Kennedy v. Bremerton pertains to high school football coach Joseph Kennedy and his practice of engaging in public prayer after school games. In their 6-3 ruling, the court held that Kennedy was within his constitutional rights, as the "free exercise and free speech clauses of the First Amendment protect an individual engaging in a personal religious observance from government reprisal; the Constitution neither mandates nor permits the government to suppress such religious expression" ("Kennedy v. Bremerton School District").

As of 2023, the case is under review by a federal judge.

WHAT IS MEANT BY "DEVOTIONAL"?

While doctrinal and devotional instruction are closely related, there is a distinction between the two. In the case of doctrinal instruction, the purpose is essentially teaching the core and fundamental beliefs of a system in such a way that students learn about and grow to accept these values as their own. Devotional instruction, on the other hand, could be described as instruction that goes beyond simply encouraging acceptance of a belief system and instead fosters a growth or development of that belief.

According to *The Encyclopedia of Christian Literature*, a devotional practice is one that may stimulate an individual's "access to and experience with the transcendent" (Kurian and Smith 2010), and devotional literature is that which stimulates "the production, sustenance, and direction of the unique interior Christian self, whether solely in relation to the divine or including also service to fellow believers, neighbor, and/or world" (Kurian and Smith 2010).

As numerous court cases and legal opinions have already determined, any such instruction in a public school class would be a clear violation of the Establishment Clause.

So, for example, a teacher could present students with the words of a prayer, as a way of demonstrating how a particular civilization or culture viewed its relationship to its god or gods, but the teacher would not be permitted to speak to the spiritual value or truth of the prayer. Similarly, a class might read a Christian allegory in a literature class and analyze it for the moral or ethical lesson it explores, but the instruction could not go beyond the scope of this sort of discussion, such as by asking students to accept the religious aspect of the work as true or spiritually significant.

A teacher in Ohio was dismissed from his position for crossing the boundary between discussion and devotion, among other reasons. John Freshwater, an 8th-grade science teacher, was released from his employment contract in 2008 for allegedly teaching creationism, actively participating in meetings of the Fellowship of Christian Athletes by offering "healing" services, and "preaching about Christianity while discussing the meaning of Good Friday and Easter" ("The Free Library," n.d.). Freshwater also allegedly used an electrostatic device known as a Tesla Coil to "mark the shape of a cross into the arms" of students, at least one of whom suffered "red welts, blistering, swelling, and blanching" ("201012–1-Recommendation_of_the_Referee.Pdf," n.d.), though Freshwater said he did not mean to burn a cross on any student's arm but rather meant to leave "a temporary X on the skin" as part of a science demonstration (Urbina 2010).

In Freshwater's case, much of the devotional instruction appeared to have been intentional, as school officials reported that his science classroom was "adorned with at least four copies of the Ten Commandments and several other posters that included verses from Scripture," and another teacher in the school said that Freshwater "advised students to refer to the Bible for additional science research" (Urbina 2010). However, a teacher might inadvertently provide devotional "instruction" when discussing religion in an ostensibly academic way, simply through his or her word choice, tone, or sharing of personal experience.

A teacher may not, for example, pray in the presence of students during the normal course of the school day. According to guidelines published by the U.S. Department of Education, "When acting in their official capacities as representatives of the State, teachers, school administrators, and other school employees are prohibited by the First Amendment from encouraging or discouraging prayer, and from actively participating in such activity with students" ("Guidance on Constitutionally Protected Prayer and Religious Expression in Public Elementary and Secondary Schools" 2020). The concern is that teachers, as authority figures within the school, serve as guides for student activity and behavior. When students see a teacher engaging in prayer, they might perceive an implicit encouragement or even directive to pray as well. Such encouragement, even if unintentional, would be in violation of the First Amendment's Establishment Clause.

See also: *Abington School District v. Schempp* (1963); Bible Instruction, Teaching in Schools; Creationism; *Lemon v. Kurtzman* Supreme Court Decision; Prayer in School; Religious Pluralism Teaching; Religious Texts as Literature and Research Sources

Further Reading

Alexander, Dan. "Chatham Schools: Accusing Us of Muslim Indoctrination Is 'Baseless.'" New Jersey 101.5. June 27, 2018. https://nj1015.com/nj-district-confident-it-will-win-lawsuit-over-islam-lesson/.

Barmakian, Ed. "Chatham Mom's 'Establishment' Case vs Chatham School District is 'Vacated' by Appellate Court; Sent Back to Lower Court." TAPinto: Chatham. Last modified August 3, 2022. Accessed April 28, 2023. https://www.tapinto.net/towns/chatham/sections/education/articles/chatham-mom-s-establishment-case-vs-chatham-school-district-is-vacated-by-appellate-court-sent-back-to-lower-court.

The Free Library. "S. v. Public school teacher in Ohio faces possible firing over religion in class." Retrieved April 28 2023 from. https://www.thefreelibrary.com/Public+school+teacher+in+Ohio+faces+possible+firing+over+religion+in...-a0182613987.

"Guidance on Constitutionally Protected Prayer and Religious Expression in Public Elementary and Secondary Schools." Policy Guidance. U.S. Department of Education (ED). January 16, 2020. https://www2.ed.gov/policy/gen/guid/religionandschools/prayer_guidance.html.

"Hilsenrath v. School District of the Chathams et al Court Docket Sheet." Docket Bird. n.d. Accessed July 9, 2020. https://www.docketbird.com/court-cases/Hilsenrath-v-School-District-of-the-Chathams-et-al/njd-2:2018-cv-00966.

"Hilsenrath v. SCHOOL DISTRICT OF THE CHATHAMS et al, No. 2:2018cv00966—Document 22 (D.N.J. 2018)." Justia Law. n.d. Accessed July 9, 2020. https://law.justia.com/cases/federal/district-courts/new-jersey/njdce/2:2018cv00966/365028/22/.

Hochron, Adam. "Teaching or Converting? NJ Schools' Islam Lessons Challenged." New Jersey 101.5. January 30, 2018. https://nj1015.com/teaching-or-converting-nj-schools-islam-lessons-challenged/.

Katz, Matt. "Allegations of Islam Indoctrination in Public Schools Spread to New Jersey." WNYC. April 10, 2017. https://www.wnyc.org/story/allegations-islam-indoctrination-public-schools-spread-nj/.

"Kennedy v. Bremerton School District." SCOTUSblog. Last modified June 27, 2022. Accessed April 28, 2023. https://www.scotusblog.com/case-files/cases/kennedy-v-bremerton-school-district-2/.

Kurian, George Thomas, and James D. Smith III. *The Encyclopedia of Christian Literature*. Lanham, MD: Scarecrow Press, 2010.

Meyrat, Auguste. "How Public Schools Indoctrinate Kids without Almost Anyone Noticing." The Federalist. October 26, 2018. https://thefederalist.com/2018/10/26/public-schools-indoctrinate-kids-without-almost-anyone-noticing/.

"Religious Doctrine in the Science Classroom." Anti-Defamation League. n.d. Accessed July 9, 2020. https://www.adl.org/resources/tools-and-strategies/religious-doctrine-science-classroom

"School Dist. of Abington Tp. v. Schempp, 374 U.S. 203 (1963)." Justia Law. n.d. Accessed July 9, 2020. https://supreme.justia.com/cases/federal/us/374/203/.

"School District of Abington Township, Pennsylvania v. Schempp." Oyez. n.d. Accessed July 9, 2020. https://www.oyez.org/cases/1962/142.

"201012–1-Recommendation_of_the_Referee.Pdf." n.d. Accessed July 9, 2020. https://ncse.ngo/files/pub/legal/freshwatertermination/201012-1-Recommendation_of_the_Referee.pdf.

Urbina, Ian. "Teacher with Bible Divides Ohio Town." *New York Times*, January 19, 2010. https://www.nytimes.com/2010/01/20/education/20teacher.html.

Zuckerman, Josh. "NJ Parents Take Legal Action against School Using False Claims of Islamic 'Indoctrination.'" National Coalition against Censorship. April 3, 2017. https://ncac.org/news/blog/nj-parents-take-legal-action-against-school-on-false-basis-of-islamic-indoctrination.

E

Edwards v. Aguillard (1987)

Edwin W. Edwards, Governor of Louisiana, et al., Appellants v. Don Aguillard et al. (*Edwards v. Aguillard*), 482 U.S. 578, is a Supreme Court case concerning the teaching of evolution and Creationism in public schools. The case, argued in December 1986 and decided June 19, 1987, involved a Louisiana statute requiring that "creation science" be taught in any public school where evolution is taught.

The teaching of evolution had been banned in several states until 1968, when the Supreme Court, in *Epperson v. Arkansas*, overturned a statute that prohibited its teaching. In 1981, the "Balanced Treatment for Creation-Science and Evolution-Science Act" was signed into law in Louisiana by Governor Edwin Edwards, mandating that if evolution is taught in a public school, creation science must be taught alongside it. A suit was brought against the state by high school biology teacher, Donald Aguillard, along with other teachers, parents, and religious leaders, on grounds that the law lacked a secular purpose and endorsed religious beliefs. The federal district court and then an appeals court ruled against the state before it finally went to the Supreme Court.

The Supreme Court applied the "Lemon Test" (see *Lemon v. Kurtzman*) as a guide for deciding this case. The first prong of the Lemon Test asks, does the law advance a secular purpose? Was it the Government's intent to endorse or disapprove of religion? Determining the intent and motive behind legislation, however, is often complicated. The state claimed that the law had a secular purpose: the promotion of academic freedom. The Court found that argument unconvincing, holding that the law did not advance the freedom of teachers to choose what to teach, nor did it advance the goal of teaching all evidence. In fact, they found that the law served to "diminish academic freedom by removing the flexibility to teach evolution without also teaching creation science even if the teachers determined that such curriculum results in less effective and comprehensive scientific instruction" (*Edwards v. Aguillard* 1987). The main author and legislative backer of the bill, Senator Bill P. Keith, repeatedly expressed his own religiously driven objections to evolution during legislative hearings, insisting he preferred that neither creationism nor evolution would be taught.

The Court found without merit "the contention that the Act furthers a 'basic concept of fairness' by requiring the teaching of all of the evidence on the subject." According to the majority, the law provided a discriminatory preference for teaching creation science and against teaching evolution. The statute, for instance, called for the development of curriculum guides and resource services for creation science but not for evolution. The act also provided unequal protection for creation science teachers, forbidding school boards "to discriminate against anyone who 'chooses to be a creation scientist' or teach creationism, while failing to protect those who choose to teach other theories or who refuse to teach creation science" (*Edwards v. Aguillard*). The act also restricted membership on the resource services panel to "creation scientists."

The majority opinion, written by Justice John Brennan joined by Justices Marshall, Blackmun, Powell, Stevens, and O'Connor (all but part II), held that the statute created an equivalence between scientific evidence and religious belief. The Court concluded that the objective of the law was to discredit evolution while promoting the belief that a supernatural being created humankind. Ultimately, the Court acknowledged that teaching a variety of scientific theories about human origins can be done with clear secular intent. "But because the primary purpose of the Creationism Act is to endorse a particular religious doctrine, the Act furthers religion in violation of the Establishment Clause" (*Edwards v. Aguillard* Page 482 U. S. 594).

Justice Antonin Scalia, joined by Chief Justice William Rehnquist, wrote a dissenting opinion defending Louisiana's assertion that the law had a sincere secular purpose—to promote a "balanced understanding of the origins of life"—and was not solely religious. "Our task," wrote Scalia, "is not to judge the debate about teaching the origins of life, but to ascertain what the members of the Louisiana Legislature believed." The dissenting opinion drew heavily on the testimony of Senator Keith, who believed that evidence for creation science is as strong as, if not stronger than, evolution but was being shortchanged by the schools. The dissent, in fact, attempted to turn the case on its head, suggesting that teaching evolution violates the Establishment Clause, calling evolution a cornerstone of secular humanism, a form of religion itself. The dissent also questioned the validity of the Lemon Test overall, noting the difficulties in determining legislative intent, when laws often have multiple and often conflicting motivations behind them.

An amicus brief filed by 72 Nobel laureates in the sciences and 17 science academies in support of Aguillard warned about the danger of conflating science with religion:

> Scientific education should accurately portray the current state of substantive scientific knowledge. Even more importantly, scientific education should accurately portray the premises and processes of science. Teaching religious ideas mislabeled as science is detrimental to scientific education: It sets up a false conflict between science and religion, misleads our youth about the nature of scientific inquiry, and thereby compromises our ability to respond to the problems of an increasingly technological world.

Justice Brennan also shared a concern that since attendance in public schools is mandatory, and thus, impressionable young schoolchildren are a captive audience, vigilance is needed to avoid entanglement with religious beliefs.

See also: First Amendment; *Lemon v. Kurtzman* Supreme Court Decision

Further Reading

Edwin W. Edwards, in his official capacity as Governor of Louisiana, et al., Appellants, v. DON AGUILLARD, et al., Appellees. No. 85–1513. Amicus Curiae Brief of 72 Nobel Laureates, 17 State Academies of Science, and 7 Other Scientific Organizations, In Support of Appellees Robert A. Klayman, Walter B. Slocombe[*], Jeffrey S. Lehman, Beth Shapiro Kaufman, Caplin & Drysdale, Chartered, One Thomas Circle, N.W., Washington, D.C., 2005 (202) 862–5000, Attorneys for Amici Curiae (La.Rev.Stat.Ann. §§ 17:286.1–17:286.7; West 1982).

Text of U.S. Supreme Court Decision: Edwards v. Aguillard: Argued December 10, 1986—Decided June 19, 1987. *Journal of Church and State* 29, no. 3 (Autumn 1987): 607–34.

Equal Access Act (Title 20)

By definition, a public school is a facility and entity that is paid for, and therefore effectively "owned," by the people in a given community, typically funded by a portion of the community's property tax revenue. As the school is a common resource, it would stand to reason that any one person or group wishing to use the school for any reason would be afforded the same rights and privileges as any other party wishing to do the same.

But on multiple occasions throughout American history, public school boards and other administrators have denied certain people or groups' use of school facilities while permitting use by others. This selective approval sometimes has resulted in situations that run afoul of the First Amendment, particularly as it pertains to free speech, and government endorsement or establishment of religion.

A school board might, for example, approve a student-led chess club to meet in classroom space during a school's lunch period but deny a Bible study club. Such a decision would, as the U.S. Supreme Court has held, essentially stifle the free speech rights of the Bible study club. On the other hand, one might argue that allowing a religiously oriented club to meet in school space might constitute a tacit endorsement of that religion, thereby violating the First Amendment's Establishment Clause.

To address this sort of situation, in 1984, Congress passed and President Ronald Reagan signed into law the "Equal Access Act."

In short, the law requires that any secondary school that receives federal funding and that has a "limited public forum" must not "deny equal access or a fair opportunity to, or discriminate against, any students who wish to conduct a meeting" ("20 U.S. Code § 4071—Denial of Equal Access Prohibited," n.d.). The law defines a "limited public forum" as existing whenever a school provides an opportunity for one or more non-curriculum-related student groups to meet during noninstructional time ("20 U.S. Code § 4071—Denial of Equal Access Prohibited," n.d.). So, in the previous example, because the school permitted one non-curriculum-related group (a chess club) to meet in classroom space during the lunch period, it would have to allow the religious group (Bible study club) to meet as well.

While the Equal Access Act appears to give blanket approval to any and all groups wishing to use school space, the language of the law does include some limitations.

To qualify as a student group protected under this law, (1) the group's meetings must be voluntary and student initiated; (2) the meeting must not be sponsored by the school, a government, or its agents, such as teachers and administrators; (3) any staff or faculty member in attendance at a religious meeting must be there only in a nonparticipatory capacity; (4) group meetings must not interfere with educational activities; and (5) nonschool persons may not direct or regularly attend the meetings ("20 U.S. Code § 4071—Denial of Equal Access Prohibited," n.d.).

For example, if students attempted to hold a prayer meeting in the front entryway of a school during a class period, the law would not apply, as the meeting would be during instructional time and would interfere with regular school operations, so the school would be within its rights to stop the meeting. Similarly, if a teacher recruited students for a lunchtime Bible study club and opened meetings with a prayer, the law would offer no protection because the club is not student initiated and the school representative in attendance is directing the meeting (and because the teacher is a representative of the school guiding students in prayer, such a club would also very likely be ruled as a violation of the Establishment Clause) (see "First Amendment").

ORIGINS AND EARLY YEARS OF THE EQUAL ACCESS ACT

In the 1980s, religious conservatives in America were engaged in a concerted effort to push back against Supreme Court rulings that they saw as removing religion from public schools (see *"Abington School District v. Schempp* (1963)"). These rulings had forbidden school-sponsored prayer and Bible reading and, in the opinion of several leading figures of the conservative movement, had contributed to the moral decline of American society.

Inspired by a 1981 Supreme Court case, *Widmar v. Vincent*, in which the Court struck down a policy at the University of Missouri at Kansas City that prohibited religious groups from meeting on university grounds, Republicans proposed the new law, and with bipartisan support from Democrats, many of whom did not want to appear anti-religion, the bill was easily passed.

The law faced its first major constitutional challenge in 1990, when the school administration at Westside High School in Omaha, Nebraska, denied a request from a group of students to form a Christian club. The administration argued that allowing the club would violate the Establishment Clause. The Supreme Court ruled that approving the club would not be a violation, though, because, under the language of the Equal Access Act, the club would be non-curriculum, student initiated and not directed by a school official ("Board of Educ. v. Mergens, 496 U.S. 226 (1990)," n.d.; "Board of Education of Westside Community Schools v. Mergens by and through Mergens," n.d.).

While the Equal Access Act was originally conceived to be a legal tool to protect religious groups that wish to use school facilities, it has ended up being pivotal to the formation of several secular clubs as well, specifically clubs that support the LGBTQ+ community (Blount 2006). Senator Orrin Hatch (R-Utah), one of the sponsors of the original bill, objected to such clubs being protected by the act and claimed at one point that school boards had a moral obligation to keep LGBTQ+ clubs out of schools. Hatch once told Utah governor Mike Leavitt that a gay and lesbian club using the Equal Access Act as a legal shield was "an unintended consequence" of the law (Sahagun 1996; Spangler 1996).

EQUAL ACCESS ACT IN ACTION

While the language of the Equal Access Act clearly prohibits schools from picking and choosing which clubs can meet in their facilities, some schools have still sought to bar certain groups, whether religious or secular.

In most cases, such a prohibition is unlawful; however, there is one potential scenario where it is not: should a school wish to prohibit the meeting of a particular non-curriculum-related club without violating the Equal Access Act, the school can amend its policy to prohibit *all* non-curriculum clubs. In doing so, the school would technically be giving all such groups equal access, in that they all would have none.

Some school districts have ended up taking this drastic step since the passage of the Equal Access Act. These decisions were usually met with significant resentment and discontent within the school community and, in some cases, protracted legal battles.

In 1996, for example, the Salt Lake City School District Board of Education voted to ban all extracurricular clubs rather than approve a gay-straight alliance club. Some Utah residents and state officials argued that a gay-straight alliance club would be a threat to the moral and religious fabric of the community and that the club would serve as a way for adult members of the gay community to "recruit" children (Sahagun 1996). The American Civil Liberties Union (ACLU) filed a lawsuit against the district in 1998, claiming that the ban violated the Equal Access Act because it was not truly universally applied, since some non-curriculum clubs were still allowed to meet, and that the policy was evidence of a "broader, unwritten, but very real policy prohibiting the expression of gay-positive viewpoints in any school setting," which resulted in a violation of students' right to free speech ("East High Gay/Straight Alliance v. Board of Education and East High School PRISM Club v. Cynthia L. Seidel (1999)" 2000). In 2000, the school board reversed its decision, and the ACLU withdrew its challenge (Tanner 2018).

In another case, in 2001, a school district in Southern California changed its policy to prohibit social and public service clubs from meeting on campus during the school day to avoid having to recognize a Christian club at one of its high schools. The decision was criticized by church group advocates, as were some of the many students affected by the change; nonetheless, under the Equal Access Act, the policy was legal and constitutional (Garrison and Borgatta 2001). The ban lasted only three months, however, because several members of the school board came to believe that the students' education would suffer if they were not able to participate in the types of service clubs that were included under the policy (Garrison and Borgatta 2001).

Despite more than 30 years of case law and legal precedent that clearly define what is required of the Equal Access Act, some schools continue to face challenges over policies that appear to violate the law, whether intentional or not.

As recently as 2019, a school in Dutchess County, New York, denied a student's application to start a Christian club. The student, a 9th grader at Roy C. Ketcham High School, argued that the decision was inconsistent with the school's goal of celebrating diversity and even cited the text of the Equal Access Act as the legal basis for her forming the club.

The student's family enlisted the help of the First Liberty Institute, a Texas-based legal firm that specializes in defending religious liberty. In a letter to the district, First Liberty reiterated the student's claim that a Christian club was protected under the Equal Access Act and ordered the school to stop denying her application. The district reversed its denial, and the club was allowed to meet, starting in January 2020 ("In Reversal, Dutchess School District Allows Student to Start Religious Club" 2019; O'Kane 2020).

See also: *Abington School District v. Schempp* (1963); First Amendment; Student-Initiated Prayer, Clubs

Further Reading

Blount, Jackie M. *Fit to Teach: Same-Sex Desire, Gender, and School Work in the Twentieth Century*. Albany: SUNY Press, 2006.

"Board of Education of Westside Community Schools v. Mergens by and through Mergens." Oyez. n.d. Accessed July 9, 2020. https://www.oyez.org/cases/1989/88-1597.

"Board of Educ. v. Mergens, 496 U.S. 226 (1990)." Justia Law. n.d. Accessed July 9, 2020. https://supreme.justia.com/cases/federal/us/496/226/.

"East High Gay/Straight Alliance v. Board of Education and East High School PRISM Club v. Cynthia L. Seidel (1999)." ACLU of Utah. Accessed October 5, 2000. https://www.acluutah.org/legal-work/resolved-cases/item/206-east-high-gay-straight-alliance-v-board-of-education-and-east-high-school-prism-club-v-cynthia-l-seidel (URL no longer active).

Garrison, Jessica, and Tina Borgatta. "Schools Ban Meetings of Service Clubs—Los Angeles Times." *Los Angeles Times*, June 15, 2001. https://www.latimes.com/archives/la-xpm-2001-jun-15-me-10853-story.html.

"In Reversal, Dutchess School District Allows Student to Start Religious Club." *Daily Freeman*, December 26, 2019. https://www.dailyfreeman.com/2019/12/26/in-reversal-dutchess-school-district-allows-student-to-start-religious-club/.

O'Kane, Caitlin. "School District Reverses Decision to Deny Teen's Christian Club at New York Public High School." CBS News. February 28, 2020. https://www.cbsnews.com/news/christian-club-denied-high-school-originally-no-religious-club-reverse-decision-outpouring-of-support-letters/.

Sahagun, Louis. "Utah Board Bans All School Clubs in Anti-Gay Move—Los Angeles Times." *Los Angeles Times*, February 22, 1996. https://www.latimes.com/archives/la-xpm-1996-02-22-mn-38753-story.html.

Spangler, Jerry. "Leavitt Joins Growing Chorus against a Gay Club at East." *Deseret News*, February 10, 1996. https://www.deseret.com/1996/2/10/19224399/leavitt-joins-growing-chorus-against-a-gay-club-at-east.

Tanner, Courtney. "How a Ban on Extracurricular Clubs in Salt Lake City Schools Led to 'an Important Milestone in Gay Rights' 20 Years Ago." *Salt Lake Tribune*, August 4, 2018. https://www.sltrib.com/news/education/2018/08/02/utah-high-school-blocked/.

"20 U.S. Code § 4071—Denial of Equal Access Prohibited." LII/Legal Information Institute. n.d. Accessed July 9, 2020. https://www.law.cornell.edu/uscode/text/20/4071.

Everson v. Board of Education of the Township of Ewing (1947)

Everson v. Board of Education of the Township of Ewing (1947) is a Supreme Court case concerning a New Jersey township statute authorizing the use of public funds to pay for transportation to and from private schools, including religious schools. The case raises several questions concerning both the First and the Fourteenth Amendments.

The case began when Ewing Township in New Jersey initiated a policy authorizing the reimbursement to parents for money spent on public transportation to and from school, whether those were public schools or private, the vast majority of private schools being Catholic schools. The appellant, Arch R. Everson, was a district taxpayer who filed suit challenging the statute on grounds that to reimburse parents for transportation to Catholic schools meant forcing district taxpayers to support and maintain religious schools and, thus, violated the First Amendment's Establishment Clause.

The Supreme Court handed down a 5–4 decision on February 10, 1947, in which it affirmed the strict separation of church and state while declaring that the township's statute did not violate the First Amendment. The majority opinion states:

> The "establishment of religion" clause of the First Amendment means at least this: Neither a state nor the Federal Government can set up a church. Neither can pass laws which aid one religion, aid all religions, or prefer one religion over another. Neither can force nor influence a person to go to or to remain away from church against his will or force him to profess a belief or disbelief in any religion. No person can be punished for entertaining or professing religious beliefs or disbeliefs, for church attendance or non-attendance. No tax in any amount, large or small, can be levied to support any religious activities or institutions, whatever they may be called, or whatever form they may adopt to teach or practice religion. Neither a state nor the Federal Government can, openly or secretly, participate in the affairs of any religious organizations or groups and vice versa. In the words of Jefferson, the clause against establishment of religion by law was intended to erect "a wall of separation between church and State." (Everson, Black 330 U.S. 1, 15–16)

It is notable that Black's decision cites Madison's "Remonstrance" and Jefferson's "Virginia Statute" as well as Jefferson's letter to the Danbury Baptist Association, from which the "wall of separation" language originates. Still, the Court determined that in this case, separation of church and state had not been violated. Justice Black wrote for the majority, famously stating that "the First Amendment has erected a wall between church and state. That wall must be kept high and impregnable, we could not approve the slightest breach. New Jersey has not breached it here."

Justice Black saw the statute as having a secular purpose and put forth what would come to be known as the "child benefit" theory, arguing that transportation is a form of "public welfare" extended "to all its citizens without regard to their religious belief." Therefore, a transportation benefit to the child, in his view, was similar to all other public services—police crossings guards, firemen, and sidewalks—that also benefit the child attending school. The Supreme Court revisited the child benefit test in 1968 in *Board of Education of Central School District v. Allen* when the Court upheld a policy whereby textbooks were purchased for and loaned to parochial school students. The Court concluded, "The law merely makes available to all children the benefits of a general program to lend school books free of charge," thus rendering students the beneficiary, not the schools.

Justice Robert H. Jackson wrote a dissenting opinion arguing there was no way to separate church and state in this case: "Catholic education is the rock on which the whole structure rests, and to render tax aid to its Church school is indistinguishable to me from rendering the same aid to the Church itself." The schools, he argued, give students "regular religious instruction conforming to the religious tenets and modes of worship of the Catholic Faith." Justice Jackson also pointed out that the schools' superintendent was a Catholic priest. Justice Wiley B. Rutledge also joined the dissenting opinion arguing that subsiding transportation was no different from subsidizing teacher salaries and other related expenses.

The *Everson* decision kicked off a rigorous debate regarding the distance between church and state and the original intent of the First Amendment. Some hold that strict separationists on the Court follow a version of the Establishment Clause history that can be misleading and question their reading of the Founders' intent (Drakeman 2010; Frank 1951). The non-preferentialist viewpoint holds that religion and state need not be entirely isolated, so long as no religion is shown preference. Law professor James M. O'Neill called the strict separationist view as espoused in Everson and other contemporary cases, "the greatest threat to our civil liberties in recent times," declaring, "No possible good can come to either religion or education by continuing to rely upon incantation addressed to the ghost of an imaginary constitutional amendment" (O'Neill 1947). Attorney Leo Pfeffer, the day's leading advocate for strict separation, wrote a spirited defense of the *Everson* decision in *Church, State and Freedom*, arguing that the non-preferentialist interpretation subverted the First Amendment.

Everson v. School District also involved questions related to the Fourteenth Amendment. In fact, the case is at the center of the process known as incorporation, whereby federal powers, such as First Amendment protections, were extended to state and local laws. In applying the Establishment Cause to a state statute for the first time, the Supreme Court asserted its reach into new territory. Moreover, prior to *Everson*, there were limited instances when church-state separation questions came into play in state and local affairs. *Everson*, in effect, opened the gates to an infinitely wider range of cases in which the First Amendment would be questioned.

See also: First Amendment

Further Reading

Annotation 2, First Amendment. Find Law, "Financial Assistance to Church-Related Institutions Under the First Amendment" https://constitution.findlaw.com/amendment1/annotation02.html.

Board of Education v. Allen 392 U.S. 236 (1968). n.d. https://caselaw.findlaw.com/us-supreme-court/392/236.html.

Corwin, Edward S. *A Constitution of Powers in a Secular State*. Charlottesville, VA: Michie, 1951.

Drakeman, Donald L. *Church, State, and Original Intent*. New York: Cambridge University Press, 2010. http://site.ebrary.com/id/10360053.

Dreisbach, Daniel. "Everson and the Command of History." In *Everson Revisited: Religion, Education, and Law at the Crossroads*, J. R. Formicola and H. Morken (eds.). Lanham, MD: Rowman and Littlefield, 1997, 609.

Everson v. Board of Education Ewing Township, 330 U.S. 1 (1947). n.d. https://caselaw.findlaw.com/us-supreme-court/330/1.html#15.

Formicola Jo Renee, Hubert Morken, William Bentley Ball, Angela C. Carmella, and Derek H. Davis. *Everson Revisited: Religion, Education, and Law at the Crossroads*. Lanham, MD: Rowman and Littlefield, 1997.

Frank, John. "Corwin: A Constitution of Powers in a Secular State." *DePaul Law Review* 1, no. 1 (November 1, 1951): 156.

George, Robert P. "Protecting Religious Liberty in the Next Millennium: Should We Amend the Religion Clauses of the Constitution." Loyola of Los Angeles Law Review 32, Rev. 27 (1998). https://digitalcommons.lmu.edu/llr/vol32/iss1/3.

O'Neill, J. M. "Church, Schools, and the Constitution." *Commentary Magazine*, June 1947 (01T00:09:00–04:00 1947). https://www.commentary.org/articles/j-oneill/church-schools-and-the-constitution/.

O Neill, J. M. *Religion and Education under the Constitution*. New York: Harper & Brothers, 1949.

Pfeffer, Leo. "Church and State: Something Less Than Separation." *University of Chicago Law Review* 19, no. 1, Article 2 (1951). https://chicagounbound.uchicago.edu/cgi/viewcontent.cgi?article=5727&context=uclrev.

Pfeffer, Leo. *Church, State, and Freedom*. First edition. Boston: Beacon Press, 1953.

Evolution, Teaching

Biological evolution refers to change in living organisms over time, typically through changes in heritable traits of biological populations over successive generations. In some cases, one species evolves into another species altogether, sometimes over millions of years. For some, evolution, and this last dimension in particular, poses a threat to religious beliefs about the creation of life and the universe, leading to backlash against the teaching of evolution in public schools.

The primary mechanism of evolution is natural selection, whereby, given genetic variation within a population, certain traits can confer greater likelihood of survival and reproductive fitness in specific environmental conditions. At the smallest level, this means changes in allele (gene) frequency. At the greatest level, this can refer to much larger speciation events, whereby new species evolve from a common ancestor. Microevolution typically refers to the relatively small variations or adaptations within a population, whereas macroevolution refers to major changes such as the extinction or generation of new species.

Sir Charles Darwin first proposed the theory of evolution in the mid-nineteenth century, building on a number of critical scientific advances of the day. For example, Charles Lyell's work in geology allowed for much more realistic estimates of the earth's antiquity, and Carolus Linnaeus developed a standardized system of taxonomy.

Darwin's ideas about evolution began to emerge after his voyage on the *Beagle*, which included a pivotal stop in the Galapagos Islands. There, Darwin not only observed general similarities between flora and fauna of the isles and the mainland but also noted variation. He collected 13 varieties of finches, clearly all members of a related group, but with easily observable differences in the form of their beaks, pointing toward one of the key mechanisms of evolution, isolation of populations, where they might be subject to varying environmental pressures. Darwin would later conclude that the Galapagos finches all descended from a common mainland ancestor, but faced with different habitats on each island, certain traits such as beak shapes and sizes meant greater likelihood of survival and reproduction. With parallel but distinct processes of genetic inheritance taking place on each island, and with little to no exchange between the isolated populations, over time, these populations diverged to the point of splitting into different species of finches. Darwin soon realized he had discovered the process he would call descent with modification by means of natural selection, specifically, adaptive radiation.

It is important to note that Darwin's theory developed in conversation not only with other members of the scientific community but also with breeders who helped Darwin conceptualize the mechanisms of selection. It is also worth noting that Darwin sat on his findings for years, hesitant to publish until a young, relatively unknown naturalist named Alfred Russell Wallace sent him a manuscript titled, *On the Tendency of Varieties to Depart Indefinitely from the Original Type*. It presented ideas rather similar to Darwin's, who was urged by colleagues to publish quickly. In 1859, Darwin published the *On the Origin of Species, by Means of Natural Selection*, followed in 1871 by *The Descent of Man*, which made clear that humans evolved in the same way as other species and over a very long period of time.

Around the same time as the publication of *Origin of Species*, but unbeknownst to Darwin and his colleagues, botanist (and monk) Gregor Mendel discovered the particulate nature of inheritance and mutation as a source of change, that is, the field of genetics. By the 1930s, genetics saw the development of mathematical models for variations in genetic structure that could be used to predict time (i.e., molecular or genetic clock). By the 1940s–1950s, as knowledge about genetics and DNA expanded, it fused with Darwinian theory to form what is known as neo-Darwinian theory.

The theory of evolution is supported by extensive record of archeological and paleontological evidence. The earliest fossil evidence for life on Earth dates back nearly 3.5 billion years (Schopf et al. 2018). The hominin fossil record begins over 5 million years ago with early bipedal forms appearing shortly after humans split with chimpanzees (c. 7mya). The earliest hominins were followed by Australopithecines, a genus represented by celebrated discoveries in the Great Rift System of East Africa (e.g., "Lucy") and in the caves of southern Africa. Multiple forms of early Homo species have also been identified, most notably *Homo habilis, Homo erectus*, and *Homo ergaster*, in addition to early forms of *Homo sapiens*, including Neanderthals and our own immediate ancestors. Most of these species appear to have originated in Africa and expanded into the Middle East, Asia, and Europe. Archaeological evidence for the use of stone tools, fire, and cave art represent increasingly complex human technology and, thus, the evolution of intelligence and culture.

There is considerable debate within the field about how to interpret this evidence. For example, with a limited sample size, it can be difficult to know when similar specimens represent two distinct species or variation within a species. It can also be difficult to determine when a change in the fossil record represents a replacement event, the intermingling of populations, or both. Despite these debates, there is broad consensus within the scientific field that fossils, archaeological evidence, and genetic data prove the evolution of bipedal hominids between 5 and 7 million years ago.

The theory of evolution, however, has faced resistance since the publication of *Origin of Species*. Pushback comes largely from religious quarters stemming from evolution's apparent contradiction of the biblical version of creation. According to philosopher of science Francisco J. Ayala, Darwin showed that "the directive organization of living beings can be explained as the result of a natural process, natural selection, without any need to resort to a creator or other external agent" (1994: 4). By the late nineteenth century, religious leaders and others warned that these new ideas about humans evolving independent of divine guidance would lead to the rise of immoral society. One clergy member at the time wrote, "[T]he Church would crash, the moral fabric of society would be torn apart, and civilized man would return to savagery" (Desmond and Moore 1992: 34). Similar concerns are still expressed in modern times. After the 1999 Columbine school shootings, Congressman Tom Delay said that such violence was inevitable as long as "our school systems teach children that they are nothing but glorified apes, evolutionized out of some primordial soup of mud."

Some of the resistance to Darwin's ideas actually stems not so much from his theory of biological evolution but rather in the way it was co-opted by so-called social Darwinists who projected the concept of evolution onto society, arguing that certain peoples and cultures were superior, justifying colonialism at the time. Darwin's own cousin, Francis Galton, used Darwin's concept of selection to advance ideas about eugenics. William Jennings Bryan, who famously argued against the teaching of human evolution in the Scopes Trial, was driven in large part by his rejection of social Darwinism and "survival of the fittest" models that he deemed racist (Fraser 2016; Williams 1936).

Classrooms have long been battlegrounds for science and religion. In 1925, the Scopes Trial, fought over the teaching of evolution in Tennessee schools, seemed like a victory for Darwinism and evolution, but in some ways, the opposite was true. In the years following the trial, Mississippi and Texas rapidly advanced efforts to prohibit the teaching of evolution, and Tennessee's Butler Law banning evolution was not repealed until 1967. Public sentiment about teaching evolution would not shift, in fact, until the late 1950s when, during the height of the Cold War, the Soviets launched Sputnik, alarming Americans into a sense that the United States had fallen behind in science and technology. The National Science Foundation funded the Biological Science Curriculum Studies, and by 1963, three new textbooks included evolution; it was soon back in most school curricula.

Recent years, however, have seen renewed efforts to inhibit the teaching of evolution. In some cases, religious groups have tried to persuade lawmakers to restrict the teaching of evolution and/or insert religion into science classrooms by exploiting misconceptions about the scientific method (McKay 2013). Anti-evolutionists have also attempted to attack evolution on evidentiary grounds, arguing, for instance, that if one species had morphed into another, the fossil record should reflect a greater number of intermediary forms. Eugenie Scott (2009), director for the National Center for Science Education, identifies four recurring themes in the ways anti-evolutionists operate. One theme is that if students or their parents object to a district teaching evolution, they can opt out. A second is the idea that teaching Creationism and evolution is a matter of fairness (i.e., "equal time"). For example, in *Edwards v. Aguillard*, the Supreme Court examined a Louisiana law requiring that if evolution be taught, Creationism must be given equal time. In Minnesota (*LeVake v. Independent School District 656*), a high school biology teacher claimed the district was discriminating on the basis of religion and impinging on his free speech when he was blocked from teaching "evidence both for and against the theory of evolution." The Court rejected this claim, citing extensive legal precedent requiring teachers to comply with their employing district's curriculum.

The third theme builds on the fairness approach, suggesting that teaching the controversy encourages students to evaluate all the "evidence," whereby they can hone their critical thinking skills. In 2005, the Cobb Country School District required that warning labels be placed on textbooks stating, "[T]his textbook contains material on evolution. Evolution is a theory, not a fact, regarding the origin of living things. This material should be approached with an open mind, studied carefully, and critically considered." When the school district was sued (*Selman v. Cobb*), the Court ruled that the disclaimers violated the Establishment Clause and ordered the stickers removed. The fourth approach involves the selection of text books, where inclusion of evolution has been controversial, and the quality of its treatment in textbooks varies considerably.

In the landmark case *Kitzmiller v. Dover School District*, a Pennsylvania district court ruled against teaching Intelligent Design (ID) and using an ID textbook, *Of Pandas and People*. The suit originated when the school district required that a statement endorsing ID be read in biology classes. Evidence presented at the *Dover* trial demonstrated that ID has immediate roots in traditional creationism. For example, it was revealed that early drafts of *Of Pandas and People* made regular reference to "creationism" and "creator," terms that were replaced with "intelligent design" and "intelligent designer" in the published version of the book. In December 2005, federal district judge John E. Jones III issued a 139-page decision ruling that ID cannot be taught in public school because it "cannot uncouple itself from its creationist, and thus religious, antecedents." "ID is a religious and not a scientific proposition," wrote Judge Jones, and "it is unconstitutional to teach ID as an alternative to evolution in a public school science classroom."

See also: Edwards v. Aguillard (1987); Scopes Trial

Further Reading

Ayala, Francisco, John Howland Campbell, J. William Schopf, and Los Angeles. "Darwin's Revolution." In *Creative Evolution?!* IGPP Center for the Study of Evolution University of California. Boston: Jones and Bartlett Publisher, 1994. https://trove.nla.gov.au/version/44298451.

Darwin, Charles. *On the Origin of Species by Means of Natural Selection, or the Preservation of Favoured Races in the Struggle for Life*. London: John Murray, 1859.

Davis, Percival, and Dean H. Kenyon. *Of Pandas and People*. Foundation for Thought & Ethics. Dallas, TX: Haughton Pub Co, 1993.

Desmond, Adrian, and James R. Moore. *Darwin*. Penguin UK, 1992.

"Expert Witness (Kenneth Miller): The Scientists Who Testified against Intelligent Design." *Nature* 438, no. 7064 (2005): 11, 1p.

Fraser, James W. *Between Church and State: Religion and Public Education in a Multicultural America*. Second edition. Baltimore, MD: Johns Hopkins University Press, 2016.

Gould, Stephen Jay. *Ever Since Darwin: Reflections in Natural History*. New York: W. W. Norton & Company, 1992.

Gould, Stephen Jay. *The Structure of Evolutionary Theory*. Cambridge, MA: Belknap Press: An Imprint of Harvard University Press, 2002.

LeVake, Rodney v. Independent School District 656 (2000). May 8, 2001. https://talkcurriculum.files.wordpress.com/2014/09/judgement-levake-plaintiff-appellant-and-independent-school-district-656-defendants.pdf.

McKay, Casey. "Tactics, Strategies, & Battles—Oh My! Perseverance of the Perpetual Problem Pertaining to Preaching to Public School Pupils & Why It Persists." *University of Massachusetts Law Review* 8, no. 2 (2013): 442–64. https://scholarship.law.umassd.edu/umlr/vol8/iss2/3.

Miller, Kenneth. *Finding Darwin's God: A Scientist's Search for Common Ground between God and Evolution*. New York: Cliff Street Books, 1999.

Schopf, J. William, Kouki Kitajima, Michael J. Spicuzza, Anatoliy B. Kudryavtsev, and John W. Valley. "SIMS Analyses of the Oldest Known Assemblage of Microfossils Document Their Taxon-Correlated Carbon Isotope Compositions." *Proceedings of the National Academy of Sciences of the United States of America* 115, no. 1 (January 2, 2018): 53–58. https://doi.org/10.1073/pnas.1718063115. https://www.pnas.org/content/pnas/115/1/53.full.pdf.

Scott, Eugenie C. *Evolution vs. Creationism: An Introduction*. Second edition. Berkeley: University of California Press, 2009.

Selman, Jeffrey Michael v. Cobb Co. School District, 449 F.3d 1320 (2006). n.d. https://ncse.ngo/files/pub/legal/selman/appeal/amicus_briefs_P/20050606_American_Jewish_Congress_amicus_brief__selman_P.pdf.

Faith-Based Initiative

In the context of American federal policy, the term "faith-based initiative" most commonly refers to the White House program office established by President George W. Bush in 2001, the Office of Faith-Based and Community Initiatives (OFBCI).

The program was created by executive order on January 29, just nine days after Bush was inaugurated, and was followed with a second executive order establishing Centers for Faith-Based and Community Initiatives in 11 federal agencies. As Bush described at the OFBCI National Conference in 2008, the mission of these offices was to "lower the legal and institutional barriers that prevented government and faith-based groups from working as partners" ("President Bush Attends Office of Faith-Based and Community Initiatives' National Conference" 2008).

Bush, a devout Christian, had run on a platform that emphasized his religious faith and had even pledged in campaign literature to "[h]elp charities and faith-based groups serve those in need" ("George W. Bush for President 2000 Campaign Brochure" 2000). Specifically, he planned to "reform laws and remove regulations" that discouraged faith-based charities from providing services and to make it possible for "private and religious groups" to "compete to provide services in federal, state and local social programs" ("George W. Bush for President 2000 Campaign Brochure" 2000).

In the view of the Bush administration, an existing tangle of complicated rules and regulations that effectively shut out faith-based organizations (FBOs) was inherently unfair and a waste of taxpayer dollars that "cut off the poor from successful programs." "Federal funds," argued Bush, "should be awarded to the most effective organizations—whether public or private, large or small, faith-based or secular—and all must be allowed to compete on a level playing field" ("President Bush's Faith-Based and Community Initiative," n.d.). This applied to education as well, and in an effort to support struggling schools, the Federal Office of Faith-Based and Neighborhood Partnerships teamed up with the U.S. Department of Education and the Corporation for National and Community Service to create the Together Tomorrow School Improvement Challenge.

RESPONSES TO THE INITIATIVE

The public reaction to the establishment of the OFBCI was mixed. While many people and organizations lauded the program as a victory for the cause of religious freedom, others believed that the program threatened to violate the Establishment Clause of the First Amendment by essentially permitting tax dollars to fund religious organizations.

Richard Cizik, vice president for governmental affairs for the National Association of Evangelicals, argued that a government funding system that did not provide money to any FBO was, in effect, discriminatory. Bush's faith-based initiative program, he said, provided equality between religious and secular social service providers ("President and His Faith— The Faith-Based Initiative Controversy," n.d.).

Some African American religious figures viewed the program as a significant step toward combating poverty and as an "endorsement" of historically black churches. Sam Davis, pastor of the Beulah Grove Baptist Church in Augusta, Georgia, called the program a "confirmation," adding, "I believe that God is getting ready to redistribute the wealth to our economically hurting communities, and I am just grateful to President Bush" (D. H. Davis 2001).

Not all religious leaders were in support of the program, however. C. Welton Gaddy, for example, a Baptist minister and president of the Interfaith Alliance, took the position that the program was patently unconstitutional. He said in a 2004 interview with PBS, "[I]t presents problems related to the institutional separation of religion and government. The faith-based initiative effectively makes houses of worship and pervasively sectarian institutions employees of the federal government" ("President and His Faith—The Faith-Based Initiative Controversy," n.d.).

Several secular organizations expressed similar concerns. In addition to calling the program a violation of the "separation of church and state," the American Civil Liberties Union (ACLU) said the program was a "prescription for discrimination" because federal funding could go to organizations that are permitted to use people's religious beliefs and positions in making hiring decisions and in prioritizing how they deliver social services. Americans United for Separation of Church and State echoed the ACLU's sentiment, adding that the program could inadvertently fund proselytizing and open the door to federal regulation of religion ("Faith-Based Fiat" 2003).

Objections to the program did not end with constitutional concerns. Gaddy and several other religious leaders expressed concern that FBOs would be putting themselves in a compromising position by taking government money. Another concern voiced by some, such as the prominent evangelical figures Pat Robertson and Jerry Falwell, was that the program might result in the government funding "unconventional religious groups, such as the Church of Scientology and the Nation of Islam" (D. H. Davis 2001). Robertson called the program a potential "Pandora's box" that could rise up to "bite [religious] organizations as well as the federal government" (D. H. Davis 2001).

WHAT IS THE IMPACT OF THE INITIATIVE ON EDUCATION?

While Bush's faith-based initiative did not directly address matters of education, it set the stage for later programs and initiatives that did.

In 2001, Congress passed the No Child Left Behind (NCLB) Act, and in 2002, the president signed it into law. In an effort to improve the overall quality of education in America, and thereby make the American education system more competitive globally, the law called for an increase in the federal government's role in ensuring academic achievement at the state and school levels. This increased involvement included setting mandatory achievement standards for schools nationwide, measuring performance within smaller demographic groups (e.g., by race, disability, and socioeconomic status), rewarding high-performing schools with increased funding, and restructuring schools that consistently underperformed.

Under NCLB, schools that did not make adequate yearly progress were required to offer children in low-income families the opportunity to receive supplemental educational services (SES), such as tutoring and remediation. These services were to be provided outside of the regular school day and could be provided by public or private organizations, including faith-based and community-based organizations (M. R. Davis 2005).

With the encouragement of the Department of Education's faith-based office, religious groups that ordinarily would not have attempted to seek out federal funding began to apply to be state-approved supplemental educational service providers. According to the Department of Education, in January 2003, only 2% of state-approved SES providers were faith based, but by the end of 2004, that percentage increased to 15 (M. R. Davis 2005).

Religious groups that offered supplemental services, such as tutoring, were required to avoid "inherently religious activities" when working with students and to tutor students regardless of their religious beliefs. They could provide their tutoring services in church or other religious buildings but could not encourage students to attend religious services (M. R. Davis 2005).

The required separation between FBOs' religious missions and their tutoring practices was of little comfort to some, though. Barry W. Lynn, for example, the executive director of Americans United for Separation of Church and State, accused Bush of being on a "crusade to bring about an unprecedented merger of religion and government" ("Faith-Based Fiat" 2003). Lynn described the situation presented by faith-based tutoring programs as a "convenient way for religious organizations to get access to a large number of new potential churchgoers" (M. R. Davis 2005).

States vary widely on their interpretation of the faith-based initiatives in relation to schools. In 2014, Ohio governor John Kasich signed into law HB483, creating Community Connectors, a roughly $10 million program to bring mentors into Ohio's schools. The program initially required that all applications include as partners a school district (or charter school) plus a business and a place of worship or FBO in order to qualify, though this requirement would later be modified after the ACLU and other raised objections (Cleveland.com 2014). In a video announcing the program's launch, Kasich said, "The Good Lord has a purpose for each and every [student] and you're helping them to find it." Other states adhere to much stricter standards of church-state separation. New Jersey Office of Faith Based Initiatives, for instance, maintains information about grant opportunities on its website but lists schools as ineligible.

Aware of potential conflicts related to the First Amendment, the Government Accounting Office (GAO) offers clear guidelines on what is permissible with regard to FBO's use of direct government funds. Government funds may not be used to support inherently religious activities such as prayer, religious instruction, or proselytization. Any inherently religious activities offered by FBOs must be performed separately in time or location from services that receive federal assistance. Government funds may only be used to support the nonreligious social services FBOs provide, and they must be clear to keep separate accounting (GAO HHS.org). FBOs cannot discriminate on the basis of religion when providing services (GAO 2006: 13[3]).

THE FUTURE OF THE INITIATIVE

Following the end of the Bush administration, the OFBCI continued under President Barack Obama but with a new name: the Office of Faith-based and Neighborhood Partnerships. Obama's executive order on the matter reaffirmed the importance of faith-based and community organizations in addressing the needs of "low-income and other underserved persons and communities" ("Amendments to Executive Order 13199 and Establishment of the President's Advisory Council for Faith-Based and Neighborhood Partnerships" 2009).

The office remained in place until the election of Donald Trump. Trump did not appoint a director to the office, and in 2018, he issued his own executive order revoking both Bush and Obama's executive orders and establishing the White House Centers for Faith and Opportunity Initiatives ("Executive Order on the Establishment of a White House Faith and Opportunity Initiative" 2018). The language of Trump's executive order, while different from those of his predecessors, expresses similar support for faith-based and community service organizations, indicating that their effort are "essential to revitalizing communities" and welcoming opportunities for partnerships between such organizations and the federal government ("Executive Order on the Establishment of a White House Faith and Opportunity Initiative" 2018).

See also: First Amendment; School Vouchers

Further Reading

"Amendments to Executive Order 13199 and Establishment of the President's Advisory Council for Faith-Based and Neighborhood Partnerships." Whitehouse.Gov. February 5, 2009. https://obamawhitehouse.archives.gov/the-press-office/amendments-executive-order-13199-and-establishment-presidents-advisory-council-fait.

Cleveland.com. "Schools Need a Religious Partner If They Want Any of Gov. Kasich's Student Mentorship Money." December 12, 2014. Accessed June 19, 2020. https://www.cleveland.com/metro/2014/12/schools_need_a_religious_partn.html.

Davis, Derek H. "EDITORIAL: President Bush's Office of Faith-Based and Community Initiatives: Boon or Boondoggle?" *Journal of Church and State* 43, no.3 (2001): 411–22.

Davis, Michelle R. "Religious Groups Jump at Chance to Offer NCLB Tutoring—Education Week." *Education Week*, June 22, 2005. https://www.edweek.org/ew/articles/2005/06/22/41faith.h24.html.

"Executive Order on the Establishment of a White House Faith and Opportunity Initiative." The White House. May 3, 2018. https://trumpwhitehouse.archives.gov/presidential-actions/executive-order-establishment-white-house-faith-opportunity-initiative/.

"Faith-Based Fiat." Americans United for Separation of Church and State. January 2003. https://www.au.org/church-state/january-2003-church-state/featured/faith-based-fiat.

"George W. Bush for President 2000 Campaign Brochure." 4President.Org. 2000. http://www.4president.org/brochures/georgewbush2000brochure.htm.

"President and His Faith—The Faith-Based Initiative Controversy." PBS—*Frontline*. n.d. Accessed July 9, 2020. https://www.pbs.org/wgbh/pages/frontline/shows/jesus/president/faithbased.html.

"President Bush Attends Office of Faith-Based and Community Initiatives' National Conference." The White House (Archives). June 2008. https://georgewbush-whitehouse.archives.gov/news/releases/2008/06/20080626-20.html.

"President Bush's Faith-Based and Community Initiative." The White House (Archives). n.d. Accessed July 9, 2020. https://georgewbush-whitehouse.archives.gov/government/fbci/president-initiative.html#:~:text=The%20Initiative%20in%20Action,FBCOs%20in%20providing%20social%20services.

United States Government Accountability Office. GAO Report to Congressional Requesters, "Faith-based and Community Initiative: Improvements in Monitoring Grantees and Measuring Performance Could Enhance Accountability." 2006. https://www.gao.gov/assets/gao-06-616.pdf.

"White House Faith-Based and Community Initiative." n.d. https://georgewbush-whitehouse.archives.gov/government/fbci/president-initiative.html.

Falwell, Jerry

One of the most influential American religious figures in the latter half of the twentieth century, Rev. Jerry L. Falwell Sr., is someone whose reputation often preceded him. Founder of Liberty University, a prominent Christian university in Lynchburg, Virginia, and one of the founders of the powerful conservative political action group, the Moral Majority, Falwell was roundly praised by Evangelicals, often vilified by progressives, and stood as a central leader in the religious cultural revolution of the 1970s and 1980s.

Jerry Falwell and his fraternal brother Gene were born on August 11, 1933, in Lynchburg, Virginia. The youngest children of Carey and Helen Falwell née Beasley, Jerry and his brother, arrived 8 years after their brother Lewis and 16 years after their sister Virginia. A fifth Falwell child, Rosha, was born in 1921 but died of peritonitis in 1931 (Falwell 1997).

The death of Rosha put an emotional strain on the Falwell family, and, in particular, on Carey Falwell, who later in 1931 would take the life of his own brother, Garland, in an act that police reports indicate was in "self defense" (Falwell 1997).

In his autobiography, Jerry Falwell remarks that the years following Rosha and Garland's deaths were, for his father, a time of "melancholy and grief," which appeared to be—at least temporarily—alleviated by the birth of Jerry and Gene. Falwell notes that his father "seemed to come to life again," adding that "though sin and the Enemy continued working in [his] father's heart, he was too busy and too productive to take much notice" (Falwell 1997).

The language of sin and salvation permeates much of Falwell's autobiographical work, in particular, when he discusses his father. Falwell describes his father as an "agnostic who hated preachers and refused to enter the doors of a church" (Falwell 1997), and he attributes much of the misfortune that plagued his father and his father's family as being the work of the "Enemy" (Falwell 1997), a more general moniker for the biblical figure Satan. Falwell viewed his upbringing as taking place in a household that was quite literally "a battleground between the forces of God and the power of Satan" (Applebome 2007) but attributed the beginning of faith journey to his mother, who was a Christian, and, indirectly, to his experience in elementary school (Falwell 1997).

Falwell attended Mountain View Elementary School in Lynchburg, where he and his classmates attended chapel, listened to recited Bible passages, sang hymns, and gained, as he put it, "a respect for God, the Bible, the church, and for all things that were holy" (Falwell 1981)—this, despite his not yet being a Christian. In his later years, Falwell would look back on the spiritual experiences and feel "a deep sense of loss for the children in elementary school today" (Falwell 1997).

Despite Falwell's experience at Mountain View and his exposure to his mother's faith, Falwell did not become a Christian until the night of January 20, 1952, at the age of 18, when he made the decision to accept

Jesus as his Savior at the Park Avenue Baptist Church in Lynchburg. In 1956, Falwell founded his own congregation, the Thomas Road Baptist Church and, in the same year, began hosting the "Old Time Gospel Hour," a nationally syndicated radio and television ministry dedicated to bringing people to Christianity (Falwell 1997).

Falwell's efforts to evangelize and educate expanded significantly in 1967 when he established the Lynchburg Christian Academy, a Christian K–12 day school, and, in 1971, when he founded Liberty University, an accredited Christian university, both in Lynchburg ("Dr. Jerry Falwell—Biography," n.d.).

In the decade that followed, Falwell would find himself increasingly disturbed and frustrated by what he saw as a crisis of American immorality. The 1973 U.S. Supreme Court ruling on *Roe v. Wade*, which found state laws prohibiting abortions before the third month to be unconstitutional, was particularly troubling for Falwell, who saw the decision as clearly immoral and one which would "bring sweeping spiritual consequences" (Falwell and Hannity 2014). Falwell attributed some of the attitudes that gave rise to *Roe v. Wade* to a decline of American culture as a whole. He believed that young people were learning "to disrespect the family as God has established it," to view the Bible as "just another book of literature," to see the world as one with "no absolutes," and to turn their backs on their American heritage (Falwell 1981).

Central to this cultural decline, Falwell believed, was "a public-school system that is permeated with secular humanism" (Falwell 1981). Public school textbooks, Falwell asserted, had been scrubbed of instruction on "basic values," such as morality, individualism, patriotism, and the benefits of a free-enterprise system, adding that it was almost as if the texts were "designed to negate what philosophies previously had been taught" (Falwell 1981).

The solution, Falwell believed, was a return to a more faith-based education. In 1984, the U.S. Senate debated proposed constitutional amendments that would have permitted individual or group prayer in public schools, a practice that had been ended two decades prior. Falwell along with the Moral Majority—a political action group he founded in 1979—was a staunch advocate of bringing prayer back into the schools. While Falwell did not claim that increases in crime, drugs, and pornography were the direct result of prayer being banned in school, he did note that the two coincided. If public schools could not provide an education more grounded in the moral values and Judeo-Christian philosophies that were prominent in classes in the past, Falwell believed that parents would have no choice but to place their children in private Christian schools, where they could get an education more aligned with their beliefs.

Although Falwell advocated for prayer in school, he noted in his autobiography that he believed that the prayers should be "voluntary, nonsectarian, and that no public official should write or mandate a prayer. Further, no child should be intimidated or embarrassed for not participating" (Falwell 1997). What was important, he believed, was that students be allowed to make a choice (Falwell 1997).

Jerry Falwell died on May 15, 2007, at the age of 73. His son, Jerry Falwell Jr., succeeded him as president of Liberty University and has continued his father's work as a champion of evangelical Christian values and public policy (Applebome 2007).

See also: *Abington School District v. Schempp* (1963); Creationism; First Amendment; Intelligent Design; Moral Majority; Prayer in School; Scopes Trial; Secularism and Secular Humanism

Further Reading

Applebome, Peter. "Jerry Falwell, Leading Religious Conservative, Dies." *New York Times*, May 15, 2007.

"Dr. Jerry Falwell—Biography." Liberty University. n.d. https://www.liberty.edu/aboutliberty/index.cfm?PID=6921.

"Engel v. Vitale." Oyez. n.d. Accessed August 23, 2020. https://www.oyez.org/cases/1961/468.

Falwell, Jerry, Sr. *Listen, America!* New York: Bantam Books, 1981.

Falwell, Jerry, Sr. *Falwell: An Autobiography*. Lynchburg, VA: Liberty House, 1997.

Falwell, Macel, and Sean Hannity. *Jerry Falwell: His Life and Legacy*. New York: Howard Books, 2014.

"Jerry Falwell Helps Found the Moral Majority." The Association of Religion Data Archives. n.d. http://www.thearda.com/timeline/events/event_46.asp.

"Liberty University." Liberty University. n.d. https://www.liberty.edu/.

Packard, William. *Evangelism: From Tents to TV*. New York: Paragon House, 1988.

Pingry, Patricia A. *Jerry Falwell, Man of Vision*. Milwaukee: Ideals, 1980.

"Roe v. Wade, 410 U.S. 113 (1973)." Justia Law. n.d. Accessed August 23, 2020. https://supreme.justia.com/cases/federal/us/410/113/.

Strober, Gerald S., and Ruth Tomczak. *Jerry Falwell: Aflame for God*. Nashville: Nelson, 1979.

Tamney, Joseph, and Stephen Johnson. "Explaining Support for the Moral Majority." *Sociological Forum* 3, no. 2 (1988): 234–55.

White, Eileen. "President Reagan Backs Constitutional Change on Prayer in School." *Education Week* 1, no. 33 (1982). https://www.edweek.org/education/president-reagan-backs-constituional-change-on-prayer-in-school/1982/05.

First Amendment

The First Amendment to the U.S. Constitution is part of the Bill of Rights, which guarantees a range of individual rights and freedoms while limiting the power of the federal government. The First Amendment reads, "Congress shall make no law respecting an establishment of religion, or prohibiting the free exercise thereof; or abridging the freedom of speech, or of the press; or the right of the people peaceably to assemble, and to petition the government for a redress of grievances."

The U.S. Constitution was first proposed in 1787 and debated over the following year in state conventions. Much of the debate was between Federalists, who believed in a strong central government, and Anti-Federalists, who had concerns about too powerful a centralized government and demanded protections for individual rights and freedoms. The Constitution was ratified in 1788 but with the caveat that amendments outlining explicit protections for individual rights and limiting government power would quickly follow. The first 10 amendments, constituting the Bill of Rights, was ratified in 1791.

The First Amendment begins with what are sometimes referred to as the religious clauses: the Establishment Clause and the Free Exercise Clause. These clauses, particularly the latter, were heavily influenced by Enlightenment ideas of Locke and others (Spellburg 2014). James Madison's *Memorial and Remonstrance against Religious Assessments* and Thomas Jefferson's *Bill for Establishing Religious Freedom in Virginia* were important precursors to the First Amendment. Several years later, in 1802, Jefferson would write the Letter to Baptists of Danbury, Connecticut, where he declared that the First Amendment erected a "wall of separation" between church and state, coining what would become a popular term expressing this idea. This was a significant intellectual development, and in the words of religious historians Gaustad and Schmidt, "for the first time in Western civilization, citizens of a nation could claim as their fundamental right their religious beliefs to be nobody's business but their very own" (2002: 127).

The First Amendment's first clause, "Congress shall make no law respecting an establishment of religion," is commonly known as the Establishment Clause. This clause prohibits the government from favoring one religion over another while limiting the government's power to compel religious thought or behavior. The second clause, called the Free Exercise Clause, prevents Congress from making any law "prohibiting the free exercise thereof." This clause was designed to protect freedom of conscience. Initially, under the Constitution's principles of dual sovereignty, Article VI and the First Amendment did not extend these guarantees to the states. Not until the Fourteenth Amendment was passed in 1868 was "equal protection of the law" ensured in the states.

These two clauses of the First Amendment sit side-by-side so as to create two complementary yet sometimes competing principles that would hold each other in balance, anticipating the infinite dilemmas that could arise. Indeed, the meaning of the First Amendment's Establishment and Free Exercise Clauses and the tension between these two have been debated innumerable times in American courts. In the first Supreme Court case testing the Free Exercise Clause, *Reynolds v. United States* (1878), Chief Justice Morrison Waite relied on the writings of Jefferson and Madison. In this case, the Court drew a distinction between freedom of religious belief and freedom of religious conduct: the former, the right to think or believe what one likes, is protected absolutely. Protections for religious practices and conduct, on the other hand, can be limited.

As the First Amendment pertains to religion and schools, questions include, inter alia, school prayer, Bible study, subsidies for tuition, transportation and other costs associated with attending religious schools, the display or religious symbols in schools, and school dress codes that impact religious apparel (all addressed in distinct entries in this volume).

The question of school prayer was examined in *Engel v. Vitale* (1962), a case involving a New York State law requiring public schools to open the day with a religious prayer. The prayer was nondenominational, and students were allowed to opt out if they found it objectionable. Nonetheless, the law was challenged as a violation of the Establishment Clause (as applied to the states via the Fourteenth Amendment). The Court ruled 8–1 that the law did violate the First Amendment, asserting that the opt-out provision was insufficient to prevent government interference with religion. In a dissenting opinion, Justice Stewart took a narrower view of the First Amendment, arguing that its intent was more literal, to prohibit the establishment of a state-sponsored church like the Church of England and no more. He argued that an interpretation of the Establishment Clause as prohibiting all types of government involvement with religion is too expansive and that the nondenominational nature of the prayer and "absentee" provision was sufficient to avoid a First Amendment violation. In *Abington v. Schempp* (1963), the Court again ruled that Pennsylvania's daily school Bible-reading requirements represented a First Amendment violation.

The First Amendment also comes into play when tax dollars make their way to religious schools, either directly or indirectly. In *Board of Education v. Allen* (392 U.S. 236, 1968) the question was raised whether the state could loan textbooks to parochial school students. The Court invoked the so-called child benefit theory, arguing that since the intent of loaning books was to further the education of all children, it "does not alone demonstrate an unconstitutional degree of support for a religious institution." In *Everson v. Board of Education*, the question of subsidized transportation to religious schools was examined.

Another dilemma arises when it comes to teaching *about* religion in public schools. This question was also addressed in *Abington v. Schempp*, when Justice Brennan in a concurring opinion emphasized the importance of religious literacy in education: "The holding of the Court today plainly does not foreclose teaching about the Holy Scriptures or about the differences between religious sects in classes in literature or history. Indeed, whether or not the Bible is involved, it would be impossible to teach meaningfully many subjects in the social sciences or the humanities without some mention of religion" (see *Abington School District v. Schempp*). In some cases, there are tensions between First Amendment rights and protections; for example, instances where non-establishment restrictions may limit freedom of speech. Does, for instance, the First Amendment prohibit a teacher from any discussion of religion or that teacher's right to freely express their own religious views?

The debate surrounding how to interpret the First Amendment's religion clauses, broadly speaking, falls into two camps. On one side, there are so-called strict separationists who believe the intent of the Establishment Clause is to mandate complete separation between religious and state institutions and, when in conflict, prioritizing the non-establishment provision over the principle of Free Exercise Clause. On the other side are the non-preferentialists or accommodationists who argue that the intent of the Establishment Clause was not strict separation but rather to ensure that no one religion never enjoyed preferential status over others. Many non-preferentialists consider the separationist view often favored by the courts as hostile toward religion and advocate for government provision of at least nondenominational support for religion. When looking to the Founders, non-preferentialists take a "watch what they do, not what they say" approach, arguing that despite the seminal writings of Jefferson and Madison cited regularly in court decisions, their actions suggest a different stance and should be given equal weight. Madison, for instance, declared national days of prayer as president, while Jefferson signed a treaty funding Christian missions to Native Americans (Drakeman 2009). There are also opponents of strict separation who embrace preferentialist views, pushing for legislation to establish the Christian nature of the United States. For example, the National Reform Association, a conservative evangelical group founded in 1864, pushed for an amendment to the Constitution to "indicate that this is a Christian nation, and will place all the Christian laws, institutions and usages of our government on an undeniable equal bases in the fundamental law of the land" (Handy 1971: 100). And again in the 1940s and 1950s, the National Association of Evangelicals called for an amendment declaring, "[T]his nation divinely recognizes the authority of the law of Jesus Christ, Savior and Ruler of Nations through whom are bestowed the blessings of Almighty God" (Kramnick and Moore 2005: 148).

See also: *Abington School District v. Schempp* (1963); *Everson v. Board of Education of the Township of Ewing* (1947); Virginia Statute for Religious Freedom

Further Reading

Abington Township, School District of v. Schempp 374 US 203 (1963). n.d. https://supreme.justia.com/cases/federal/us/374/203/.

Appeal from the United States District Court for the Eastern District of Pennsylvania. No. 142. Argued February 27–28, 1963 374 U.S. 203 June 17, 1963.

Drakeman, Donald L. *Church, State, and Original Intent.* Cambridge University Press, 2009.

Engel v. Vitale 370 U.S. 421 (1962). n.d. https://h2o.law.harvard.edu/collages/3118.

Gaustad, Edwin S. and Schmidt, Leigh. *The Religious History of America: The Heart of the American Story from Colonial Times to Today.* New York: HarperCollins, 2002.

Handy, Robert. *A Christian America: Protestant Hopes and Historical Realities*. First edition. Oxford, New York: Oxford University Press, 1971.

Kramnick, Isaac, and R. Laurence Moore. *The Godless Constitution: A Moral Defense of the Secular State*. Updated edition. New York: W. W. Norton & Company, 2005.

Middle Tennessee State University. First Amendment Encyclopedia. n.d. https://mtsu.edu/first-amendment/article/1218/thomas-jefferson.

Spellberg, Denise. *Thomas Jefferson's Qur'an: Islam and the Founders*. New York: Vintage, 2014.

U.S. Bill of Rights. n.d. https://billofrightsinstitute.org/founding-documents/bill-of-rights/.

U.S. Congress Constitution Annotates: Interpretation and Analysis of the U.S. Constitution, First Amendment. n.d. https://constitution.congress.gov/constitution/amendment-1/.

Focus on the Family

Focus on the Family describes itself as a "global Christian ministry dedicated to helping families thrive" through providing "help and resources for couples to build healthy marriages that reflect God's design, and for parents to raise their children according to morals and values grounded in biblical principles" ("About Focus on the Family," n.d.).

The organization's statement of values is grounded in what it refers to as six guiding philosophies, or "pillars," which stand in opposition to "humanistic notions" that are prevalent in modern American society. These pillars are the preeminence of evangelism, the permanence of marriage, the value of children, the sanctity of human life, the importance of social responsibility, and the value of male and female ("About Focus on the Family," n.d.).

FOUNDING AND BACKGROUND

Focus on the Family was founded in 1977 by psychologist, radio host, and author James Dobson ("Focus on the Family," n.d.). Based in Colorado Springs, the organization first began airing the radio broadcast *Let's Get Acquainted* as a weekly program, on March 26, which is recognized as the "anniversary date" of the founding of the organization ("About Focus on the Family," n.d.).

Beginning as a "response to the sexual revolution" of the 1960s and 1970s, Focus on the Family evolved into a formidable "media empire" that included magazines, films, books, and additional radio and video projects (Ainsworth and Harward 2019).

Dobson led Focus on the Family for more than 30 years before stepping down as chairman in 2009. The organization indicated that Dobson's resignation was part of a "succession plan," with Dobson stating in a press release, "One of the common errors of founder-presidents, is to hold to the reins of leadership too long, thereby preventing the next generation from being prepared for executive authority" ("Dr. Dobson Steps down as Chairman of Focus on the Family" 2009).

Focus on the Family is currently headed by Dobson's personally selected successor, Jim Daly ("About Focus on the Family," n.d.).

PAST ACTIVITIES

As part of its ministry, Focus on the Family has long been involved in matters of religion in public education. It has advocated for the return of prayer to the school system but only that which is led by students. Teacher-led prayer, the organization contends, could result in Christian students being led to pray to other figures, such as "Allah, Buddha, or the goddess Sophia" (quoted in "Right Wing Organization: Focus on the Family," n.d.).

Focus on the Family also has been a vocal advocate of private schooling and homeschooling. While not explicitly discouraging parents from enrolling their children in public schools, Focus on the Family has cautioned that, in public schools, "teachers may promote agendas that contradict values taught at home," such as sex education that emphasizes the use of "condoms and contraception while ignoring or minimizing the importance of responsibility, abstinence, and connecting sexuality to a value system" (Reisser 1997).

RECENT ACTIVITIES

One of Focus on the Family's recent initiatives to advocate for the inclusion of religion in school is its annual "Bring Your Bible to School Day" ("Bring Your Bible to School," n.d.). Observed on the first Thursday of every October, students "engage in a visual celebration of religious freedom by . . . bringing their personal Bibles to school and initiating conversations about how God's love has changed their lives" (Daly 2019).

This outward expression of religious faith is protected by the First Amendment, as long as the students do not "disrupt class or other activities" (Concannon 2019). According to Candi Cushman, Focus on the Family's director of education issues and initiatives, in at least three cases, two in 2014 and one in 2016, "schools prohibited students from sharing Bible verses, praying, and reading the Bible, respectively" (Concannon 2019). In all three cases, the prohibition stemmed from "misunderstandings by school teachers or administrators on how to apply settled law around religious expression in public schools," and in each incident, "the school districts involved issued apologies and clarified policy for district employees" (Concannon 2019).

See also: First Amendment; Prayer in School; Religion and Sexual Education, Teaching in Schools; Secularism and Secular Humanism; Student-Initiated Prayer, Clubs

Further Reading

"About Focus on the Family." Focus on the Family. n.d. Accessed July 9, 2020. https://www.focusonthefamily.com/about/.

Ainsworth, Scott H., and Brian M. Harward. *Political Groups, Parties, and Organizations That Shaped America: An Encyclopedia and Document Collection*. 3 Vols. Santa Barbara: ABC-CLIO, 2019.

"Bring Your Bible to School." Focus on the Family. n.d. Accessed August 23, 2020. https://www.focusonthefamily.com/bring-your-bible/.

Concannon, Cavan. "Every Day Is Already 'Bring Your Bible to School Day.'" Religion and Politics. October 1, 2019. https://religionandpolitics.org/2019/10/01/every-day-is-already-bring-your-bible-to-school-day/.

Daly, Jim. "Jim Daly: It's Bring Your Bible to School Day . . . " Fox News. October 3, 2019. https://www.foxnews.com/opinion/jim-daly-bring-bible-school-day.

"Dr. Dobson Steps Down as Chairman of Focus on the Family." Catholic News Agency, February 27, 2009. http://www.catholicnewsagency.com/news/dr._dobson_steps_down_as_chairman_of_focus_on_the_family.

"Focus on the Family." *Christianity Today*. n.d. Accessed July 9, 2020. https://www.christianitytoday.com/ct/topics/f/focus-on-the-family/.

Reisser, Paul. *The Focus on the Family Complete Book of Baby and Child Care*. First edition. FOTF Complete Guide. Carol Stream, IL: Tyndale House Publishers, 1997.

"Right Wing Organization: Focus on the Family." People for the American Way: Right Wing Watch. n.d. Accessed July 9, 2020. http://www.pfaw.org/pfaw/general/default.aspx?oid=4257.

Freedom from Religion Foundation

The Freedom from Religion Foundation (FFRF) is an American nonprofit organization that advocates for the total separation of church and state and works to "educate the public on matters relating to nontheism" ("What Is FFRF's Purpose?" n.d.). Its philosophy is grounded in the premise that most progress in the Western world has sprung from "persons free from religion" ("About FFRF," n.d.), resulting in changes in the modern era such as prison reform, improved treatment for the mentally ill, the abolition of capital punishment, women's suffrage, and abortion rights, among others.

Among the FFRF's primary advocacy activities are taking legal action to challenge perceived entanglements of government and religion, as well as government endorsement or promotion of religion. The foundation also publishes the newspaper *Freethought Today*, sponsors student essay competitions, conducts conventions that honor freethought activism, and recognizes public figures with an award for "plain-speaking on religion" ("What Does FFRF Do?" n.d.).

The foundation is currently headed by co-presidents Annie Laurie Gaylor and Dan Barker (Grauvogl 2009).

FOUNDING AND BACKGROUND

Annie Gaylor formed the foundation in Madison, Wisconsin, in 1976, along with her mother, Anne Nicol Gaylor, and her mother's friend John Sontarck (Robert 2015). The foundation, as Anne Gaylor once put it, began as "a dining room table cause group" but, by 1978, evolved into a national organization (Robert 2015). According to Annie Gaylor, the catalyst for the group's initial founding was when they "somehow became aware that [government officials] were opening county board meetings with prayer." The fledgling group asked the board to stop the practice, calling it unconstitutional, and believe they "would sound more powerful if [they] called [themselves] a group" (Robert 2015).

Anne Gaylor, born Lucie Anne Nicol, established her credentials as an activist well prior to her formation of the FFRF. An early feminist, in a 1967 editorial for the *Middleton Times-Tribune*, she called for the legalization of abortion, six years before the landmark U.S. Supreme Court ruling of *Roe v. Wade* (Jones 2015). Later, in the 1970s, she co-founded the Women's Medical Fund, a charity that provides financial assistance to women who want but cannot afford an abortion ("Who We Are," n.d.). Her abortion rights advocacy foreshadowed her work with the FFRF: According to her daughter, Anne Gaylor believed that the "root cause of women's oppression was religion and dogma in" secular laws (Jones 2015). This position would extend into the foundation's work, as the organization would go on to fight for various causes over the following decades in the interest of keeping the affairs of state distinctly separate from religion.

KEY ISSUES

Bible Instruction

In 2000, the FFRF received a complaint from a family in Dayton, Tennessee, alleging that the Rhea County school system was offering Bible instruction in its classrooms. The parents at the center of the complaint told the FFRF that, in addition to objecting to Bible classes being taught during the day by Bryan College students, they objected to the distribution of New Testaments in the classroom by the Gideons organization, morning Bible reading over the school's intercom followed by a moment of silence, and the posting of religious messages in classrooms ("FFRF's Letter to Rhea County Schools" 2000).

In a letter from the FFRF to Rhea County superintendent Sue Porter, foundation co-president Dan Barker cited several U.S. Supreme Court cases, including *McCollum v. Board of Education* (1948), *Tudor v. Board of Education of Rutherford* (1954), *Berger v. Rensselaer* (1993), *Wallace v. Jaffree* (1985), and *Stone v. Graham* (1980), as grounds for why such religious instruction ran afoul of constitutional provisions ("FFRF's Letter to Rhea County Schools" 2000).

Barker went on to say in this letter that "Rhea County believers are free to worship at the church of their choice, to pray, read the bible, and teach sectarian values to their children" but concluded that the school district "should remain strictly neutral on these matters, treating no student as second class, respecting the freedom of all viewpoints" ("FFRF's Letter to Rhea County Schools" 2000).

Federal judge R. Allan Edgar ruled in 2002 that the Bible classes violated the constitutional separation of church and state ("County of the

Scopes Trial Is Told to Halt Bible Classes in Schools" 2002), effectively ending the classes.

Prayer at School Functions (e.g., board meetings, sports events, graduation)

As recently as 2018, the FFRF has taken on an issue that was ostensibly addressed and resolved in the 2000 Supreme Court case *Santa Fe Independent School District v. Doe*: prayer before school-sponsored events.

In that case, the court ruled that a school may not permit the recitation of a prayer at the beginning of a football game, as it constituted a violation of the First Amendment's Establishment Clause ("Santa Fe Independent School District v. Doe," n.d.). The school district argued that the prayer was exempt from constitutional restrictions because it was student led and student initiated, but the court's opinion was that because such a prayer was authorized by the school, the policy implied a government endorsement of religion.

A similar situation arose in Blount County, Alabama, when the FFRF learned that the county school district was permitting voluntary student-led prayer over the public address system at football games held at its schools. The FFRF sent a letter to the county Board of Education, challenging the policy, citing *Santa Fe v. Doe*, and calling for it to be discontinued.

Blount County school superintendent Rodney Green personally opposed the FFRF's position, arguing that "prayer at football games has never been about making any child believe in a certain religion" but instead has been about tradition and people sharing a common interest (Gholson 2018). Nevertheless, Green instructed all school personnel to comply with the FFRF's request, indicating that it was the school's responsibility to teach students to follow the law.

The foundation's concern about prayer at school functions extends beyond the athletic field and into school board meetings as well. In December 2019, the FFRF learned that the Clark County School District, in Nevada, had started at least one meeting of the board of school trustees with a prayer. The FFRF filed a complaint, claiming that starting a school board meeting with prayer was a clear violation of the Establishment Clause. Board counsel Eleissa Lavelle responded to the FFRF complaint in January 2020, indicating that "the Board of School Trustees will no longer begin its meetings with an invocation" (Miller 2020).

Creationism and Evolution

In February 2020, the foundation took aim at a school district in New York where, it alleged, that "a biology teacher there recently began a lesson on evolution by undermining the theory" (Gymburch 2020). The foundation announced that it had been informed of the incident by a "concerned" parent. The teacher in question, Phil Lucason, was alleged to have told the student that "evolution only goes so far" and that when they take the Regents Exam, they have to "play the evolution game where evolution is the answer to everything" ("N.Y. Public School Reins in Proselytizing Teacher, per FFRF Advice" 2020). The school district quickly responded to the FFRF's concerns and assured the organization that such instructions would be curtailed.

Advocates for the teaching of alternate theories of the origins of the universe, such as creationism and intelligent design, decried the school's response as capitulation to intimidation and bullying. Writing for *Evolution News*, David Klinghoffer, a senior fellow of the Discovery Institute, defended the teacher's instruction: "The teacher wasn't teaching Genesis as science. Not at all! His point seems to be that the students should take the Regents test and answer as expected, but at the end of day, they are free to draw their own private conclusions" (Klinghoffer 2020).

CRITICISM AND CONTROVERSY

Klinghoffer is certainly not the FFRF's only critic, and the organization has drawn its share of negative attention. For example, according to Snopes.com, a website devoted to evaluating and debunking conspiracies and hoaxes, in 2015, the FFRF was the subject of a claim that gained traction online, which suggested that it was seeking to "ban Bibles from all hotel rooms" ("Are Angry Atheists Demanding a Ban on the Bible?" 2015).

The claim apparently originated with a Facebook post from the conservative Christian advocacy group American Center for Law and Justice, which read, "A radical group of atheists is demanding all hotels remove Bibles from their rooms, claiming the Bible 'may endanger your health and life'" ("Are Angry Atheists Demanding a Ban on the Bible?" 2015; Sekulow 2015).

In truth, the FFRF had requested that Bibles be removed from public university hotel rooms and had requested that hotels offer "bible-free" rooms in order to be more "hospitable to non-Christian and nonreligious clientele" ("FFRF Requests 'Bible-Free' Hotel Rooms—Freedom from Religion Foundation" 2015).

Despite such exaggerated claims about the foundation's actions being disproved, suspicion of the FFRF and its motives persists. In 2018, a *Christian Post* article condemned the organization's purposes as "evil" and rooted in its founders' worldview on the sanctity of life, specifically their position on abortion (McCullen 2018). The author of the article, Don McCullen, and other religious figures conclude that the foundation wants to "fundamentally transform America into what will become hell on earth" (McCullen 2018) and "destroy the very fabric of this Nation" (Locke 2019; Mojica 2019) by effectively removing religion from public life.

See also: Bible Study; Creationism; Devotional/Doctrinal Curriculum; *Edwards v. Aguillard* (1987); Evolution, Teaching; First Amendment; Prayer in School; Student-Initiated Prayer, Clubs

Further Reading

"About FFRF—Freedom from Religion Foundation." n.d. Accessed August 23, 2020. https://ffrf.org/about.

"Are Angry Atheists Demanding a Ban on the Bible?" Snopes.Com. December 10, 2015. Accessed August 23, 2020. https://www.snopes.com/fact-check/angry-atheists-ban-bible/.

"County of the Scopes Trial Is Told to Halt Bible Classes in Schools." *New York Times*, February 9, 2002, sec. A, p.12. https://www.nytimes.com/2002/02/09/us/county-of-the-scopes-trial-is-told-to-halt-bible-classes-in-schools.html.

"FFRF Requests 'Bible-Free' Hotel Rooms—Freedom from Religion Foundation." Freedom from Religion Foundation. December 7, 2015. Accessed August 23, 2020. https://ffrf.org/news/news-releases/item/24917-ffrf-requests-bible-free-hotel-rooms.

"FFRF's Letter to Rhea County Schools—Freedom from Religion Foundation." Freedom from Religion Foundation. September 27, 2000. Accessed August 23, 2020b. https://ffrf.org/news/news-releases/item/2549-daytonletter.

Gholson, Ron. "Freedom from Religion Foundation Threatens Lawsuit over Prayer at County Football Games." *Blount Countian*, September 26, 2018. Accessed August 23, 2020. https://www.blountcountian.com/articles/freedom-from-religion-foundation-threatens-lawsuit-over-prayer-at-county-football-games/.

Grauvogl, Ann. "Dan Barker and Annie Laurie Gaylor Are Happily God-Free." Isthmus. December 18, 2009. https://isthmus.com/news/cover-story/dan-barker-and-annie-laurie-gaylor-are-happily-god-free/.

Gymburch, Dave. "Self-Described 'Watchdog' Takes Issue with Area Educator." *Rome Daily Sentinel*, February 21, 2020. Accessed August 23, 2020. https://romesentinel.com/stories/self-described-watchdog-takes-issue-with-area-educator,92722.

Jones, Meg. "Freedom from Religion Founder Anne Nicol Gaylor Dies." *Journal Sentinel*, June 15, 2015. Accessed August 23, 2020. http://www.jsonline.com/news/obituaries/freedom-from-religion-founder-anne-nicol-gaylor-dies-b99520019z1-307404821.html.

Klinghoffer, David. "Blasphemy against Darwin in New York State! Atheist Group Intimidates School District." Evolution News, March 5, 2020. Accessed August 23, 2020. https://evolutionnews.org/2020/03/blasphemy-against-darwin-in-new-york-state-atheist-group-intimidates-school-district/.

Locke, Greg. "Pastor Greg Locke on Twitter." Twitter. October 15, 2019. Accessed August 23, 2020. https://twitter.com/pastorlocke/status/1184278972634423297.

McCullen, Don. "The True Evil Purpose of the Freedom from Religion Foundation." *Christian Post*, February 06, 2018. Accessed August 23, 2020. https://www.christianpost.com/voices/the-true-evil-purpose-of-the-freedom-from-religion-foundation.html.

Miller, Cody. "Clark County School Board Meetings to No Longer Begin with Prayer Following Complaint." KSNV. February 10, 2020. https://news3lv.com/news/local/clark-county-school-board-meetings-to-no-longer-begin-with-prayer-following-complaint.

Mojica, Adrian. "Tennessee Pastor, Freedom from Religion Foundation Spar over Ad, Book | WZTV." October 25, 2019. Accessed August 23, 2020. https://fox17.com/news/local/tennessee-pastor-freedom-from-religion-foundation-spar-over-ad-book.

"N.Y. Public School Reins in Proselytizing Teacher, per FFRF Advice—Freedom from Religion Foundation." Freedom from Religion Foundation. February 28, 2020. Accessed August 23, 2020. https://ffrf.org/news/news-releases/item/%2037133-n-y-public-school-reins-in- proselytizing-teacher-per-ffrf-advice.

Roberts, Sam. "Anne Gaylor, 88, Dies; Guarded Wall between Church and State." *New York Times*, June 16, 2015. Accessed August 23, 2020. https://www.nytimes.com/2015/06/17/us/anne-gaylor-passionate-atheist-is-dead-at-88.html.

"Santa Fe Independent School District v. Doe." Oyez. n.d. Accessed July 9, 2020. https://www.oyez.org/cases/1999/99-62.

"Santa Fe Independent School District v. Doe, 530 U.S. 290 (2000)." Justia Law. n.d. Accessed July 9, 2020. https://supreme.justia.com/cases/federal/us/530/290/.

Sekulow, Jay. 2015. "Angry Atheists Try to Ban Gideon Bibles in Public Hotel Rooms." American Center for Law and Justice. November 12, 2015. Accessed

August 23, 2020. https://aclj.org/free-speech/angry-atheists-try-to-ban-gideon-bibles-in-public-hotel-rooms.

"What Does FFRF Do?—Freedom from Religion Foundation." n.d. Accessed August 23, 2020. https://ffrf.org/faq/item/15001-what-does-%20the-foundation-do.

"What Is FFRF's Purpose?—Freedom From Religion Foundation." n.d. Accessed August 23, 2020. https://ffrf.org/faq/item/14999-what-is-the-foundations-purpose.

"Who We Are." Women's Medical Fund. n.d. Accessed August 23, 2020. https://wmfwisconsin.org/who-we-are.

I

Indigenous Faiths

When discussing religion and its relationship to public schools in America, it can be easy to focus on the more commonly known or widely observed traditions, such as Christianity, Judaism, and Islam. These religions, and other globally observed faiths, including Buddhism and Hindu, make up nearly three-quarters of what Americans observe, according to the Pew Research Center ("U.S. Demographic Groups: Religious Affiliations" 2015).

There is, however, a population in America, albeit small, that observes one of many unique Native American religions. This segment constitutes less than 0.3% of the population of the United States, but its beliefs and practices are just as constitutionally protected as those of any of the more widely observed traditions.

DEFINING NATIVE AMERICAN RELIGION

Defining "Native American religion" can be challenging because, unlike a religion such as Christianity, which is understood in a much more monolithic way, with common beliefs and rituals that span the globe, traditional Native American religions are as diverse as the many tribes that make up the population. As of 2018, the U.S. Bureau of Indian Affairs recognizes 574 distinct tribes, many of which have their own individual and unique religious beliefs and practices.

There are, however, a few traits that can be said to be "common" among Native American religions. Historian Christine Leigh Heyrman suggests that there are three generalities that can be used to better understand Native American religious tradition, especially as it existed at the time when Europeans first arrived in North America. By that time, most indigenous cultures in America had developed "coherent religious systems," most native peoples worshipped an "all-powerful, all-knowing Creator or 'Master Spirit,'" and members of most tribes believe in the "immortality of the human soul and an afterlife" (Heyrman, n.d.).

Complicating the issue, though, is that, despite having some traits in common with religions such as Christianity, "many followers of Native American spirituality do not regard their spiritual beliefs and practices as a 'religion' in the way in which many Christians do," seeing their belief, instead, as forming an "integral and seamless part" of their being ("Native American Spirituality," n.d.).

Another distinction between many Native American religions and the more commonly practiced world religions in America is that many indigenous traditions place a great emphasis on nature, with animals, plants, and even the land carrying great spiritual significance. In this way, many Native American religions could be said to be animistic, having more in common with Eastern religions, such as Shinto, Hindu, and Buddhism, than with Western faiths, such as Christianity, Judaism, or Islam.

Furthermore, while many world religions maintain their traditions through written histories and sacred texts, many tribes historically relied on an oral tradition in which religious beliefs and principles are passed down verbally.

These varied ways of understanding what is meant by "Native American religion" posed such a challenge for the earliest Europeans to arrive in America that for many centuries, such traditions were not even classified as "religion." As the American Indian Heritage Foundation puts it, "Their beliefs were not understood and the complexity of their religion was not seen" ("The History of Native American Religion," n.d.). A consequence of this lack of understanding is that many early European missionaries sought to convert Native Americans to Christianity, specifically Catholicism, in an effort to "save [their] souls" believing that "indigenous communities has no culture or religion at all" ("First Encounters: Native Americans and Christians," n.d.). The effort to convert Native Americans evolved in the seventeenth century to also include Protestant Christian traditions, including Anglicanism and Puritanism.

PROTECTING AMERICAN INDIAN RELIGIOUS FREEDOM

The view of Native Americans by Christian colonists and missionaries as "'heathens' who either accepted or resisted conversion to Christianity"

("First Encounters: Native Americans and Christians," n.d.) had long-reaching effects in American history and culture. For centuries, Native American religious traditions were viewed by many as lesser than or not equivalent to the more common world religions.

It was not until 1978, in fact, that the United States passed legislation that explicitly provided protection for Native American religions. The "American Indian Religious Freedom Act" formally required that the United States "protect and preserve for American Indians their inherent right of freedom to believe, express, and exercise" their traditional religions ("STATUTE-92-Pg469.Pdf," n.d.). These protections include "access to sites, use and possession of sacred objects, and the freedom to worship through ceremonial and traditional rites" ("STATUTE-92-Pg469.Pdf," n.d.).

One might wonder why passing this act was necessary, since the religious protections of the First Amendment of the U.S. Constitution should, ostensibly, apply to all religions. In 1979, the Native American Rights Fund addressed this very question, writing that "despite what may have been the intention" of the authors of the Constitution, "the history of [the United States] is consistent in the area of Native religions" as being disrespectful, ignorant, and suppressive of such traditions ("'We Also Have a Religion'..." 1979). Native American religious beliefs, the Fund contended, had been subjected to "suppression and persecution" from the nation's founding to the modern era, rendering the First Amendment a "meaningless promise to Native Americans" ("'We Also Have a Religion'..." 1979).

Despite the passage of the American Indian Religious Freedom Act, Native Americans have continued to face significant legal challenges when it comes to freely practicing their religion. In one of the most prominent cases in recent history, Native American groups in North Dakota voiced stern opposition to the construction of the Dakota Access Pipeline through land that they considered sacred. The Standing Rock Sioux Tribe, among others, protested construction of the underground pipeline on the grounds that should the pipeline experience a spill under the Missouri River, it would pollute water that the tribe relied on for fishing, drinking, and religious ceremonies. In 2016, the Standing Rock Sioux sued in Federal District Court to stop construction of the pipeline (Friedman 2020). Nonetheless, the pipeline was eventually constructed, being completed in April 2017.

Legal scholar Melissa Tatum, writing on the issue, contended that the construction of the Dakota Access Pipeline was just the most recent example to suggest that Native Americans "have no religious freedom unless they give up their traditional religions and adopt a Judeo-Christian one" (Tatum 2018). She cited other cases as well, such as the Supreme Court cases of *Lyng v. Northwest Indian Cemetery Protective Association* (1988), in which the court held that the U.S. Forest Service could harvest timber from religiously significant land because, while the harvesting would adversely affect the land and, by extension, Native Americans who believe the land to be sacred, the people affected "would not be coerced by the Government's action into violating their religious beliefs" ("Lyng v. Northwest Indian Cemetery, 485 U.S. 439 (1988)," n.d.), and *Employment Division v. Smith* (1990), in which the court ruled that a state could deny unemployment benefits to someone fired for using peyote, a drug that is central to some Native American religious rituals.

While Native American religious traditions have certainly come to be more widely recognized and understood within the broader American population, and, by extension, within the legal realm, as the aforementioned cases indicate, they still face many unique challenges, particularly when it comes to conflicts between tradition and federal policy.

INDIGENOUS FAITHS AND SCHOOLS

Much as the Native American population has faced hurdles when it comes to conflicts between religious tradition and U.S. economic or legal interests, the relationship between Native American religion and American schools also has been historically strained.

Of particular note is the formation at the end of the nineteenth century of Native American boarding schools. These schools were created as part of a shift in U.S. policy toward indigenous peoples, away from a "War Policy" and toward a "Peace Policy." This new policy, while seemingly innocuous in name and concept, aimed to assimilate Native Americans to a more Eurocentric ideal by eliminating their "Indianness" ("Native Americans and Freedom of Religion" 2020). To this end, many Native American families were forced to send their children to schools that were run by the federal government and Christian missionaries, where they were forbidden from speaking their native languages and taught that their cultures were inferior and where their religious practices were "forcibly replaced" with Christianity ("Boarding School—Native Words Native Warriors," n.d.).

Several repressive policies accompanied the operation of these schools, including the formation of a set of rules known as the "Code of

Indian Offenses," which banned Native American religious practices, under the threat of penalties such as withholding of food rations and incarceration ("Native Americans and Freedom of Religion" 2020).

In 1934, the commissioner of Indian Affairs, John Collier, issued a circular that called into question bans on Native American religious practices and ceremonies ("Commissioner Calls for Religious Freedom for American Indians—Timeline—Native Voices," n.d.). Collier wrote that "no interference with Indian religious life or ceremonial expression will hereafter be tolerated" ("Outlawing American Indian Religions," n.d.).

While Collier's directive did not bring an immediate end to efforts to dilute or eliminate Native American religious practices in the schools, it signaled a shift in American cultural attitudes toward Native American traditions.

More than four decades later, in 1978, the U.S. government officially recognized its role in stifling Native American religion with the passage of the American Indian Religious Freedom Act ("Native Americans and Freedom of Religion" 2020).

See also: Accommodations; First Amendment; Religious Discrimination in Schools; Religious Diversity in the United States; Virginia Statute for Religious Freedom

Further Reading

"Boarding School—Native Words Native Warriors." n.d. Accessed August 23, 2020. https://americanindian.si.edu/education/codetalkers/html/chapter3.html.

"Commissioner Calls for Religious Freedom for American Indians—Timeline—Native Voices." n.d. Accessed August 23, 2020. https://www.nlm.nih.gov/nativevoices/timeline/453.html.

"First Encounters: Native Americans and Christians." The Pluralism Project. n.d. Accessed July 9, 2020. https://pluralism.org/first-encounters-native-americans-and-christians.

Friedman, Lisa. "Standing Rock Sioux Tribe Wins a Victory in Dakota Access Pipeline Case—The New York Times." *New York Times*, March 25, 2020. https://www.nytimes.com/2020/03/25/climate/dakota-access-pipeline-sioux.html.

Heyrman, Christine Leigh. "Native American Religion in Early America, Divining America." National Humanities Center. n.d. Accessed August 23, 2020. http://nationalhumanitiescenter.org/tserve/eighteen/ekeyinfo/natrel.htm.

"The History of Native American Religion." n.d. Accessed August 23, 2020. http://indians.org/articles/native-american-religion.html.

"Lyng v. Northwest Indian Cemetery, 485 U.S. 439 (1988)." Justia Law. n.d. Accessed July 9, 2020. https://supreme.justia.com/cases/federal/us/485/439/.

"Lyng v. Northwest Indian Cemetery Protective Association." Oyez. n.d. Accessed July 9, 2020. https://www.oyez.org/cases/1987/86-1013.

"Native American Spirituality." n.d. Accessed August 23, 2020. http://www.religioustolerance.org/nataspir.htm.

"Native Americans and Freedom of Religion." National Geographic Society. April 27, 2020. http://www.nationalgeographic.org/article/native-americans-and-freedom-religion/.

"Outlawing American Indian Religions | Native American Netroots." n.d. Accessed August 23, 2020. http://nativeamericannetroots.net/diary/2063.

"STATUTE-92-Pg469.Pdf." n.d. Accessed July 9, 2020. https://www.govinfo.gov/content/pkg/STATUTE-92/pdf/STATUTE-92-Pg469.pdf.

Tatum, Melissa. "No Religious Freedom for Traditional Native Religions." The Berkley Center. February 20, 2018. https://berkleycenter.georgetown.edu/responses/no-religious-freedom-for-traditional-native-religions.

"U.S. Demographic Groups: Religious Affiliations." Pew Research Center's Religion & Public Life Project. May 12, 2015. https://www.pewforum.org/2015/05/12/chapter-4-the-shifting-religious-identity-of-demographic-groups/.

"'We Also Have a Religion': The American Indian Religious Freedom Act and the Religious Freedom Project of the Native American Rights Fund." Native American Rights Fund. Winter 1979. https://www.narf.org/nill/documents/nlr/nlr5-1.pdf.

Intelligent Design

Intelligent Design (ID) is the idea that there is a supernatural designer involved in the creation of the world, and humans in particular. It is an argument against evolutionary theory, which it sees as inadequate to explain the complexity of biological forms found on earth. One of the premier organizations promoting ID, the Discovery Institute Center for Science and Culture, describes it as a "theory that holds certain features of the universe and of living things are best explained by an intelligent cause, not an undirected process such as natural selection." The ID movement casts doubt on Darwinian evolution and offers ID as an alternate theory, with public schools as a major focal point of these efforts. ID attempts to preclude Establishment Clause violations by downplaying or denying any religious/scripturally based motivation, presenting as scientifically based, and suggesting that the "designer" in ID need not be God; the image of the watchmaker, for example, is sometimes invoked. ID has met with a strong backlash from the scientific community, which views this movement as anti-science and rooted in religion. Scientists and scholars, along with judges and elected officials who oppose ID, view it as no more than a repackaged version of traditional creationism launched following failed efforts to force it into biology classrooms in the late 1980s and 1990s (Coyne, J. 2005; Forrest and Gross 2004).

One of the foremost proponents of ID is biologist Michael Behe of Lehigh University. In his 1996 book, *Darwin's Black Box*, Behe presents the idea that the complexity of living things is indicative of conscious design. According to this theory, some biomolecular structures are "irreducibly complex." Behe, together with William Dembski (2002), gives the example of structures such as bacterial flagellum, which they deem too complex to have been produced through natural selection, the key mechanism of Darwinian evolution. In *Edge of Evolution* (2007), Behe embraces certain key Darwinian concepts, such as the common ancestry of humans and chimps, while maintaining that ultimately the random nature of Darwinian evolution fails to account for creative biological change. Supposed "non-random mutations," or mechanisms that "guide" natural selection, are necessary for explaining the development of biological complexity. In his most recent book, *Darwin Devolves* (2019), Behe argues that the Darwinian process is destructive and, thus, "a process that so easily tears down sophisticated machinery is not one which will build complex, functional systems." The ID argument has also been put forth, in print and in court, by molecular biologist Jonathan Wells (2000, 2006).

Support for ID has come from think tanks such as the Discovery Institute Center for Science and Culture and their online publication Evolutionnews.org. The stated mission of the Discovery Institute is to "to advance the understanding that human beings and nature are the result of intelligent design rather than a blind and undirected process" (Discovery Institute: Center for the Renewal of Science and Culture 1999). A leaked internal document known as the "Wedge Strategy" reveals a public relations strategy aiming to cast doubt on evolutionary science and the scientific consensus by influencing "the broadcast media, scientists, academics, congressional staff . . . and potential academic allies" (Forrest and Gross 2004). One goal is to encourage states and school boards to "teach the controversy" by including criticism of evolution in their curriculum

(Wedge Strategy). This often means teaching evolution in schools while highlighting the "problems and weaknesses" of evolutionary theory. In Utah, for example, a bill mandated that the state curriculum "stress that not all scientists agree on which theory regarding the origins of life, or the origins or present state of the human race, is correct." ID has also found some common ground with the "rhetoric of science" movement, which holds that all science is subjective and disseminated through process of persuasion. Schools have sometimes taught ID by offering electives called "Philosophy of Design."

Proponents of ID allege that scientists reject it because of its religious connotations. Eugenie Scott, author of *Evolution vs. Creationism*, responds that ID is rejected simply as bad science (Scott 2009). Many of ID's core assertions have been refuted by scientific evidence (Miller 1999, Pennock 2000; Young and Edis 2004). For instance, the assertion that certain cellular structures are too complex to have evolved has been critiqued by Molecular biologist David Levin, who points out that arguments for "irreducible complexity" in biological systems overlook the great plasticity of the evolutionary process (Levin 2008). Behe's argument bears no mention of exaptation, the process whereby nature retools or recycles structures for new function. It also overlooks the mechanism that evolutionary biologists call "scaffolding," whereby "at an earlier time in the history of the structure, there might have been components that supported function of the structure" (Scott 2009: 125).

While the scientific community has largely rejected ID, support for it has come from highest level political figures. In 2005, then President Bush and U.S. Senate majority leader Bill Frist said that ID ought to be taught alongside evolution, and in 2013, Louisiana governor Bobby Jindal expressed support for a local school board that wanted to teach ID.

The journal *Nature*, a premier forum for discussion of evolutionary theory, published an editorial in 2005 entitled "Dealing with Design," arguing that scientists have failed altogether to deal effectively with ID in allowing science and faith to be represented as a dichotomy. Science education, it is argued, could do more "to point to options other than ID for reconciling science and belief" and thus avoid the unnecessary perception that scientific truth affronts students' faith (*Nature* 2005). Jerry Coyne (2005) publishing in the same forum, disagrees, suggesting that discussion of religion has no place in the science classroom.

Kitzmiller v. Dover Area School District (M.D. Pa. 2005) is a landmark case involving a Pennsylvania district's requirement that a statement endorsing ID be read in biology classes. Evidence presented during the trial revealed that ID has immediate roots in traditional creationism. For example, early drafts of *Of Pandas and People*, a high school textbook espousing ID, made regular reference to "creationism" and "creator," terms that would be replaced with "intelligent design" and "intelligent designer" in the published version of the book. On December 20, 2005, federal district Judge John E. Jones III issued a 139-page decision ruling that ID cannot be taught in public schools because it "cannot uncouple itself from its creationist, and thus religious, antecedents." "ID is a religious and not a scientific proposition," wrote Judge Jones, and "it is unconstitutional to teach ID as an alternative to evolution in a public school science classroom."

See also: Creationism; Evolution, Teaching; Religion and Pseudoscience

Further Reading

Behe, Michael J. *Darwin Devolves: The New Science about DNA That Challenges Evolution.* Reprint edition. New York: HarperOne, 2019.
Behe, Michael J. *Darwin's Black Box: The Biochemical Challenge to Evolution.* New York: Free Press, 1996.
Behe, Michael J. *The Edge of Evolution: The Search for the Limits of Darwinism.* Reprint edition. New York: Free Press, 2007.
Coyne, George V. "Evolution and Intelligent Design. What Is Science and What Is Not." *Revista Portuguesa de Filosofia* 66, no. 4 (2010): 717–20.
Coyne, Jerry. "When Science Meets Religion in the Classroom." *Nature* 435, no. 7040 (2005): 275. https://doi.org/10.1038/435275a.
"Defying Darwin." *Science* 305, no. 5691 (2004): 1709.
Dembski, William A., and Michael Behe. *Intelligent Design: The Bridge between Science Theology.* Place of publication not identified: IVP Academic, 2002.
Discovery Institute: Center for the Renewal of Science and Culture. "The Wedge." 1999. http://www.antievolution.org/features/wedge.pdf.
Fisher, Ian, and Cornelia Dean. "In 'Design' vs. Darwinism, Darwin Wins Point in Rome." *New York Times*, January 19, 2006.
Forrest, Barbara, and Paul R. Gross. *Creationism's Trojan Horse: The Wedge of Intelligent Design.* First edition. Oxford, New York: Oxford University Press, 2004.
Heath, Erin. "Evolution after Dover." *Bioscience* 56 (2006): 300.
Holden, Constance. "School Board Sued over 'ID.'" *Science* 306, no. 5704 (2004): 2023.

Levin, David. "Review: The Edge of Evolution | National Center for Science Education." *Reports of the National Center for Science Education* 27 (2008): 38–40. https://ncse.ngo/review-edge-evolution.

Matsumura, Molleen, and Louise Mead. "Ten Major Court Cases about Evolutionism and Creationism." National Center for Science Education. 2007. http://ncse.com/taking-action/ten-major-court-cases-evolution-creationism.

Miller, Kenneth. *Finding Darwin's God: A Scientist's Search for Common Ground between God and Evolution*. New York: Cliff Street Books, 1999.

National Academy of Sciences Institute of Medicine. *Science, Evolution, and Creationism*. Washington, D.C.: Academic Press, 2008.

Nature. "Dealing with Design." 434 (2005): 1053.

Pennock, Robert T. *Tower of Babel: The Evidence against the New Creationism*. Cambridge, MA: MIT Press, 2000.

Scott, Eugenie C. *Evolution vs. Creationism: An Introduction*. Second edition. Berkeley: University of California Press, 2009.

Tammy Kitzmiller, et al. v. Dover Area School District, et al., Case No. 04cv2688 (2005). n.d.

Wells, Jonathan. *Icons of Evolution: Science or Myth*. Washington, D.C.: Regnery Publishing, 2000.

Wells, Jonathan. *The Politically Incorrect Guide to Darwinism and Intelligent Design*. Washington, D.C.; Lanham, MD: Regnery Publishing, 2006.

Young, Matt, and Taner Edis. *Why Intelligent Design Fails: A Scientific Critique of the New Creationism*. New Brunswick, NJ: Rutgers University Press, 2004.

Lemon v. Kurtzman Supreme Court Decision

The 1971 Supreme Court case, *Alton J. Lemon, et al. v. David H. Kurtzman, Superintendent of Public Instruction of the Commonwealth of Pennsylvania, et al.* (403 U.S. 602), known as *Lemon v. Kurtzman*, centered on statutes in Pennsylvania and Rhode Island that involved the provision of state aid to church-related schools. Both statutes were challenged on grounds that they violated the Establishment and Free Exercise Clauses of the First Amendment and the Due Process Clause of the Fourteenth Amendment. Subsuming the cumulative criteria historically developed by the Court, the *Lemon v. Kurtzman* decision outlined three criteria for determining whether an act violates the First Amendment, known as the "Lemon Test." According to the Court, (1) the statute must have a secular legislative purpose, (2) its principal or primary effect must be one that neither advances nor inhibits religion, and (3) the statute must not foster an excessive government entanglement with religion.

Lemon v. Kurtzman subsumed two different district court cases, one from Rhode Island and one from Pennsylvania, involving public funding for secular education in private religious schools. Rhode Island's 1969 Salary Supplement Act provided for a salary supplement paid directly to teachers in nonpublic schools to compensate for deficits in secular education. The law placed restrictions on how the funds could be used; for example, eligible teachers were required to teach only courses offered in the public schools, using the same teaching materials and reimbursement for courses containing non-secular matter was prohibited. At the time, a considerable number of Rhode Island's elementary students attended Roman Catholic schools, and this was intended as an effort to offset increasing financial burden on these schools. Pennsylvania's Nonpublic Elementary and Secondary Education Act (1968) similarly authorized the "purchase" of certain "secular educational services" from nonpublic schools. The schools were reimbursed directly by the state for teachers' salaries, as well as textbooks and instructional materials. The Pennsylvania law prohibited support for courses containing "any subject matter expressing religious teaching, or the morals or forms of worship of any sect" ("Elementary and Secondary Education Act of 1965 [20 USCS §§ 6301 et seq]," n.d.). Despite these stipulations, lower courts ruled that these acts fostered "excessive entanglement" between government and religion and had the effect of giving "significant aid to a religious enterprise" (316 F. Supp. 112).

Lemon v. Kurtzman was argued before the Supreme Court in March 1971 and decided in June 1971. The suit was brought by citizens and taxpayers alleging that these acts violated the First Amendment, with the concern that religiously affiliated schools might use these laws to promote their own particular faith. The named appellant, Alton Lemon, was the parent of a child attending public school in Pennsylvania. Appellees were state officials responsible for administering the act, along with seven church-related schools. The Court applied a three-pronged standard that would come to be known as the Lemon Test. The third of the three prongs, the entanglement test, was where the Court found the greatest difficulty. A teacher at a religious institution, held the Court, might struggle to maintain strict separation between religious and secular aspects of education, and the level of surveillance required for both curricular content and financial expenditures to ensure adherence to the Establishment Clause (e.g., inspection of financial records) would lead to excessive entanglement of church and state (*Lemon v. Kurtzman*, 615–22). Long-standing traditions of tax exemptions for places of religious worship (see *Walz v. Tax Commission*, 397 U.S. 664) were considered, but the Court held that both the Rhode Island and Pennsylvania programs had "self-perpetuating and self-expanding propensities," which create great risk of entanglement (*Lemon v. Kurtzman*, 624–25). The Court also expressed concerns that such programs could lead to intensified "political fragmentation and divisiveness on religious lines" since they likely required "permanent annual appropriations that benefit relatively few religious groups" (*Lemon v. Kurtzman*, 622–24). This was one of the major concerns expressed by Justice O'Connor, who would later argue that entanglement may give institutions "access to government or governmental powers not fully shared by nonadherents of the religion, and foster the creation of political constituencies defined along religious lines" (*Aguilar v. Felton*). In a review of the

Lemon Test, law professor Daniel O. Conkle (1988: 1147–48) suggests that in O'Connor's view, the Establishment Clause is meant to guarantee that no one be denied equal access to the political process based on their religious affiliation or beliefs.

In a decision delivered by Chief Justice Warren Burger and joined by Justices Black, Douglas, Harlan, Stewart, Marshall, and Blackmun, the Court found both statutes in violation of the First Amendment, with an 8–1 majority on the Rhode Island act and 8–0 for Pennsylvania. The Court judged that these acts themselves did not constitute the establishment of a state religion, but given the parochial school system's centrality to the religious mission of the Catholic Church, they could be seen as respecting that end and a step toward such an establishment. Ultimately, the Supreme Court found both statutes "unconstitutional under the Religion Clauses of the First Amendment, as the cumulative impact of the entire relationship arising under the statutes involves excessive entanglement between government and religion" (*Lemon v. Kurtzman*, 611–25).

The *Lemon* decision affirmed Jefferson's "wall of separation" where schools are concerned while acknowledging that this line is "a blurred, indistinct, and variable barrier depending on all the circumstances of a particular relationship" (614; see Wood and Petko 2000). The strength of Lemon has been tested during the ensuing years. The Court appeared, in *Lee v. Weisman*, to refine the Lemon Test by emphasizing the "endorsement or disapproval" question proposed by Justice O'Connor, where the key is whether the "government's action, either in actual purpose or reasonable perception, works to endorse or disapprove religious beliefs" (Conkle 1993; Schweitzer 1993). In the early 1990s, law professor Michael Paulsen went so far as to declare that "Lemon is dead," suggesting that in *Lee v. Weisman*, the Court effectively replaced the Lemon Test with a coercion test, whereby a policy does not violate the Establishment Clause so long as the government's action does not in some way coerce religious or irreligious minorities (Paulsen 1993).

See also: First Amendment

Further Reading

Conkle, Daniel O. "Comment: Lemon Lives." *Case Western Reserve Law Review* 43, no. 3 (1993): 865.

Conkle, Daniel O. "Toward a General Theory of the Establishment Clause." *Northwestern University Law Review* 82, no. 4 (1988): 1112–92.

Board of Education v. Allen, 392 U.S. 236, 243 (1968), p. 613; Walz, supra, at 674. n.d. https://supreme.justia.com/cases/federal/us/392/236/.

Elementary and Secondary Education Act of 1965 [20 USCS §§ 6301 et seq]. n.d. https://www2.ed.gov/documents/essa-act-of-1965.pdf.

Paulsen, Michael Stokes. "Lemon Is Dead." *Case Western Reserve Law Review* 43, no. 3 (January 1, 1993): 795.

Schweitzer, Thomas. "Lee v. Weisman: Whither the Establishment Clause and the Lemon v. Kurtzman Three-Pronged Test?" *Touro Law Review* 9, no. 2 (1993). https://digitalcommons.tourolaw.edu/lawreview/vol9/iss2/9.

Wood, R., and Michael Petko. "Assessing Agostini v. Felton in Light of Lemon v. Kurtzman: The Coming of Age in the Debate between Religious Affiliated Schools and State Aid." *Brigham Young University Education and Law Journal* 2000, no. 1 (2000): 1–16.

Moral Majority

The Moral Majority was a political action and advocacy group focused on mobilizing conservative Christian voters and promoting legislative agendas that worked to minimize the perceived influence of secularism on American society ("Jerry Falwell Helps Found the Moral Majority," n.d.).

During its time, the Moral Majority "lobbied for prayer and the teaching of creationism in public schools, while opposing the Equal Rights Amendment, homosexual rights, abortion, and the U.S.-Soviet SALT treaties" ("Moral Majority" 2007).

FOUNDING AND BACKGROUND

The 1970s saw a surge in America of concern among "conservative Catholics and evangelical Protestants [who] became increasingly worried about the moral direction of the United States. The U.S. Supreme Court had banned official prayers in public schools, upheld abortion rights, and protected free speech for pornographers" ("Jerry Falwell Helps Found the Moral Majority," n.d.).

In 1979, in an effort to "transcend the traditional divide between "evangelical Protestants, conservative Catholics, and neoconservative Jews," Rev. Jerry Falwell, one of the most prominent evangelical Christian leaders of the time, founded the Moral Majority in collaboration with fellow conservatives Paul Weyrich, Richard Viguerie, Terry Dolan, Howard Phillips, and Robert Billings ("Jerry Falwell Helps Found the Moral Majority," n.d.).

The early success of the Moral Majority can be measured in the context of the 1980 election, in which Republican presidential candidate Ronald Reagan won in a landslide victory against incumbent Democrat

Jimmy Carter ("1980 Presidential General Election Results," n.d.). During his campaign, Reagan had made a concerted effort to meet with and speak to religiously conservative voters, particularly those aligned with the Moral Majority. After the 1980 election, Falwell took credit, on behalf of the organization, for "a number of Republican victories across the country" (FitzGerald 1981).

PAST ACTIVITIES

In 1984, the Moral Majority's influence took center stage in the debate over two proposed constitutional amendments, both of which aimed to "undo the Supreme Court rulings that put an end to organized prayer in America's public schools" (Goodman 1984). Falwell, an advocate of prayer in school, drew attention to "the rise of such ills as crime, drug addiction and pornography since the [U.S. Supreme] court struck down school prayer" (Goodman 1984), not specifically citing a causal relationship but "invit[ing] that inference" (Goodman 1984). While left-leaning Democrats in Congress were not inclined to support the measure, they were "reluctant to offend the Moral Majority in an election year," which speaks to the weight of the organization's influence in Washington at the time (Goodman 1984).

RECENT ACTIVITIES

The Moral Majority was dissolved in 1989. Founder Rev. Jerry Falwell announced in June of that year, at a meeting of the Religious News Writers Association in Las Vegas, that the organization's mission was accomplished (Steinfels 1989), saying that "[t]he Religious Right is solidly in place. . . . Moral Majority as an organization is no longer needed" (Dart 1989).

See also: *Abington School District v. Schempp* (1963); Falwell, Jerry; First Amendment; Prayer in School; Religion and Sexual Education, Teaching in Schools; Religious Discrimination in Schools; Religious Pluralism Teaching; Secularism and Secular Humanism

Further Reading

Dart, John. "Moral Majority Has Reached Goal, Will Dissolve—Falwell." *Los Angeles Times*, June 12, 1989. https://www.latimes.com/archives/la-xpm-1989-06-12-mn-1446-story.html.

FitzGerald, Frances. "A Disciplined, Charging Army." *New Yorker*, May 18, 1981. https://www.newyorker.com/magazine/1981/05/18/a-disciplined-charging-army.

Goodman, Walter. "Strongest Effort Yet to Put Organized Prayer In Schools." *New York Times*, March 8, 1984. https://www.nytimes.com/1984/03/08/us/strongest-effort- yet-to-put-organized-prayer-in-schools.html.

"Jerry Falwell Helps Found the Moral Majority." Association of Religion Data Archives. n.d. Accessed July 9, 2020. http://www.thearda.com/timeline/events/event_46.asp.

"Moral Majority." *Columbia Encyclopedia*. Sixth edition. August 19, 2007. http://www.bartleby.com/65/e-/E-MoralMajo.html.

"1980 Presidential General Election Results." US Election Atlas. n.d. Accessed July 9, 2020. https://uselectionatlas.org/RESULTS/national.php?year=1980.

Steinfels, Peter. "Moral Majority to Dissolve; Says Mission Accomplished." *New York Times*, June 12, 1989, sec. U.S. https://www.nytimes.com/1989/06/12/us/moral-majority-to-dissolve-says-mission-accomplished.html.

National Council on Religion in Public Education

The National Council on Religion in Public Education (NCRPE) was an organization whose mission was to promote the objective study of religion in schools (Knicker 2009). Its position on religion in public education made it unique in the debate about the subject, in that, unlike the more conservative and evangelical groups involved in the discussion, it did not advocate for prayer or doctrinal instruction, and unlike the more secular and nontheist groups, it did not see religion as a necessarily inappropriate topic for instruction.

HISTORY

The NCRPE was founded in 1971, in the same climate that saw the founding of religious advocacy groups such as the Moral Majority, and Focus on the Family (see "Focus on the Family" and "Moral Majority"). In the 1970s, there was a noted surge among Americans, particularly conservative Catholics and evangelical Protestants, who were concerned that the nation was moving in the wrong moral direction ("Jerry Falwell Helps Found the Moral Majority," n.d.).

Of concern to many people in this camp were U.S. Supreme Court cases from the prior decade, such as *Abington School District v. Schempp* and *Murray v. Curlett* (1963) and *Engel v. Vitale* (1962), which effectively banned public prayer in public schools. "In the 1963 cases, the justices extended the ban to include devotional Bible readings and the Lord's Prayer" (Vile, n.d.). Writing for the majority in the *Abington* decision, though, Justice Tom Clark stated, "[I]t might well be said that one's education is not complete without a study of comparative religion on the history of religion and its relationship to the advancement of civilization. It certainly may be said that the Bible is worthy of study for its literary and historic qualities. Nothing we have said here indicates that such study of the Bible or of religion, when presented objectively as part of a secular program of education, may not be effected consistently with the First Amendment" (Boston 2010). Clark specifically explained that his opinion "did not forbid states from teaching religion in a nondevotional context" (Vile, n.d.).

ACTIVITIES AND ADVOCACY

The NCRPE "sought to carry out Justice Tom Clark's dicta that religion could be taught 'objectively' in public schools" (Knicker 2009). To this end, it encouraged state leaders to meet to promote religion studies in their respective public schools and urged colleges of education to prepare teachers for such instruction (Knicker 2009). The council also worked with several institutions to develop instructional materials and curriculum aids that could be used at the public school level.

One publication in which NCRPE members were instrumental is the informational pamphlet, "Religion in the Public School Curriculum." This pamphlet provided guidance for teachers on not simply whether they *should* teach about religion but rather *how* they should do so. Specifically, the pamphlet sought to distinguish "between the teaching of religion (religious education or indoctrination) and teaching about religion" ("Teaching about Religion—Educational Leadership," n.d.). Information from this pamphlet is still available in *Finding Common Ground: A Guide to Religious Liberty in Public Schools*, co-authored by Charles C. Haynes, former president of the NCRPE, and Oliver Thomas, a Baptist minister and constitutional lawyer, and published by the First Amendment Center.

While the council's efforts had mixed success during its time, owing in part to disagreements over what should be taught about religion, and how, toward the end of the 1980s, it did note a rise in interest among public schools in offering instruction about religion. In 1989, Haynes noted that interest in teaching about religion was "exploding," as several states, such as North Carolina, Arizona, and California, began implementing curriculum changes to include religious topics in their respective school systems (Haynes and Thomas 2007).

DISSOLUTION OF THE COUNCIL AND ITS LEGACY

The NCRPE was relatively short lived as a formal entity and began disbanding in 1992. Among the reasons for its dissolution were "fewer serious attempts to alter the First Amendment religion clauses" and the "development of constitutionally acceptable ways of dealing with religion in public school curriculum" (Knicker 2009), essentially leaving the organization with less of a distinct advocacy role.

One of the council's lasting legacies was its establishment of the academic journal, *Religion & Education*, which is still in publication as of Spring 2023. The journal is described as a journal of "analysis and comment with the purpose of advancing public understanding and dialogue on issues at the intersections of religion and education" ("Religion & Education Aims & Scope," n.d.). Subjects addressed in recent issues include teacher attitudes about religious liberty in the classroom, religion's influence on educational attainment, combating Islamophobia in public high schools, and the challenges of teaching about pluralism (Religion and Education).

See also: Abington School District v. Schempp (1963); Focus on the Family; Moral Majority; Religious Diversity in the United States; Religious Pluralism Teaching

Further Reading

Boston, Robert. *Why the Religious Right Is Wrong about Separation of Church and State*. Amherst, NY: Prometheus Books, 2010.

Haynes, Charles C., and Oliver Thomas. *Finding Common Ground: A First Amendment Guide to Religion and Public Schools*. Nashville, TN: First Amendment Center, 2007.

"Jerry Falwell Helps Found the Moral Majority." Association of Religion Data Archives. n.d. Accessed July 9, 2020. http://www.thearda.com/timeline/events/event_46.asp.

Knicker, Charles. "National Council on Religion and Public Education." In *The Praeger Handbook of Religion and Education in the United States*, edited by James C. Carper and Thomas C. Hunt, Vol. 2, 326–28. Westport, CT: Praeger, 2009.

Religion and Education. n.d. Accessed August 28, 2023. https://www.tandfonline.com/toc/urel20/current.

"Religion & Education Aims & Scope." n.d. Accessed August 23, 2020. https://www.tandfonline.com/action/journalInformation?show=aimsScope&journalCode=urel20.

"Teaching about Religion—Educational Leadership." n.d. Accessed August 23, 2020. http://www.ascd.org/publications/educational-leadership/oct02/vol60/num02/Teaching-About-Religion.aspx.

Vile, John R. "Tom Clark." n.d. Accessed August 23, 2020. https://www.mtsu.edu/first-amendment/article/1327/tom-clark.

Nontraditional Religious Identities

Within the broader discussion of the relationship between religion and public education in America, it is easy to sometimes focus on only a few select religious traditions. A quick review of the most prominent court cases and news stories on the subject reveals that, with some exceptions, the religion that is most commonly referenced is Christianity.

To an extent, this stands to reason. After all, according to the Pew Research Center's study on Religion and Public Life, in 2014, of 35,000 people surveyed, more than 70% self-identified as some type of Christian ("Religion in America: U.S. Religious Data, Demographics and Statistics," n.d.). Applied to the U.S. population, as a whole, this means that the country is home to an estimated 230 million Christians.

Yet when considering how religion fits into the public education experience, it is important to remember that under the Constitution, all religions are granted equal protection. This includes not only the other major world religions, such as Judaism, Islam, Buddhism, and Hindu, but also those faiths that might be limited to narrower segments of the population or that otherwise fall outside the mainstream traditions of most Americans.

Like Christianity, many of these religions have been at the center of societal and legal disputes over religion in public schools. As the country increasingly becomes religiously pluralistic, such disputes may become more common.

WICCA AND PAGANISM

One nontraditional religious identity that has seen a significant increase in adherents in recent decades is actually more of a combination of identities rather than a singular one: Wicca and Paganism.

According to a series of surveys conducted by Trinity College, the number of people who identify as Wiccan rose from only 8,000 in 1990 to more than 340,000 in 2008, and in 2004, the Pew Research Center found that about 1.5 million Americans identify themselves as Wiccan or Pagan (Lesley 2018).

Wicca, as a religious belief, is often associated, especially in popular media, with witchcraft, which is defined as the practice of natural magic; however, as Wiccans will point out, the two terms are not synonymous. Because natural magic is central to Wiccan belief and practice, all Wiccans can be said to be practitioners of witchcraft, but not all witches are necessarily Wiccan ("What Is Wicca" 2014). Essentially, the distinction is that while Wicca has a religious component, such as belief in and worship of a god and goddess, witchcraft does not.

Another point of confusion for those who are unfamiliar with Wicca is that while Wicca can be classified as a Pagan or neo-Pagan religion, not all who identify as Pagan practice Wicca (Wigington 2020). "Pagan," as a term, derives from Latin roots, meaning "villager" or "rustic," and was originally used as a term by Christians in the fourth century to identify people in the Roman Empire who practiced polytheism. While the word has derogatory origins, having been used throughout much of its history to refer disparagingly to a person who worshipped a false god or gods, it has come to be embraced by people who practice a variety of religions that trace roots to the pre-Judeo-Christian religions of Western Europe, including Wicca. So, similar to the relationship between Wicca and witchcraft, all Wiccans can be considered Pagans, but not all Pagans are Wiccan.

Because Wicca and Paganism are recognized as religions in the United States, their adherents are afforded the same rights of free exercise as members of any other religion, but there have been cases in which schools have attempted to limit the rights of students to openly and freely practice their faith. In 1999, for example, a school district in suburban Detroit, Michigan, announced a policy change that prohibited students from wearing pentacles ("Michigan ACLU Defends Honor Student Witch" 1999). The pentacle, a five-pointed star enclosed in a circle, is regarded as a religious symbol in Wicca, analogous to a cross in Christianity, a Star of David in Judaism, or a crescent moon in Islam.

The American Civil Liberties Union (ACLU) sued the district on behalf of Crystal Seifferly, a 17-year-old student at Lincoln Park High School and a practicing Wiccan. Seifferly had been "ordered by school authorities to remove her pentacle under threat of suspension" (Cantrell 2001). The ACLU argued that, under the First Amendment, the school could not permit Christian students to wear crosses but deny other students the right to wear a pentacle ("Michigan ACLU Defends Honor Student Witch" 1999). The court ruled in favor of Seifferly, and the school subsequently reversed the policy.

RASTAFARIANISM

Another nontraditional religion that has encountered trouble within American public schools is Rastafarianism. Rastafarianism is a monotheistic Abrahamic religion that was developed in Jamaica in the 1930s and places an emphasis on Afrocentrism and embracing a common cultural strength and identity among the African diaspora ("Rastafarians—Minority Rights Group," n.d.).

Adherents of Rastafarianism, typically referred to as Rastas, observe a variety of beliefs and practices as part of their faith, such as eating only foods that are considered "pure" (i.e., foods without artificial flavorings, artificial colors, and preservatives); shunning alcohol, coffee, and tobacco as substances that pollute the body; smoking marijuana, referred to as "ganja," as a means of spiritual purification; and refraining from cutting one's hair, in accordance with Hebrew scriptures (Leviticus 21:5) (Beyer 2019).

In 2014, a young Rasta student in Louisiana faced disciplinary action related to the length of his hair. The boy was sent home from South Plaquemines High School because his hair, worn in dreadlocks, extended beyond the collar of his shirt, a violation of the school dress code. The following week, he returned to school with his hair pinned up but was told by school officials that his hair was still in violation of school policy. He was sent home again (Gettys 2014).

As in the case of Crystal Seifferly, the ACLU stepped in to defend the student's right to express his religion. In a letter from the ACLU of Louisiana, staff attorney Candice Sirmon argued that the student could not cut his hair because of his sincerely held religious beliefs and that requiring him to do so to attend school violated both the First and Fourteenth Amendments to the U.S. Constitution, as well as an article of the Louisiana Constitution (Adelson 2014). The wearing of dreadlocks, the ACLU contended, was "akin to the wearing of a religious icon by another student" (Gettys 2014), a practice that U.S. courts had already upheld as being constitutional.

The school district ultimately relented and allowed the student to return to school, following an agreement between the superintendent and the boy's religious leader that permitted him to attend classes on the condition that he keep his hair pinned up.

SATANISM

One nontraditional religion that has stirred significant controversy since its founding is Satanism. While the terms "Satanist" and "Satanism" have existed for centuries as epithets, often used by conflicting Christian groups to describe each other's practices as heretical, the modern-day religion is a relatively recent development (Dickinson 2019).

Founded in 1966 by author, musician, and occultist Anton LaVey, the Church of Satan, the most well-known of several churches that identify as "Satanist," has been the subject of much rumor and speculation over the years. While the popular image of Satan is usually as the embodiment of evil in Christianity, a figure who stands in direct and intentional opposition to God, religious Satanism considers Satan to be a pre-Christian figure that is more a "force of nature" than a type of deity ("The Church of Satan: Quotes, Overview, Founding, Beliefs," n.d.). In fact, Satanists do not worship a deity and usually identify as either agnostic or atheist. Among Satanism's central beliefs are the notion that humanity's true nature is "that of a carnal beast, living in a cosmos that is indifferent to [human] existence" ("Official Church of Satan Website," n.d.) and that morals and values are purely subjective human constructs.

The Church of Satan, and other Satanic groups, became the subject of great suspicion and fear during a flurry of reports of ritual abuse that arose in the 1980s, commonly referred to as the "Satanic Panic." These reports alleged acts of violence and sexual abuse against children, human ritual sacrifice, and animal mutilations, acts that are all denounced by the modern Church of Satan ("Official Church of Satan Website," n.d.). These acts were said to be linked to an extensive hypothetical Satanic Cult. Rumors of such a cult eventually proved to be false, as were many of the highest profile accusations, but the image of Satanism as a religion of violence and devil worship persists, even to this day (Eddy 2015).

Given Satanism's reputation and the lack of information most people have about the religion, any activities associated with Satanism often elicit suspicion and fear, particularly when it comes to children. Such was the case in 2016 when the Satanic Temple, an organization founded in 2013 and distinct from the Church of Satan, announced that it planned to launch "After School Satan" clubs at elementary schools around the country.

According to the Satanic Temple, the initiative was intended to provide an alternative to religious clubs, such as the Good News Clubs, which the church believes "focus on indoctrination" and are instilling in children a "fear of Hell and God's wrath" ("After School Satan: Educatin' with Satan," n.d.), both of which are concepts rejected by Satanism.

In Tacoma, Washington, where an After School Satan club launched in 2016, several residents expressed their objection to the club, with some arguing that it would "take away the innocence of [the] children" (Cafazzo 2016) and one group of parents asking the Tacoma School Board to prohibit the club from using school facilities.

Under the Constitution, however, the district was obligated to allow the club to use school facilities. A 2001 Supreme Court ruling held that when a government operates a "limited public forum" (see "Equal Access Act"), such as when a school offers its facilities for use by members of the public, it may not discriminate against speech that takes place within that forum. Because the Tacoma school in question had already permitted a chapter of the Good News Club to meet in school facilities, it was required to permit the After School Satan club to use the facilities as well.

See also: Equal Access Act (Title 20); First Amendment; Religion and School Dress Code; Religious Discrimination in Schools; Religious Diversity in the United States

Further Reading

Adelson, Jeff. "Rastafarian Student Allowed Back into High School | Education | Nola.Com." NOLA.Com. August 28, 2014. https://www.nola.com/news/education/article_efd9bde9-f149-54b0-baea-0716ab3c1104.html.

"After School Satan: Educatin' with Satan." After School Satan. n.d. Accessed July 9, 2020. https://afterschoolsatan.com/.

Beyer, Catharine. "The Beliefs and Practices of Rastafari." Learn Religions. June 25, 2019. https://www.learnreligions.com/rastafari-95695.

Cafazzo, Debbie. "After-School Satan Club Draws the Curious and the Devout to Tacoma School | Tacoma News Tribune." *News Tribune*, December 14, 2016. https://www.thenewstribune.com/news/local/education/article121001243.html.

Cantrell, Gary. *Wiccan Beliefs & Practices: With Rituals for Solitaries & Covens*. Woodbury, MN: Llewellyn Worldwide, 2001.

"The Church of Satan: Quotes, Overview, Founding, Beliefs." Religious Tolerance. Accessed July 9, 2020. http://www.religioustolerance.org/satanis1.htm.

Dickinson, Kevin. "The Origins of Satanism: A Humanist History?" Big Think. June 27, 2019. https://bigthink.com/culture-religion/satanism.

Eddy, Cheryl. "A Brief History of 'Satanic Panic' in the 1980s." Gizmodo. January 20, 2015. https://io9.gizmodo.com/a-brief-history-of-satanic-panic-in-the-1980s-1679476373.

Gettys, Travis. "Louisiana School Hits Rastafarian Teen with 'Unlimited Suspension' over His Dreadlocks." RawStory. August 26, 2014. https://www.rawstory.com/2014/08/louisiana-school-hits-rastafarian-teen-with-unlimited-suspension-over-his-dreadlocks/.

Lesley, Alison. "Witches Outnumbers Presbyterians among U.S. Millennials." World Religion News. October 11, 2018. https://www.worldreligionnews.com/religion-news/witches-outnumbers-presbyterians-among-u-s-millennials.

"Michigan ACLU Defends Honor Student Witch." American Civil Liberties Union. February 10, 1999. https://www.aclu.org/press-releases/michigan-aclu-defends-honor-student-witch.

"Official Church of Satan Website." Church of Satan. n.d. Accessed July 9, 2020. https://www.churchofsatan.com/.

"Rastafarians—Minority Rights Group." MinorityRights.Org. n.d. Accessed July 9, 2020. https://minorityrights.org/minorities/rastafarians/.

"Religion in America: U.S. Religious Data, Demographics and Statistics." Pew Research Center's Religion & Public Life Project. n.d. Accessed July 9, 2020. https://www.pewforum.org/religious-landscape-study/.

"What Is Wicca." Witchcraft & Wicca. August 30, 2014. https://witchcraft.org/what-is-wicca/.

Wigington, Patti. "What Legal Rights Do Pagan Students Have in School?" Learn Religions. August 2, 2019. https://www.learnreligions.com/legal-rights-of-pagan-students-2562919.

Wigington, Patti. "Wicca, Witchcraft or Paganism—What's the Difference?" Learn Religions. January 12, 2020. https://www.learnreligions.com/wicca-witchcraft-or-paganism-2562823.

P

People for the American Way

People for the American Way (PFAW) is a self-described "progressive advocacy organization founded to fight right-wing extremism and build a democratic society that implements the ideals of freedom, equality, opportunity and justice for all" ("About Us," n.d.).

FOUNDING AND BACKGROUND

PFAW was founded in 1981 by Norman Lear (well-known television and film producer), the late congresswoman Barbara Jordan, and a group of civic, religious, and civil rights leaders. According to the PFAW "About Us" page, the organization's founding was specifically in response to the "divisive rhetoric of newly politicized televangelists" ("About Us," n.d.).

The mission statement reads, "[T]o build a democratic society that implements the ideals of freedom, equality, opportunity and justice for all" and to "defend fundamental rights, and fight to dismantle systemic barriers to equitable opportunity" ("About Us," n.d.).

Regarding religion, the organization's statement of values indicates that it "celebrate[s] freedom of religion and religious pluralism as core American values," adding that it resists "religious discrimination and the misuse of religious liberty as a basis to justify legal discrimination or harm to others" ("About Us," n.d.).

PAST ACTIVITIES

PFAW is largely known for its opposition of conservative nominees to the U.S. Supreme Court, such as Robert Bork in 1987 and Clarence Thomas in 1991 (Gibson, n.d.).

In 1987, the organization paid for a 60-second television ad, in which actor Gregory Peck criticized Bork for defending poll taxes and literacy tests "which kept many Americans from voting" and opposing the civil rights law that "ended 'whites only' signs at lunch counters" (Taylor 1987). The veracity and accuracy of the ad was immediately a point of contention among Bork's supporters, some of whom accused the ad of distorting or misrepresenting facts. In response, Arthur J. Kropp, the director of PFAW, claimed that Bork's supporters were, in fact, the ones distorting information. The ads, he said, were "fair advocacy in 'a healthy national debate on the role of courts in our society,'" adding that Bork's supporters had "distorted the advertisements in an effort to 'turn this into a dirty little exercise'" (Taylor 1987).

One of the organization's notable actions pertaining to the role of religion in public schools was its report in 1983 during congressional hearings on the Equal Access Act. PFAW conducted a survey of schools in North Carolina, which found, among other points, that prayer was conducted at various times in nearly one-third of North Carolina public schools, daily classroom prayer was a feature in over 18% of North Carolina public schools, and 15% of the schools had teacher- or principal-led "silent meditation" ("Hearings . . ." 1984). The PFAW report suggested that many schools in North Carolina were "evading and even defying U.S. Supreme Court rulings against organized religious practices in public education" ("Hearings . . ." 1984). The organization's findings contributed to the argument that public schools should "reevaluate what's going on" and "make sure any unconstitutional practices are stopped" ("Hearings . . ." 1984).

RECENT ACTIVITIES

PFAW continues to advocate for separation of church and state in the public school classroom. In a February 2007 statement from Andrew Stengel, director of the Northeast Regional Office of People for the American Way Foundation, the organization took a stand on the matter of a history teacher at Kearny High School, in Kearny, New Jersey, who allegedly taught Christian doctrine to students during an American history class. In a recording taken by a student, the teacher was heard telling students that "if they do not believe that Jesus died for their sins, they 'belong in hell'" (McGeehan 2007).

In his statement, Stengel wrote, "Public schools are no place for pulpits.... As Americans, we are free to worship as our hearts lead. Religious discrimination and religious indoctrination are not proper roles for the government, and our public schools should reflect those principles" ("PFAWF Stands with Kearny High School Student," n.d.).

See also: Equal Access Act (Title 20); First Amendment; Religious Pluralism Teaching

Further Reading

"About Us." *People For the American Way* (blog). Accessed August 23, 2020. https://www.pfaw.org/about-us/.
Gibson, James T. "People for the American Way." The First Amendment Encyclopedia. n.d. Accessed July 9, 2020. https://www.mtsu.edu/first-amendment/article/1197/people-for-the-american-way.
"Hearings on the Equal Access Act: Hearings before the Subcommittee on Elementary, Secondary, and Vocational Education of the Committee on Education and Labor, House of Representatives, Ninety-Eighth Congress, First Session, on H.R. 2732 . . . Hearings Held in Washington, D.C., on June 16, October 18, 19, and 20, 1983." U.S. Government Printing Office. 1984.
McGeehan, Patrick. "Student, 16, Finds Allies in His Fight over Religion." *New York Times*, February 20, 2007. https://www.nytimes.com/2007/02/20/nyregion/20teacher.html.
"PFAWF Stands with Kearny High School Student." People for the American Way. n.d. Accessed July 9, 2020. https://www.pfaw.org/press-releases/pfawf-stands-with-kearny-high-school-student/.
Taylor, Stuart, Jr. "Ads against Bork Still Hotly Disputed." *New York Times*, October 21, 1987, sec. A.

Pledge of Allegiance

The Pledge of Allegiance of the United States is, as the name suggests, a statement of allegiance, loyalty, or commitment, specifically to the flag of the United States. While a form of flag salute was composed by Civil War veteran Colonel George T. Balch in 1885, to coincide with the first celebration of Flag Day (Jones 2010), the form with which people are most familiar today derives from the 1892 version written by Francis Bellamy, a Christian socialist and former clergyman.

Bellamy's original pledge, composed for use in "patriotic celebrations of the 400th anniversary of Christopher Columbus's arrival in the New World" (Andrews 2018), read:

> I pledge allegiance to my flag and the republic for which it stands, one nation, indivisible, with liberty and justice for all. ("The Pledge of Allegiance," n.d.b)

The phrase "my flag" was replaced with "the Flag of the United States" in 1923, in response to concern that "foreign-born people might have in mind the flag of the country of their birth instead of the United States flag" ("The Pledge of Allegiance," n.d.a), and a year later, the phrase "of America" was added after "United States."

The final revision to the Pledge came in 1954, in response to the perceived threat of Communism to the American way of life. The Soviet Union had articulated an objective of "elimination of religion" ("Revelations from the Russian Archives: Anti-Religious Campaigns," n.d.), so at the urging of President Dwight D. Eisenhower, the phrase "under God" was added to the Pledge to position the United States as the ideological opposite of its global rival. This version, which is the official Pledge today, reads:

> I pledge allegiance to the flag of the United States of America, and to the republic for which it stands, one nation under God, indivisible, with liberty and justice for all. ("U.S.C. Title 4—FLAG AND SEAL, SEAT OF GOVERNMENT, AND THE STATES," n.d.)

WHY IS IT RELEVANT TO A DISCUSSION OF RELIGION IN SCHOOL?

The first constitutional objections to the Pledge of Allegiance arose not in response to the addition of the phrase "under God" but to the requirement that the Pledge be said at all. In 1935, two children, Lillian and William Gobitis, were expelled from a Pennsylvania public school for refusing to salute the flag. The Gobitis children were Jehovah's Witnesses and, as such, believed that saluting the flag was forbidden by their faith ("Minersville School District v. Gobitis," n.d.).

According to the Jehovah's Witness publication, *School and Jehovah's Witnesses*, adherents to the faith "view the flag salute as an act of worship" and maintain that they "cannot conscientiously give what [they] view as worship to anyone or anything except [their] God, Jehovah" ("Flag Salute, Anthems and Voting," n.d.).

The U.S. Supreme Court ruled in an 8–1 decision that the Gobitis children's rights, specifically those under the First and Fourteenth Amendments, were not infringed by compulsory recitation of the Pledge ("Minersville School District v. Gobitis," n.d.). (This ruling was later reversed by a 1943 ruling, which held that "the Free Speech clause of the First Amendment prohibits public schools from forcing students to salute the American flag and say the Pledge of Allegiance" (Bomboy 2020).

Following the addition of the phrase "under God," the Pledge was subject to further constitutional objections and legal scrutiny:

> In the 1990s, the American Civil Liberties Union defended students who faced punitive action for refusing to recite the Pledge in school. ("The Pledge of Allegiance and Legal Challenges in Education" 2017)

In 2004, a California parent Michael A. Newdow, an avowed atheist, challenged a policy of the Elk Grove Unified School District that required students to recite the Pledge, on behalf of his daughter, on the grounds that the reference to God was tantamount to a state endorsement of religion ("The Pledge of Allegiance and Legal Challenges in Education" 2017). The Supreme Court ruled unanimously in favor of the school district, finding that Newdow "did not have standing to bring suit because he did not have sufficient custody over his daughter," adding that there was nothing unconstitutional about requiring teachers to lead the Pledge.

In 2010, a challenge similar to Newdow's was denied, when two federal appeals courts ruled that "the Pledge of Allegiance does not violate the Establishment Clause because Congress' ostensible and predominant purpose was to inspire patriotism" and "both the choice to engage in the recitation of the Pledge and the choice not to do so are entirely voluntary" (Bomboy 2020).

WHERE DOES IT STAND NOW?

While the U.S. Supreme Court has ruled that the inclusion of the phrase "under God" does not constitute an endorsement of religion, and that students are welcome to either recite the Pledge or abstain, legal challenges persist at the state level.

In 2014, a group of parents, teachers, and the American Humanist Association brought suit against the Acton-Boxborough Regional School District, claiming that the phrase "under God" in the Pledge was a violation of the state constitution's Equal Protection Clause. In the same year, a family in New Jersey, again, along with the American Humanist Association, filed a similar suit against the Matawan-Aberdeen Regional School District, seeking to "eliminate the use of the words 'under God' from Pledges taken at public schools" (Bomboy 2020). The school district cited a New Jersey state law that schools lead a daily recitation of the Pledge, adding that students were not required to participate. In both cases, the courts ruled in favor of the school districts.

See also: Accommodations; American Civil Liberties Union; First Amendment

Further Reading

Andrews, Evan. "Who Created the Pledge of Allegiance?" History.Com. August 22, 2018. https://www.history.com/news/who-created-the-pledge-of-allegiance.

Bomboy, Scott. "The History of Legal Challenges to the Pledge of Allegiance." National Constitution Center. June 14, 2020. https://constitutioncenter.org/blog/the-latest-controversy-about-under-god-in-the-pledge-of-allegiance.

"Flag Salute, Anthems and Voting." Watchtower Online Library. n.d. Accessed July 9, 2020. https://wol.jw.org/en/wol/d/r1/lp-e/1101983034.

Jones, Jeffrey Owens. *The Pledge : A History of the Pledge of Allegiance.* New York: Thomas Dunne Books/St. Martin's Press, 2010. https://archive.org/details/pledgehistoryofp0000jone.

"Minersville School District v. Gobitis." Oyez. n.d. Accessed July 9, 2020. https://www.oyez.org/cases/1940-1955/310us586.

"The Pledge of Allegiance." The American Legion. n.d.a. Accessed July 9, 2020. https://www.legion.org/flag/pledge.

"The Pledge of Allegiance." USHistory.Org. n.d.b. Accessed July 9, 2020. https://www.ushistory.org/documents/pledge.htm.

"The Pledge of Allegiance and Legal Challenges in Education." Findlaw. September 29, 2017. https://education.findlaw.com/student-rights/the-pledge-of-allegiance-and-legal-challenges-in-education.html.

"Revelations from the Russian Archives: Anti-Religious Campaigns." Library of Congress. n.d. Accessed July 9, 2020. https://www.loc.gov/exhibits/archives/intn.html.

"U.S.C. Title 4—FLAG AND SEAL, SEAT OF GOVERNMENT, AND THE STATES." n.d. Accessed July 9, 2020. https://www.govinfo.gov/content/pkg/USCODE-2011-title4/html/USCODE-2011-title4-chap1.htm.

Prayer in School

Prayer, as an act, is a behavior that most people in the United States would likely be able to visualize or describe, if asked to do so. About half of all Americans report engaging in some form of daily prayer, with groups such as Jehovah's Witnesses, Evangelical and Historically Black Protestants, Mormons, Muslims, and Catholics reporting some of the highest numbers of adherents who pray every day ("Frequency of Prayer. . ." 2014).

Yet defining the act of prayer in clear and objective terms is no simple task. Evangelical Christian organizations, such as the Billy Graham Evangelistic Association, define "prayer" as a "spiritual communication between man and God," likening the act of prayer to a "child's conversation with his father" ("What Is Prayer?" n.d.). One can find similar understandings in Jewish practice, where prayer can be described as an act that "builds the relationship between God and human beings" ("Judaism: Prayer and Blessings in Judaism" 2009), and in Islam, where prayer is one of the faith's five pillars and is used by Muslims to "remember their Lord, express their love and respect for Him and invoke and strive to express their gratitude towards Him" (Hussain 2019).

Even in faith traditions that do not necessarily recognize the existence of a singular almighty deity to whom one would direct prayer, such as Buddhism, or in those that recognize multiple gods or multiple manifestations of God, such as Hinduism, Shinto, and some Native American faiths, people can be said to engage in many "prayer-like activities, such as vows and invocations" (O'Brien 2018) as well as requests for help and expressions of gratitude, recitation of mantras, and focused meditation.

From a more empirical position, prayer can be described as a "discursive act," which seeks to bridge "human limitation and the spiritual realm," and in which the participant becomes "conscious of mortal existence" (Baquedano-Lopez 1999). It is often linked to ritual and celebration and serves as a way for members of a given cultural group to bond with one another, both within a contemporary community and throughout generations.

Regardless of how one comes to understand the meaning of the word "prayer," one element that is consistent across definitions is that prayer involves a communication, and thereby invokes a relationship, with something that exists beyond human experience. This sort of relationship is core to nearly all religions, which indicates why the subject of prayer in a public school is such a point of concern for those who concern themselves with constitutional interpretation: as an act of faith, does prayer belong in a public school classroom, and if so, in what capacity and to what end?

CONSTITUTIONAL CONCERNS

At issue in the discussion of the role of prayer in public schools is whether having prayer in school violates the Constitution, specifically the First Amendment, and even more narrowly the Free Exercise and the Establishment Clauses.

The text of the First Amendment reads, "Congress shall make no law respecting an establishment of religion, or prohibiting the free exercise thereof" ("The Bill of Rights: A Transcription" 2015). The language of this portion of the amendment raises several questions: If a school were to make prayer a mandatory part of the school day, would this imply an establishment of a religion? If there were a penalty for students and staff who chose *not* to pray, would that constitute a prohibition of free exercise? On the other hand, if a school were to prohibit or ban prayer on its grounds or during the school day, would that also limit a student or teacher's right to free exercise of their faith? Would it infringe even further on the First Amendment by "abridging the freedom of speech" of some individuals? ("The Bill of Rights: A Transcription" 2015) (see "The First Amendment").

These questions have been at the heart of several landmark Supreme Court decisions and have been central to some of the most well-known religious social movements of the twentieth century, particularly the rise of the evangelical Christian right in the 1970s and 1980s, with groups such as the Moral Majority being founded specifically to lobby for prayer and the teaching of Creationism in public schools ("Moral Majority" 2007) (see "Moral Majority").

MANDATORY PRAYER AND MOMENTS OF SILENCE

Of most direct concern for those on both sides of the issue is whether schools can authorize, lead, or require that students participate in prayer. This question has been addressed multiple times at the Supreme Court level.

In the case of *Engel v. Vitale* (1962), for instance, the Court addressed the concerns of several organizations that challenged a policy by the New York State Board of Regents that authorized schools to begin each day with a short, voluntary prayer. Similarly, in *Abington School District v. Schempp* (1963), the Schempp family filed suit against the schools over a policy that required the reading of at least 10 passages from the Bible at the beginning of each school day.

In both cases, the Supreme Court ruled that the practices in question did, as the complaints alleged, violate the First Amendment, in that both effectively resulted in a government sponsorship or advocacy of a particular religion. The Court consolidated its *Schempp* ruling with another case, *Murray v. Curlett* (1963), in which a group of Maryland atheists challenged a policy that provided for opening public school days with a reading from the Bible and recitation of the Lord's Prayer (see "*Abington School District v. Schempp* (1963)").

A related concern that has also been addressed by the Supreme Court is whether schools can provide time for students to engage in silent prayer, whether the students are required to participate or not. In *Wallace v. Jaffree* (1985), Ishmael Jaffree, a parent of three children in public schools in Mobile, Alabama, filed a complaint alleging that the schools were conducting "regular religious prayer services or other forms of religious observances" ("Wallace v. Jaffree," n.d.). The case eventually came to address the constitutionality of Alabama state statutes that permitted periods of silence during the school day for "meditation" or "voluntary prayer" and that authorized teachers to lead "willing students" in prayer.

As in the other cases pertaining to school-sanctioned or teacher-led prayer, the Court ruled that Alabama's prayer and meditation statutes did, indeed, violate the First Amendment, as it did not serve any demonstrably secular purpose.

Worth noting is that there are still multiple state statutes in effect that permit or even require moments of silence.

As recently as 2014, 13 U.S. states had mandatory moment of silence laws: Alabama, Arkansas, Georgia, Illinois, Indiana, Massachusetts, Nevada, Oklahoma, Rhode Island, South Carolina, Tennessee, Texas, and Virginia.

Another 18 states do not require mandatory moments of silence during the school day but have passed legislation that permits such moments, usually at the discretion of school district leaders, administrators, or individual teachers: Arizona, Connecticut, Delaware, Florida, Kansas, Kentucky,

Louisiana, Maryland, Maine, Michigan, Minnesota, New Mexico, New York, North Carolina, North Dakota, Ohio, Pennsylvania, and Utah.

These statutes, as written, typically indicate that teachers may not engage in any activity during these silent periods that could be construed as instructing or advocating for a particular religion.

A few states have laws that still allow for some form of prayer in school but with language that prohibits any devotional or doctrinal instruction from accompanying said prayers:

> Montana's state code allows for a teacher or administrator to "open the school day with a prayer," but also states that "[i]nstruction may not be given advocating sectarian or denominational doctrines." ("20-7-112. Sectarian Publications Prohibited and Prayer Permitted, MCA," n.d.)

Similarly, the Mississippi state code allows for "any teacher or school administrator" to "permit the voluntary participation by students or others in prayer" ("2010 Mississippi Code," n.d.). And again, as in the Montana legislation, the code indicates that schools and teachers are not authorized "to prescribe the form or content of any prayer" ("2010 Mississippi Code," n.d.).

New Hampshire's legislation on this matter is unique in that it not only allows for a school district to "authorize the recitation of the traditional Lord's prayer in public elementary schools" but also includes language stating that pupil participation is voluntary and that the recitation of the prayer must be in the context of illustrating to pupils the importance their freedoms and not to "influence an individual's personal religious beliefs in any manner" ("Section 194:15-a Lord's Prayer in Public Elementary Schools," n.d.).

PRAYER AT OFFICIAL FUNCTIONS AND EVENTS

While prayer within schools and during the school day is the practice most overtly at issue, some cases have dealt with prayer that occurs beyond the hours of the school day, such as at extracurricular and official functions.

In *Lee v. Weisman* (1992), for example, a parent in Providence, Rhode Island, sought to stop a rabbi from opening a middle school graduation ceremony with a prayer, invocation, or benediction. The rabbi had been invited by the school principal. The Supreme Court narrowly ruled in a 5-4 decision that having the rabbi lead prayer at the graduation at the principal's request constituted a violation of the Establishment Clause ("Lee v. Weisman," n.d.).

This ruling stands in contrast to an earlier ruling in *Marsh v. Chambers* (1983), when a Nebraska state legislator challenged the practice of opening legislative sessions with a prayer led by a chaplain, whose presence was paid for by public funds. In this case, the majority opinion held that the practice of opening a legislative session with a prayer was one that dated back to the First Continental Congress and was, therefore, "part of the fabric of [American] society" ("Marsh v. Chambers," n.d.), intended not to establish a religion but to recognize a widely held belief and custom of the American people.

One way that schools have attempted to avoid running afoul of constitutional prohibitions is to have any sort of prayer be student-led, thereby putting the school in a more hands-off role; however, even this practice has proved to be problematic.

In 2000, in the case of *Santa Fe Independent School District v. Doe*, the Supreme Court held that the district's policy permitting student-led, student-initiated prayer at football games violated the Establishment Clause. While the district argued that students were permitted to lead prayer as they saw fit, as an exercise of their First Amendment right to free speech, the Court found that a prayer delivered on school grounds, at a school function, using the school's public address system, and under the supervision of school faculty, could not be characterized as protected private speech and that the school's policy "explicitly and implicitly" encouraged public prayer ("Santa Fe Independent School District v. Doe, 530 U.S. 290 (2000)," n.d.).

RECENT DEVELOPMENTS: *KENNEDY V. BREMERTON SCHOOL DISTRICT*

In June 2022, the U.S. Supreme Court ruled on a case regarding high school football coach Joseph Kennedy and his right to engage in personal prayer on school grounds. During his tenure at Bremerton High School, Kennedy, who was hired in 2008, frequently engaged in a brief, silent prayer on the football field at the conclusion of games. While he sometimes prayed alone, he was also sometimes joined by players from his team, along with coaches and players from opposing teams.

In 2015, after incidents that led to the district directing Kennedy to avoid "on-the-job prayer with players in the . . . football program, both in the locker room prior to games as well as on the field immediately following games," the district opted to not hire him for the next season, citing his failure to follow district policy regarding religious expressions and claiming that he had "failed to supervise student-athletes after games" (Kennedy v. Bremerton School District, No. 21–418 (June 27, 2022)).

Kennedy sued in federal court after he was dismissed from his position, alleging that the district "violated the First Amendment's Free Speech and Free Exercise Clauses" (Kennedy v. Bremerton School District, No. 21–418 (June 27, 2022)).

Kennedy said, "that he 'never told any student that it was important they participate in any religious activity,' and that he 'never pressured or encouraged any student to join' his postgame midfield prayers" (Kennedy v. Bremerton School District, No. 21–418 (June 27, 2022)).

The Supreme Court held in a 6–3 decision that the district had erred, holding that "a high school football coach praying on-field after a football game was protected speech under the First Amendment" ("Kennedy v. Bremerton School District," n.d.).

In her dissent, Justice Sonya Sotomayor cited the district's claim that "[d]uring the time following completion of the game, until players are released to their parents or otherwise allowed to leave the event, Mr. Kennedy, like all coaches, is clearly on duty and paid to continue supervision of students" (Kennedy v. Bremerton School District, No. 21–418 (June 27, 2022)).

Sotomayor suggested in her dissent that the ruling weakened precedent, writing, "Today's decision goes beyond merely misreading the record. The Court overrules *Lemon v. Kurtzman*, 403 U. S. 602 (1971), and calls into question decades of subsequent precedents that it deems 'offshoot[s]' of that decision. . . . [and] rejects longstanding concerns surrounding government endorsement of religion" (Kennedy v. Bremerton School District, No. 21–418 (June 27, 2022)).

See also: *Abington School District v. Schempp* (1963); First Amendment; Moral Majority

Further Reading

Baquedano-Lopez, Patricia. "Prayer." *Journal of Linguistic Anthropology* 9, no. 1/2 (1999): 197–200. Accessed August 23, 2020. http://www.jstor.org/stable/43102465.

"The Bill of Rights: A Transcription." National Archives. November 4, 2015. https://www.archives.gov/founding-docs/bill-of-rights-transcript.

"Frequency of Prayer—Religion in America: U.S. Religious Data, Demographics and Statistics." Pew Research Center. 2014. https://www.pewforum.org/religious-landscape-study/frequency-of-prayer/.

Hussain, Amjad M. "Prayer in Islam." The British Library. September 23, 2019. https://www.bl.uk/sacred-texts/articles/prayer-in-islam.

"Judaism: Prayer and Blessings in Judaism." BBC (Archive). August 13, 2009. https://www.bbc.co.uk/religion/religions/judaism/worship/prayer_1.shtml.

"Kennedy v. Bremerton School District." Ballotpedia. n.d. Accessed December 11, 2022. https://ballotpedia.org/Kennedy_v._Bremerton_School_District#cite_note-9th-3.

"Kennedy v. Bremerton School District, No. 21–418 (June 27, 2022)." n.d. Accessed December 11, 2022. https://www.supremecourt.gov/opinions/21pdf/21-418_i425.pdf.

"Lee v. Weisman." Oyez. n.d. Accessed August 23, 2020. https://www.oyez.org/cases/1991/90-1014.

"Marsh v. Chambers." Oyez. n.d. Accessed July 9, 2020. https://www.oyez.org/cases/1982/82-23.

"Moral Majority." *Columbia Encyclopedia*. Sixth edition. August 19, 2007. http://www.bartleby.com/65/e-/E-MoralMajo.html.

O'Brien, Barbara. "Do Buddhists Pray? Yes, and No, and Maybe." Learn Religions. January 4, 2018. https://www.learnreligions.com/do-buddhists-pray-449582.

"Santa Fe Independent School District v. Doe." Oyez. n.d. Accessed July 9, 2020. https://www.oyez.org/cases/1999/99-62.

"Santa Fe Independent School District v. Doe, 530 U.S. 290 (2000)." Justia Law. n.d. Accessed July 9, 2020. https://supreme.justia.com/cases/federal/us/530/290/.

"Section 194:15-a Lord's Prayer in Public Elementary Schools." n.d. Accessed July 9, 2020. http://www.gencourt.state.nh.us/rsa/html/xv/194/194-15-a.htm.

"20–7-112. Sectarian Publications Prohibited and Prayer Permitted, MCA." Accessed July 9, 2020. https://leg.mt.gov/bills/mca/title_0200/chapter_0070/part_0010/section_0120/0200-0070-0010-0120.html.

"2010 Mississippi Code : TITLE 37—EDUCATION : Chapter 13—Curriculum; School Year and Attendance. 37-13-4-1. Voluntary Prayer at School-Related Student Events." Justia Law. n.d. Accessed August 23, 2020. https://law.justia.com/codes/mississippi/2010/title-37/13/.

"Wallace v. Jaffree." Oyez. n.d. Accessed July 9, 2020. https://www.oyez.org/cases/1984/83-812.

"Wallace v. Jaffree, 472 U.S. 38 (1985)." Justia Law. n.d. Accessed July 9, 2020. https://supreme.justia.com/cases/federal/us/472/38/.

"What Is Prayer?" Billy Graham Evangelistic Association. n.d. Accessed July 9, 2020. https://billygraham.org/answer/what-is-prayer/.

R

Religion and Pseudoscience

The term "pseudoscience" refers to beliefs, practices, and explanatory models that are presented as science but that do not meet the threshold of established scientific standards. Pseudoscience also presents data, interpretations, and arguments that can appear to be scientific but are not based on rigorous scientific methods of analyzing and explaining evidence and often violate basic rules of science. Oxford Reference defines "pseudoscience" as "studies and their results based on dubious or spurious science; slipshod methods; false premises, axioms, and assumptions; sensational presentation of findings; predetermined outcomes; and various combinations of the above" (Oxford Reference 2023).

Certain features are common to most forms of pseudoscience. Pseudoscientific claims are sometimes built on the existence of "new fundamental forces"; for example, Rupert Sheldrake's theory of morphic resonance relies on the existence of psychic forces that he terms "inherited memory" (Sheldrake.org; Sheldrake 1981). Claims such as these are typically rejected by scientists because they are untestable by any scientific standards.

Pseudoscience also has a proclivity to fall into the logical fallacy known as *post hoc ergo propter hoc*, where proximity of events is conflated with causality. For example, prayers preceding the occurrence of an improbable event are interpreted as evidence for divine intervention. But the conventions of science urge us to seek the most parsimonious explanation for natural phenomenon, that is, Occam's razor, while pseudoscience often relies on spurious correlations, leaps of faith, and "hidden variable theories." For example, Robert Russell, founder and director of the Center for Theology and the Natural Sciences at the Graduate Theological Union in Berkeley, California, argues that because genetic mutations are random, they must be the hand of God directing evolution.

Differentiating between pseudoscience and science is sometimes construed as the "demarcation problem." Demarcating the line between pseudoscience and science can be complicated by the fact that the former is attempting to present itself as the latter (Lombrozo 2017). In the *Stanford Encyclopedia of Philosophy*'s entry on Pseudoscience, it suggests, "[t]here is much more agreement on particular cases of demarcation than on the general criteria that such judgments should be based upon"; in other words, we know when it is not science, but the specific criteria used to make this determination could be more clearly defined. One approach to demarcation employs the falsifiability test, whereby a statement, at least in theory, must be capable of being proven false with observable data if it is to be deemed scientific. According to the seminal work of philosopher of science Karl Popper, "[S]tatements or systems of statements, in order to be ranked as scientific, must be capable of conflicting with possible, or conceivable observations." Other critical criteria used in assessing whether or not a claim is scientific are: Does it rely on the authority of the individual making the argument as opposed to the evidence they present in support of their claim? Are claims tested against physical evidence and revised in light of new data? Can experiments designed to test the validity of a claim be replicated?

In schools, church-state conflicts can arise when pseudoscientific "evidence" is presented to students as "proof" of supernatural events described in the Bible. Rather than being treated as articles of faith, biblical miracles such as Creation and the Great Flood are presented as real phenomena using quasi-scientific methods, and religious teachings are included in curricula under the guise of legitimate science (Hansson 2013; Mahner 2013). The most visible controversy involving pseudoscience is the debate surrounding Evolution and Intelligent Design. Creationism and Intelligent Design can be regarded as pseudoscience since they embody explanations involving supernatural forces that do not follow the laws of nature (Honey 2015; Numbers 2006; Ruse 2014). One example is the so-called Young Earth Science, or Young Earth Creationism (YEC). A basic tenet of YEC is that a global flood, as described in Genesis 6–9, is a historical fact and the age of Earth is between 6,000 and 10,000 years. Employing explanatory tools available at the time, late-eighteenth–early-nineteenth-century naturalists such as Georges Cuvier subscribed to a model of "catastrophism," whereby geological changes were sudden and dramatic. By the mid-nineteenth century, Hutton's slow, grinding

Uniformitarianism indicated a much older age for Earth, and current dating methods (e.g., radiometric measures) all indicate an age of roughly 4.54 billion years for Earth. In other words, scientific evidence clearly refutes the pseudoscientific assertions.

In some cases, creationists co-opt valid scientific data in efforts to validate pseudoscientific ideas. For example, the Institute for Creation Research conducted an eight-year study called Radioisotopes and the Age of the Earth (RATE) in which they claimed to test the validity of the radioisotopic dating of rocks, a critical tool in the scientific reconstruction of evolution's timeline. Vardiman, Snelling, and Chaffin (2005) conclude that the evidence indicating over 500 million years' worth of radioactive decay is valid but maintain that during Creation and the Flood, decay rates must have been accelerated by a factor of 1 billion, employing a circular logic that the biblical narrative is true and, thus, the facts must fall in line. Given the outlandish claims regarding time, this work has been all but ignored by the mainstream scientific community. Scholars such as Randall Isaac, who are dedicated specifically to navigating questions of faith and science, however, have made a point to expose RATE as classic pseudoscience (Isaac 2007). Popular "Science Guy," Bill Nye, has also made a point to engage directly with questions involving pseudoscience (Nye, n.d.).

Still, despite the preponderance of evidence proving the great age of Earth and the universe, acceptance of pseudoscientific and paranormal beliefs continues to grow. Teachers, supervisors, and all involved with curriculum design need to have clear criteria of inclusion that protect students against unreliable and disproven teachings. The problem is particularly pervasive in the age of social media where information, true or not, can be rapidly disseminated unchecked. In addition, pseudoscientific ideas about religion and science are widely circulated in popular media. Films such as *Is Genesis History* urge the viewer to follow "over a dozen scientists as they explore the science behind the history recorded in Genesis" (IsGenesisHistory.com). Other examples of religiously based pseudoscience conflicting with science as taught in schools include assertions about relics, such as the Shroud of Turin and other attempts to provide scientific support for miracles (Keener 2011).

Scholars and educators have shared useful ideas about how to teach students to distinguish between science and pseudoscience. Some have suggested introducing examples of pseudoscience into the classroom as a way to contrast them with legitimate science. This is not to be confused with the "Teach the Controversy" approach espoused by creationists, which scholars like Scott (2009) and Grayling (2014) warn gives pseudoscience equal footing and equal time with science while casting doubt on scientifically documented aspects of evolution. Rather, by incorporating case studies into their lectures, instructors can teach students the critical thinking skills needed to distinguish between science and pseudoscience and provide the tools to recognize and refute claims (Lilienfeld 2005, 2012; Martin 1994; Schmaltz and Lilienfeld 2017). Students can learn to identify certain clear signs that expose an assertion as pseudoscientific, for example: the use of psychobabble, or terms that sound quasi-scientific but are misused and/or misleading; heavy dependence on anecdotal evidence; extraordinary claims lacking extraordinary evidence to support them; claims that are non-falsifiable; assertions that contradict established scientific facts; lack of serious peer review; and claims that are repeated in the face of evidence to the contrary (Schmaltz and Lilienfeld 2017). Bringing supernatural views into the classroom allows students to perform critical testing exercises and thereby discover firsthand the logical flaws of pseudoscience. This, in turn, helps students develop the ability to evaluate pseudoscientific claims for themselves (Honey 2015; Martin 1994).

See also: Creationism; Intelligent Design

Further Reading

Dolby, R. G. A. "Science and Pseudoscience: The Case of Creationism." *Journal of Religion and Science* 22 (1987): 195–212.

Gardner, M. *Fads and Fallacies in the Name of Science*. New York: Dover, 1957.

Hansson, Sven Ove, M. Pigliucci, and M. Boudry (eds.). "Defining Pseudoscience and Science." In *Philosophy of Pseudoscience Reconsidering the Demarcation Problem*, 61–77. Chicago: Chicago University Press, 2013.

Honey, P. Lynne. "Why I Teach the Controversy: Using Creationism to Teach Critical Thinking." *Frontiers in Psychology* 6, no. 793 (2015): 1–5. https://doi.org/10.3389/fpsyg.2015.00793.

Isaac, Randall. "Assessing the RATE Project Essay Review." *Perspectives on Science & Christian Faith* (June 2007): 143–6. https://www.asa3.org/ASA/education/origins/rate-ri.htm.

IsGenesisHistory.com. https://isgenesishistory.com/product/feature-film/?msclkid=a6cc38d575ab11a43cbe5cad6d0019a3

Keener, Craig S. *Miracles: 2 Volumes: The Credibility of the New Testament Accounts*. Pck edition. Grand Rapids, MI: Baker Academic, 2011.

Koerber S., D. Mayer, C. Osterhaus, K. Schwippert, and B. Sodian. "The Development of Scientific Thinking in Elementary School: A Comprehensive Inventory." *Child Development* 86 (2015): 327–36.

Laudan, Larry. "The Demise of the Demarcation Problem." In *Physics, Philosophy and Psychoanalysis: Essays in Honour of Adolf Grünbaum*, edited by R. S. Cohen and L. Laudan, 111–27. Boston Studies in the Philosophy of Science. Dordrecht: Springer Netherlands, 1983. https://doi.org/10.1007/978-94-009-7055-7_6.

Lilienfeld, Scott O. "Public Skepticism of Psychology: Why Many People Perceive the Study of Human Behavior as Unscientific." *American Psychologist* 67, no. 2 (2012): 111–29. https://doi.org/10.1037/a0023963.

Lilienfeld, Scott O. "The 10 Commandments of Helping Students Distinguish Science from Pseudoscience in Psychology." *APS Observer* 18, no. 9 (September 1, 2005): 39–40, 49–51.

Lilienfeld, Scott O., R. Ammirati, and M. David. "Distinguishing Science from Pseudoscience in School Psychology: Science and Scientific Thinking as Safeguards against Human Error." *Journal of School Psychology* 50 (2012): 7–36.

Lombrozo, Tania. "What Is Pseudoscience?" NPR. May 8, 2017.

Mahner, Martin. "Science and Pseudoscience: How to Demarcate after the (Alleged) Demise of the Demarcation Problem." In *Philosophy of Pseudoscience: Reconsidering the Demarcation Problem*, 29–43. Chicago: Chicago University Press, 2013.

Martin, Michael. "Pseudoscience, the Paranormal, and Science Education." *Science & Education* 3, no. 4 (October 1, 1994): 357–71. https://doi.org/10.1007/BF00488452.

Numbers, Ronald L. *The Creationists: From Scientific Creationism to Intelligent Design*. No. 33. Harvard University Press, 2006.

Nye, Bill. "Pseudoscience." Official Website of Bill Nye, the Science Guy. n.d. Accessed June 21, 2020. https://www.billnye.com/the-science-guy/pseudoscience.

Oxford Reference. Oxford: Oxford University Press, 2023. https://www.oxfordreference.com/.

Pigliucci, Massimo, and Maarten Boudry. *Philosophy of Pseudoscience: Reconsidering the Demarcation Problem*. Chicago: University of Chicago Press, 2013.

Ruse, Michael. "Creationism." *Encyclopedia of Life Sciences* (2014). https://doi.org/10.1002/9780470015902.a0005867.pub2.

Schmaltz, Rodney M., and Scott O. Lilienfeld. "Editorial: Novel Approaches to Teaching Scientific Thinking: Psychological Perspectives." *Frontier Psychology* 8 (2017): 820.

Scott, Eugenie C. *Evolution vs. Creationism: An Introduction*. Second edition. Berkeley: University of California Press, 2009.

Sheldrake, Rupert. *A New Science of Life: The Hypothesis of Formative Causation*. Second edition. Los Angeles: J.P. Tarcher, 1981.

Vardiman, Larry, Andrew A. Snelling, and Eugene F. Chaffin (eds.). *Radioisotopes and the Age of the Earth*. Vol. 2. El Cajon, CA: Institute for Creation Research, 2005.

Wigington, Patti. "Wicca, Witchcraft or Paganism—What's the Difference?" Learn Religions. January 12, 2020. https://www.learnreligions.com/wicca-witchcraft-or-paganism-2562823.

Religion and School Dress Code

School dress codes typically require and/or prohibit specific attire in the school. Dress codes can come into conflict with First Amendment protections that guarantee freedom of speech and expression as well as freedom to exercise religion, particularly when religions suggest or require of their adherents dress codes of their own that contradict the dress codes of the school. Dress codes can also conflict with the Fourteenth Amendment, which guarantees equal protection under the law. This can be particularly problematic when schools either prohibit or require attire that are encouraged or forbidden by religious law or practice. For example, a dress code might ban headwear such as hijabs, turbans, and kippot, as well as accessories such as jewelry with religious symbols or even hairstyles. Dress codes can affect not only students but school staff and faculty as well.

In 1969, the Supreme Court examined the question of dress codes and the First Amendment in *Tinker v. Des Moines Independent Community School District*. The case involved students who were sent home from school for wearing black armbands to protest the Vietnam War. Though religion was not a factor in *Tinker*, the landmark case addressed the issue of attire as a form of expression versus the school's right to enforce a ban on certain articles of clothing. In this and similar cases, schools assert that uniforms have positive effects such as suppressing inequalities and preventing disruptions. The Court held that while dress codes are not inherently unconstitutional, in this case, it violated the students' First Amendment rights, adding, students "do not shed their Constitutional rights to freedom of speech or expression at the schoolhouse gate" (*Tinker v. Des Moines Independent Community School District*). In *Hearn and United States v. Muskogee PSD* (2004), a Muslim student was suspended from school for wearing a hijab in violation of a dress code prohibiting headwear. The U.S. Department of Justice's Civil Rights Division, which enforces federal statutes prohibiting discrimination based on religion, intervened, arguing that the school district had violated Hearn's Fourteenth Amendment rights to equal protection when it applied a dress code in a manner that was inconsistent and discriminatory on the basis of religion. Assistant Attorney General R. Alexander Acosta said:

> No student should be forced to choose between following her faith and enjoying the benefits of a public education.... We certainly respect local

school systems' authority to set dress standards, and otherwise regulate their students, but such rules cannot come at the cost of constitutional liberties. Religious discrimination has no place in American schools.

Ultimately, the school district agreed to modify its policy, permitting Hearn to wear the hijab and requiring the district to make similar accommodations for any student with sincere religious objection to the dress code (U.S. Dept of Justice.gov 2004).

Similarly, in 2011, a 14-year-old student and Junior Reserve Officers' Training Corps (ROTC) cadet, Demin Zawity, was prohibited from participating in a homecoming parade because she wore a hijab. The Council on American Islamic Relations (CAIR) advocated on her behalf, writing to Secretary of Defense Leon Panetta; as a result, the army changed its policy to allow religious headwear in training programs. *Arocha v. Needville Independent School District* (2010) was a case involving the religious rights of a kindergartner who wore his hair to school braided in the style of his American Indian heritage. When the 5-year-old boy was disciplined with in-school suspension for violating the district's requirement that boys wear short hair, the American Civil Liberties Union (ACLU) of Texas filed a lawsuit on his behalf. The U.S. District Court for the Southern District of Texas ruled that the district had violated both the First Amendment and Texas' own Religious Freedom Restoration Act (RFRA), by punishing the student for expressing his religious heritage, a decision upheld in a federal appeals court.

In *Menora v. Illinois High School Association*, Jewish basketball players were prohibited from wearing yarmulkes during a game, the reason being given that the headwear posed a danger should it fall off during play. The district court defended their right to wear religious garb, asserting that forcing students to choose between observing the rules of their faith and participating in a sport infringed on their right to free exercise of religion. An appeals court vacated the district court's decision and remanded the case, invoking the "false conflict" concept and suggesting that the conflict could have been avoided by simply doing a better job to secure the headwear. Still, there was no compelling case that the safety risk was serious enough to overcome the First Amendment rights—no one had ever suffered injury from a loose yarmulke (Carpenter 1987).

Dress codes are not only prohibitive but can also be compulsory, requiring students to wear articles of clothing that could offend their religious values. For instance, schools may require shorts or tops for gym class that are more revealing than permitted by certain religious standards of modesty (see Drake 2017).

One frequently, if inconsistently, used standard in First Amendment cases involving discrimination is the "strict scrutiny" test. To pass the strict scrutiny test, the law in question must fulfill two criteria: (1) their intended effect is to further a "compelling governmental interest" and (2) they have been "narrowly tailored to achieve that interest" (Law.Cornell.edu). The "strict scrutiny" principle was articulated by Justice Sandra Day O'Conner in her dissenting opinion in *Goldman v. Weinberger*, a Supreme Court case involving dress codes and religion in the military. The Supreme Court ruled that the interests of the military prevailed over those of a rabbi whose religion compelled him to wear a yarmulke. Justice O'Conner dissented, writing, "Since the Bill of Rights is expressly designed to protect the individual against the aggregated and sometimes intolerant powers of the state, the government must show that the interests asserted will in fact be substantially harmed by granting the type of exemption requested by the individual." Justice O'Conner stressed that the onus is on the state to demonstrate compelling state interest and least restrictive means in order to justify its denial of a person's freedom of expression.

Professor of Constitutional and First Amendment Law Dale Carpenter has argued that courts should consistently apply one standard test that strikes a balance between government interests in enforcing a dress code and a person's fundamental right to practice his or her sincerely held religion (Carpenter 1987: 602). Pointing to case law, Carpenter suggests that the Court has already developed a three-part test based on strict scrutiny. First, the claimant must demonstrate a burden on religiously motivated conduct (i.e., their free exercise of religion is inhibited). Second, to justify the burden placed on the claimant, the state must prove, with evidence, a compelling interest in enforcing the rule. Finally, the state must also show that the law's intended effect cannot be met with less restrictive means.

Many states now have laws, essentially their own version of RFRA, that require public schools to demonstrate a "narrow and compelling interest" when enforcing regulations that substantially burden religious activity or practice. Any dress code must remain neutral toward religion, and thus, the language of any dress code or policy must not specifically target any religion or religious practice for adverse treatment (Idleman 2001). And if secular accommodations are afforded by the code or policy (e.g., medical exemptions), similar exemptions must be made for religious practice. Finally, the policy or code cannot be designed in a manner whereby it effectively targets religious but not secular conduct (ADL.org, see also *Church of the Lukumi Babalu Aye, Inc. v. Hialeah*, 508 U.S. 520 (1993)). Protections against religious discrimination in schools may also be enforced under Titles IV and IX of the 1964 Civil Rights Act. Schools too can do their part by considering the religious needs of students when drafting dress codes in the first place (see Idleman 2001).

See also: First Amendment

Further Reading

ACLU.org. "Fifth Circuit Upholds Religious Rights of American Indian Kindergartner." July 9, 2010. https://www.aclu.org/press-releases/fifth-circuit-upholds-religious-rights-american-indian-kindergartner.

Anti-Defamation League. "Dress Codes." 2018. https://constitutioncenter.org/blog/constitution-check-do-school-uniform-policies-violate-the-first-amendment/.

Carpenter, Dale E. "Free Exercise and Dress Codes: Toward More Consistent Protection of a Fundamental Right." *Indiana Law Journal* 63, no. 601 (1987): 601.

Carreón-Sánchez, Sulema, and Pheobe Schlanger. "Religion Equity and School Dress Codes." 2018. https://www.idra.org/resource-center/religion-equity-and-school-dress-codes/.

Drake, Aliya. "PE Dress Codes Leave Many Muslim Students on the Bench." 2017. http://neatoday.org/2017/10/23/muslim-students/.

EYVINE HEARN, et al. Plaintiffs and UNITED STATES OF AMERICA, Plaintiff Intervenor, v. MUSKOGEE PUBLIC SCHOOL DISTRICT 020, et al., Defendants. C.A. No. CIV 03 598-S. n.d. https://www.justice.gov/sites/default/files/crt/legacy/2010/12/15/musk.pdf.

Gilhooley, Diane. "Dress Codes and Religious Discrimination in Educational Institutions." August 7, 2008. https://www.timeshighereducation.com/news/dress-codes-and-religious-discrimination-in-educational-institutions/403131.article.

Haynes, C. C., S. Chaltain, J. E. Ferguson, D. L. Hudson, and O. Thomas. *The First Amendment in Schools: A Guide from the First Amendment Center*. Alexandria, VA: Association for Supervision and Curriculum Development, 2003.

Idleman, Scott C. "Religious Freedom and the Interscholastic Athlete." *Marquette Sports Law Review* 12 (2001): 295–345. http://scholarship.law.marquette.edu/sportslaw/vol12/iss1/10.

Menora v. Illinois High School Association, 683 F.2d 1030 (7th Cir. 1982).

State Religious Freedom Restoration Acts (RFRA) Map. 1st Amendment Partnership. 2018. Washington, D.C. http://1stamendmentpartnership.org/wp-content/uploads/RFRA-Map.jpg.

U.S. Department of Justice. "Combating Religious Discrimination and Protecting Religious Freedom." Washington, D.C. 2015. https://www.justice.gov/crt/combating-religious-discrimination-and-protecting-religious-freedom-12.

U.S. Department of Justice Civil Rights Division. "Religious Freedom in Focus." Vol. 3. April 2004.

Religion and Sexual Education, Teaching in Schools

Sexual Education, often referred to as Sex Ed., is a general term used to describe curricula pertaining to human sexual health and sexuality. The teaching of Sex Ed in public schools in the United States has faced opposition from people who tend to view it as morally corrupting and in conflict with religiously conservative values. Topics typically taught in Sex Ed classes include sexual anatomy and reproductive health along with various aspects of human sexual behavior. Comprehensive Sex Ed refers to programs that include instruction on safe sex and sexually transmitted diseases (STDs), as well as birth control methods such as oral contraceptives and the use of condoms, in some cases involving the distribution of condoms.

Proponents and opponents of Sex Ed disagree on multiple points, such as the age at which children should start receiving Sex Ed and the amount of detail revealed, particularly with regard to topics dealing with human sexuality and behavior. Opponents of Sex Ed claim that teaching about sex promotes early sexual activity and promiscuity in youth. Proponents of Sex Ed argue the opposite: that providing students with information about sex is the most effective method for preventing teen pregnancy, while students deprived of information about prevention are more likely to have unwanted pregnancies. They also point to Sex Ed as the most effective way to reduce the spread of STDs.

Opposition to Sex Ed has taken various forms over time, but common to all of these programs is the objective of encouraging students to delay sexual activity until marriage. Certain conservative opponents of Sex Ed, such as the Heritage Foundation and Ascend (formerly called the National Abstinence Education Association), assert that abstinence programs provide greater foundation for personal responsibility as well as enduring marital commitment (The Heritage Foundation 2002). Still, most opposition to Sex Ed invokes religious beliefs about chastity and sexual relations outside of wedlock.

Opposition to Sex Ed in public schools today often takes the form of Abstinence-Only Education (AOE), sometimes referred to as Abstinence-Only-Until-Marriage, or Abstinence-Centered Education. AOE teaches that abstaining from sexual relations is the only effective and morally acceptable approach to premarital relations and usually omits information about family planning, contraception, and safe sex typically taught in Comprehensive Sex Ed courses. Abstinence-only initiatives have been promoted through legislation such as the Adolescent Family Life Act (AFLA), Community-Based Abstinence Education (CBAE), and Title V, Section 510 (42 U.S.C. Section 710) of the Personal Responsibility and Work Opportunity Reconciliation Act of 1996 (Section 912). Though it is usually state and local governments that make decisions about Sex Ed, over $2 billion in federal funding has been spent on AOE programs both in the United States and abroad (Trenholm et al. 2007).

Support for AOE has typically fluctuated with each administration, first gaining momentum under Reagan and peaking in 2008 under George W. Bush. AOE took a sharp turn as Obama shifted away from it and toward evidence-based programs like Personal Responsibility Education Program (PREP) and the Teen Pregnancy Prevention Program (TPPP) (Department of Health and Human Services, n.d.). Again, this turned around under Trump administration, which, in 2018, announced that funding would be geared toward programs that emphasize abstinence or "sexual risk avoidance" while naming an AOE advocate as Chief Staff for the Department of Health and Human Services (HHS). The Biden-Harris administration is currently shifting back toward Comprehensive Sex Ed.

The states vary considerably on this issue. According to the Guttmacher Institute (2018), 39 states require that sex education, when taught, include abstinence instruction and 29 of those states require that AOE be emphasized. Twenty states and District of Columbia, on the other hand, require that when sex education is taught, information on contraception be provided. Nineteen states require that instruction emphasize sex only within marriage. But AOE approaches that directly inhibit the dissemination of information about sexual health could be in violation of the First Amendment's Free Speech Clause.

AOE also raises questions related to the Establishment Clause. Many of the assertions made by opponents of Sex Ed about its inappropriateness are based on Christian values and thus appear to favor one religion's values in formulating curricula in public schools. Organized opposition to Sex Ed in public schools generally emanates from the religious right. In the early 1980s, Jerry Falwell's Moral Majority and Beverly LaHaye's Concerned Women for America (CWA) pushed to ban sex education programs in public schools. Opposition to Sex Ed also came from Pat Robertson, founder of the Virginia-based Christian Coalition, and organizations such as Focus on Family. According to Phyllis Schlafly and the Eagle Forum, "[T]he major goal of nearly all sex education curricula being taught in the schools is to teach teenagers (and sometimes children) how to enjoy fornication without having a baby and without feeling guilty" (Eagle Report 1981). Millions of dollars of Title V, 510 funding have been distributed to religious organizations such as the Tennessee-based Life Choices, Inc.; Colorado's Life Network; and New Jersey–based Several Sources Foundation for the purposes of promoting AOE (https://www.lifechoicestn.org; SIECUS, n.d.). Many such organizations couch their mission in religious terms; for example, James Dobson's Focus on the Family claims that AOE "follows God's plan for sexuality and reflects a biblical vision of marriage and family" (Focus on the Family, n.d.).

Ultimately, Comprehensive Sex Ed and AOE share the overlapping goals of preventing unwanted pregnancy and transmission of STDs. A report released in 2008 by the Heritage Foundation, "Abstinence Education: Assessing the Evidence," based on 21 studies of abstinence education programs, concluded that data show "abstinence programs are effective in deterring teens from becoming sexually active, thereby reducing the risk of STDs, teen pregnancy, etc." (Heritage Foundation 2002). However, multiple studies on the effect of such programs indicate that Comprehensive Sex Ed is considerably more effective in preventing pregnancy and the spread of STDs. A five-year study on the effectiveness of AOE submitted to the HHS in 2007 found that youth in the program were no less likely to engage in premarital sex and were less likely than the control group youth to perceive condoms as effective at preventing STDs (Trenholm et al. 2007). A University of Washington (UW) study in 2008 found that Sex Ed programs that omitted information about birth control showed a 50% higher risk of teen pregnancy when compared to students who did receive this information. The UW study also refuted the assertion that informing students about birth control leads to increased sexual activity and promiscuity (Kohler, Manhart, and Lafferty 2008). A study funded by the National Institute of Child Health and Human Development and conducted by researchers at Johns Hopkins University also found no indication that Sex Ed leads to increased sexual activity.

A comprehensive review of data collected in 2005 (Stanger-Hall and Hall 2011) revealed that AOE as a state policy did not result in reduced teenage pregnancy and, in fact, may have the adverse effect. The Texas Abstinence Education program, for instance, features curricula based on a "sexual risk-avoidance method that empowers youth to voluntarily avoid sexual activity before marriage" (Texas.gov, n.d.). Researchers examining areas of Texas where AOE is taught found that teen pregnancy rates, though falling, remain considerably higher than the national average (e.g., 58% in the Fort Worth cluster). During the 2015–2016 school year, roughly one quarter of Texas public school districts offered no sex education at all; still, the Centers of Disease Control and Prevention ranked Texas fifth highest in the nation in teen birth rates that year (Texas.gov, n.d.; Texas Tribune 2017). By contrast, California, where Comprehensive Sex Ed is taught and students have access to contraception, has lowered its teenage birth rate by 74% from 1991 to 2012 (Amin et al. 2017).

Studies also indicate that the failure of AOE to prevent pregnancy and STDs may result from the dissemination of inaccurate information. A 2004 congressional committee report revealed "major errors and distortions of public health information" in AOE curricula (Stanger-Hall and Hall 2011). The report concludes that these programs leave teens uninformed about reproductive biology and in failing to impart the tools needed to make educated decisions may actually promote irresponsible, high-risk behavior.

The scientific components of Sex Ed curricula, such as human reproductive biology and STD prevention, need not be coupled with social studies. Researchers such as Stanger-Hall and Hall (2011) have proposed integrating comprehensive sex and STD education into the biology curriculum in middle and high school science classes, while a parallel social studies curriculum with expert instructors could cover behavioral components such as family planning and reducing risk, as per the Teen Pregnancy Prevention Initiative and the Precaution Adoption Process Model advocated by the National Institutes of Health.

Some research suggests that removing moral valuation from Sex Ed and focusing instead on the maturity of teens and their ability to handle the consequences of sexual relations is a more effective approach. A study by researchers at the University of Pennsylvania and the University of Waterloo in Canada, as well as a study by the Ontario Institute for Cancer Research, found that abstinence education given to middle schoolers significantly reduced sexual activity (Jemmott, Jemmott, and Fong 2010). Investigators employed an interactive curriculum designed to encourage 6th and 7th graders to delay having sex, largely by focusing on ways to resist peer pressure and role-playing activities while avoiding definition of abstinence as waiting until marriage. Two years after completing the program, 67% of the students taught in this way delayed having sex, compared to 48% of students in a control group who received basic health information only.

See also: First Amendment

Further Reading

Amin, Raid, Julie Zemaitis Decesare, Jennifer Hans, and Kay Roussos-Ross. "Epidemiologic Surveillance of Teenage Birth Rates in the United States, 2006–2012." *Obstetrics & Gynecology* 129, no. 6 (June 2017): 1068–77. https://doi.org/10.1097/AOG.0000000000001897.

Department of Health and Human Services. "Adolescent Health." n.d. https://www.hhs.gov/ash/oah/adolescent-development/reproductive-health-and-teen-pregnancy/teen-pregnancy-and-childbearing/teen-pregnancy-prevention-program/index.html.

Eagle Forum. "Eagle Forum." Eagle Report 1981. n.d. Accessed June 25, 2020. https://eagleforum.org/.

Focus on the Family. n.d. https://www.focusonthefamily.com/socialissues/education/why-abstinence-education-its-right-and-it-works/why-abstinence-education-its-right-and-it-works.

Guttmacher Institute. "Sex and HIV Education." State Laws and Policies, as of May 1, 2018. Accessed June 25, 2020. https://www.guttmacher.org/.

The Heritage Foundation. "The Effectiveness of Abstinence Education Programs in Reducing Sexual Activity among Youth." April 8, 2002. https://www.heritage.org/education/report/the-effectiveness-abstinence-education-programs-reducing-sexual-activity-among.

Jemmott, John B., Loretta S. Jemmott, and Geoffrey T. Fong. "Efficacy of a Theory-Based Abstinence-Only Intervention over 24 Months: A Randomized Controlled Trial with Young Adolescents." *Archives of Pediatrics & Adolescent Medicine* 164, no. 2 (01 2010): 152–59. https://doi.org/10.1001/archpediatrics.2009.267.

KFF. "Abstinence Education Programs: Definition, Funding, and Impact on Teen Sexual Behavior." June 1, 2018. https://www.kff.org/womens-health-policy/fact-sheet/abstinence-education-programs-definition-funding-and-impact-on-teen-sexual-behavior/.

Kohler, Pamela K., Lisa E. Manhart, and William E. Lafferty. "Abstinence-Only and Comprehensive Sex Education and the Initiation of Sexual Activity and Teen Pregnancy." *Journal of Adolescent Health* 42, no. 4 (April 1, 2008): 344–51. https://doi.org/10.1016/j.jadohealth.2007.08.026.

Life Choices https://www.lifechoicestn.org/.

National Coalition against Censorship. "Timeline of Abstinence-Only Education in U.S. Classrooms." n.d. https://ncac.org/resource/timeline-of-abstinence-only-education-in-u-s-classrooms.

Office of Planning Research and Evaluation. "Personal Responsibility Education Program (PREP) Multi-Component Evaluation." 2011–2021. https://www.acf.hhs.gov/opre/research/project/personal-responsibility-education-program-prep-multi-component.

O'Neill, Elyse. "Religion and Sex: The Politics of Abstinence-Only Sex Education." *Berkeley Political Review*, May 14, 2016. https://bpr.berkeley.edu/2016/05/14/religion-and-sex-the-politics-of-abstinence-only-sex-education/.

People for the American Way. "Teaching Fear: The Religious Right's Campaign against Sexuality Education." September 1996. http://www.pfaw.org/report/teaching-fear-the-religious-rights-campaign-against-sexuality-education/.

The Pew Forum on Religion and Public Life. "Faith-Based Funding Backed, but Church-State Doubts Abound." April 10, 2001. https://www.pewresearch.org/wp-content/uploads/sites/4/legacy-pdf/15.pdf.

Planned Parenthood. "How Sex Education Gets Funding." n.d. https://www.plannedparenthoodaction.org/issues/sex-education/how-sex-education-funded.

SIECUS. "SIECUS: Sex Ed for Social Change." n.d. Accessed June 25, 2020. https://sexeducationcollaborative.org/organizations/siecus-sex-ed-social-change.

Stanger-Hall, Kathrin F., and David W. Hall. "Abstinence-Only Education and Teen Pregnancy Rates: Why We Need Comprehensive Sex Education in the U.S." *PLOS ONE* 6, no. 10 (October 14, 2011): e24658. https://doi.org/10.1371/journal.pone.0024658.

Strayhorn, Joseph M., and Jillian C. Strayhorn. "Religiosity and Teen Birth Rate in the United States." *Reproductive Health* 6, no. 14 (2009). doi:10.1186/1742-4755-6-14.

Texas.gov. "Texas Abstinence Education Program." n.d. https://hhs.texas.gov/doing-business-hhs/provider-portals/health-services-providers/texas-abstinence-education-program.

Texas Tribune. "Study: A Quarter of Texas Public Schools No Longer Teach Sex Ed." 2017. https://www.texastribune.org/2017/02/14/texas-public-schools-largely-teach-abstinence-only-sex-education-report/.

Trenholm, Christopher, Barbara Devaney, Ken Fortson, Lisa Quay, Justin Wheeler, and Melissa Clark. "Impacts of Four Title V, Section 510 Abstinence Education Programs." 2007. https://aspe.hhs.gov/report/impacts-four-title-v-section-510-abstinence-education-programs.

Religion and Sports Competition

Although it is primarily an academic endeavor, the American high school experience is inextricably tied to sports. The National Collegiate Athletics Association (NCAA) estimates that nearly 8 million students participate in some form of high school athletics ("Estimated Probability of Competing in College Athletics" 2015).

Because these students are competing under the auspices of their respective schools, most of which are public entities, they are entitled to the same religious protections on the court or field as they are in the classroom.

But determining how to protect a student's religious rights in a football game or cross-country race is a slightly different and, in some ways, more challenging task than doing so in a history class. Consideration must be given to the effective performance and safety of both the student athlete and all the other athletes involved in the competition.

In an effort to devise rules that are equitable to all student athletes, schools and state athletic associations sometimes develop policy that is potentially unconstitutional.

RELIGIOUS GARMENTS AND HAIRSTYLES

Many world religions include, as part of their professions of faith, requirements for what their adherents can wear or how they must groom themselves.

In Judaism, for instance—depending on the denomination—men are expected to wear one of several types of head coverings, such as kippot (also referred to as yarmulkes), or shtreimels (a type of fur hat), and married Orthodox women are usually expected to cover their hair with a hat, wig, or scarf ("Jewish Clothing," n.d.).

In several Muslim traditions, women are expected to wear some type of head or body covering, such as a hijab (a headscarf and one of the least concealing garments), a niqab (a facial veil worn with a headscarf that leaves the area around the eyes clear), or a burka (a full-body garment that is the most concealing), among others ("What's the Difference between a Hijab, Niqab and Burka?" 2018).

In the Sikh tradition, all adherents, men and women, are required to wear what are known as the "Five K's": *kesh* (uncut hair, including facial hair), *kanga* (a wooden comb), *kara* (an iron bangle worn on the wrist), *kachera* (a type of cotton undergarment), and *kirpan* (a sword or dagger) ("Wearing the 5K's..." 2019).

These are only a few examples, but they serve to indicate the obligation that many people are faced with when it comes to demonstrating their religious faith.

The question that sometimes arises in the context of public schools is whether a school can prohibit a student from wearing a religious garment in a sports competition. The answer, although by no means simple, is probably not but maybe.

The McLellan Online Free Speech Library, a resource produced in cooperation with the Michigan State University College of Law, addressed the question of whether a school could require a student to remove her hijab prior to participating in a cross-country running competition. According to the library, because the hijab is a symbol of the student's religion, requiring a student to remove it to compete is, most likely, a violation of the Free Exercise Clause of the First Amendment ("Can a School Make a Student Take Off a Hijab to Compete in a Sporting Event?" n.d.).

The National Federation of State High School Associations, the body that sets standards for high school athletic uniforms and headwear, offers some guidance on the matter but does not offer a hard-and-fast rule. In its rules for high school soccer, for example, it indicates that individual state high school athletic associations may permit players to wear head coverings for religious reasons, as long as the garment is securely affixed to the player's head and poses no danger to any other player and is worn for religious reasons ("Soccer Rules Changes—2018–19" 2018). While this policy clearly invites states to permit religious headgear, it does not explicitly require it.

In order to permit student athletes to wear religious garments, while maintaining a consistent standard for athletic uniforms, states may require students or schools to seek a waiver prior to competition. With such a policy in place, students who fail to apply for waivers could be barred from participating in competition.

This very circumstance occurred in 2019, when a student in Ohio was disqualified from a cross-country race for wearing a hijab without completing the proper paperwork. The student, Noor Alexandria Abukaram, did not learn about her disqualification until after she had completed the race.

Abukaram's situation attracted state and national attention, prompting the Ohio State Senate to draft Senate Bill 288, which "prohibits schools and interscholastic organizations from adopting rules banning the wearing of religious apparel during athletic events" (Feldkamp 2020). The bill was passed and took effect as law in May 2022.

SCHEDULING AROUND RELIGIOUS HOLY DAYS AND TIMES

Another issue that public schools need to consider when it comes to student religious beliefs and athletic competitions is the schedule and timing of competitions and related events.

Most high school athletic events take place in the afternoons and evenings during the week, from Monday to Friday. While this schedule does not conflict with the religious observance of most Americans, for some, such as Orthodox Jews, it can pose a considerable problem because it conflicts with the Sabbath.

Both Judaism and Christianity recognize a weekly Sabbath, a day of religious observance that, among those who adhere to tradition, is usually set aside for prayer, reflection, attendance at religious service, and abstinence from work. For most Christians, the Sabbath is observed on Sunday, and even among the most religiously observant Christians, many still perform some form of labor, whether they are working at a job, taking care of work around the home, or engaging in some sort of physical recreation (Piper 2019). In traditional Judaism, however, the Sabbath (*Shabbat* in Hebrew) takes place during the time between sunset on Friday and nightfall on Saturday. And while a religious Christian might still perform some sort of work on the Sabbath, for observant Jews, most work is prohibited ("Shabbat," n.d.).

Among tasks that are prohibited on the Sabbath in Jewish tradition are traveling, buying and selling, the use of electricity, and the transporting of an object from the private to public domain, or transporting any object in the public domain ("Shabbat," n.d.). For an observant Jewish student athlete, attending and competing in a competition that takes place after sunset on a Friday would likely include several of these acts and, as such, would be prohibited.

In fact, in some cases, Jewish student athletes in America have had to choose between competing and adhering to their religious beliefs. In 2012, for example, the boys' basketball team at the Robert M. Beren Academy in Houston was set to compete in the state semifinals in Dallas but had to miss the tournament. Beren Academy is an Orthodox Jewish day school, and the semifinal game was scheduled for 9 p.m., on a Friday (Pilon 2012).

The school is a member of the Texas Association of Private and Parochial Schools (TAPPS), the organization that runs the tournament the Beren Academy team was to be a part of. Their tournament is separate from the larger one for the state's public schools. Beren Academy filed an appeal with the TAPPS, but it was denied, and the team slot in the tournament was ultimately filled by another team (Pilon 2012).

While the Beren Academy situation fell out of the purview of public schools, as it and all of its opponents in the tournament were private schools, the circumstance is one that could potentially affect students' abilities to compete in public school events, such as when an observant Jewish student attends a public school or in state leagues in which public and private schools compete together.

Sarah Barringer Gordon, a professor of law and history at the University of Pennsylvania, said that she expected conflicts between religious beliefs and sports schedules to become more common as "pluralism works its way through American sports" (Popke 2012).

As matters stand, there is no law prohibiting schools from scheduling athletic competitions on days such as the Sabbath; the most commonly recommended solution is for schedules to be designed with sensitivity toward students' religious obligations and for schools and athletic associations to start, as Gordon put it, "rethinking who their constituencies are" (Popke 2012).

See also: Accommodations; Religion and School Dress Code; Religious Discrimination in Schools; Religious Diversity in the United States; Student-Initiated Prayer, Clubs

Further Reading

"Can a School Make a Student Take Off a Hijab to Compete in a Sporting Event?" n.d. Accessed July 9, 2020. https://mclellanlib.com/questions/wearing-hijab-during-sport-event.

"Estimated Probability of Competing in College Athletics." NCAA. March 2, 2015. http://www.ncaa.org/about/resources/research/estimated-probability-competing-college-athletics.

Feldkamp, Justin. "Noor Alexandria Abukaram Becomes Face of Senate Bill 288." 13abc.Com. June 25, 2020. https://www.13abc.com/content/news/Noor-Alexandria-Abukaram-becomes-face-of-Senate-Bill-288-571497261.html.

Hirt, David. "New Ohio Law Prohibits Restrictions Against Students Wearing Religious Apparel While Competing." JDSUPRA. Last modified June 1, 2022. Accessed April 28, 2023. https://www.jdsupra.com/legalnews/new-ohio-law-prohibits-restrictions-7279089/.

"Jewish Clothing." My Jewish Learning. n.d. Accessed July 9, 2020. https://www.myjewishlearning.com/article/jewish-clothing/.

Pilon, Mary. "In Texas, the Sabbath Trumps the Semifinals." *New York Times*, February 28, 2012. https://www.nytimes.com/2012/02/28/sports/jewish-schools-team-refusing-to-play-during-sabbath-loses-trip-to-state-semifinals.html.

Piper, John. "Advice for Christians Who Work Sundays." Desiring God. November 1, 2019.

Popke, Michael. "Jewish School Forfeits Tourney Game to Observe Sabbath—Athletic Business." February 2012. Accessed August 23, 2020. https://www.athleticbusiness.com/jewish-school-forfeits-tourney-game-to-observe-sabbath.html.

"Shabbat." Judaism 101. n.d. Accessed July 9, 2020. http://www.jewfaq.org/shabbat.htm.

"Soccer Rules Changes—2018–19." 2018. NFHS. February 20, 2018. https://www.nfhs.org/sports-resource-content/soccer-rules-changes-2018-19.

"Wearing the 5K's (Kara, Kesh, Kirpan, Kacheras, Kanga)." Sikh Dharma International. March 26, 2019. https://www.sikhdharma.org/the-5-ks-kara-kesh-kirpan-kacheras-kanga/.

"What's the Difference between a Hijab, Niqab and Burka?" BBC. August 7, 2018. https://www.bbc.co.uk/newsround/24118241.

Religion in Performances

Some of the most common artistic expressions in which public school students engage are music and the dramatic arts. Students in schools nationwide take part in classes and programs such as marching band, orchestra, theater, and choir.

In the context of these programs, students often perform songs, plays, and musicals that invoke the religious in one way or another. A high school, for example, might perform an annual concert in late December, in which students perform songs such as George Handel's "Hallelujah Chorus" or the African American spiritual, "Go Tell It on the Mountain." Both these songs are replete with religious meaning and lyrics.

Such performances raise several important questions: Are the songs religious in a devotional sense? Can they be performed in the proper context? What should or must a school do in the face of objections from the community?

DOES "SACRED" MUSIC HAVE A PLACE IN PUBLIC SCHOOLS?

The National Association for Music Education has faced these questions head-on, producing a position statement on sacred music in schools. The association's position on the matter is "that the study and performance of religious music within an educational context is a vital and appropriate part of a comprehensive music education. The omission of sacred music from the school curriculum would result in an incomplete educational experience" ("Sacred Music in Schools," n.d.).

This position aligns with Supreme Court rulings, such as *Abington School District v. Schempp* (1963), in which the Court ruled that "one's education is not complete without a study of comparative religion or the history of religion and its relationship to the advancement of civilization" ("School Dist. of Abington Tp. v. Schempp, 374 U.S. 203 (1963)," n.d.) (see "*Abington School District v. Schempp* (1963)").

Educator and composer Adam Paltrowitz wrote that when someone is performing a piece "with a sacred text in a non-religious setting," such as a student chorus or orchestra performing a piece during a schoolwide assembly, "it is no longer being used for religious purposes; the song then becomes a piece of art, just as taking a painting off of a church wall and bringing it into the classroom for art students to learn from would not be religious" (Paltrowitz 2016).

But concern about religious music in public schools has been a perennial concern among American parents.

The Freedom from Religion Foundation claims that in its more than 30 years, it has received more complaints about the "promotion of religion" in music classes and in team sport than any other type of complaint (Gaylor, n.d.).

The foundation suggests that, when evaluating whether a musical selection is academically appropriate, one should consider the educational value of the song, what ages are studying the music, whether the school or district uses religious holiday titles for its performances, whether there is a balance between secular and religious music in a performance program, whether religious symbols are used in the performance, and if the music teacher, band leader, or choral director actively promotes a particular religion rather than music comprehension and mastery (Gaylor, n.d.).

LEGAL HISTORY OF SACRED MUSIC IN PUBLIC SCHOOLS

Legal challenges to religious music date back to the 1970s, according to the National Association for Music Education. In 1977, in Sioux Falls, South Dakota, two public school kindergarten classes rehearsed and performed a Christmas assembly that includes a call-and-response dialogue between the teacher and students in the class, which consisted the lines:

> Teacher: Of whom did heav'nly angels sing, /And news about His birthday bring?
> Class: Jesus.
> Teacher: Now, can you name the little town/Where they the Baby Jesus found?
> Class: Bethlehem.
> Teacher: Where had they made a little bed/For Christ, the blessed Saviour's head?
> Class: In a manger in a cattle stall.
> Teacher: What is the day we celebrate As birthday of this One so great?
> Class: Christmas. ("Florey v. SIOUX FALLS SCH. DIST. 49–5, 464 F. Supp. 911 (D.S.D. 1979)," n.d.)

A parent of one of the pupils lodged a complaint with the Sioux Falls School District about the program, taking exception to both the previously cited dialogue and the singing of songs such as "Silent Night," which he argued had inherently religious themes and purposes ("Florey v. SIOUX FALLS SCH. DIST. 49–5, 464 F. Supp. 911 (D.S.D. 1979)," n.d.). The challenge eventually made its way to the Eighth U.S. Court of Appeals, where the court ruled that the school's policy on using religiously themed music in its assembly was not "promulgated with religious purposes in mind" ("Sacred Music in Schools," n.d.).

In a later case, a U.S. District Court judge dismissed a lawsuit against Salt Lake City's West High School, over Christian songs sung by the school choir. The plaintiff in that matter was a student at West High School who argued that the songs were "sung prayers" and constituted a violation of the Establishment Clause. The court said that the music had "a purpose in education beyond the mere words or notes in conveying a mood, teaching cultures and history, and broadening understanding of arts" and that the music's purpose was primarily secular ("Bauchman, by and through Bauchman v. West High, 900 F. Supp. 254 (D. Utah 1995)," n.d.; "Sacred Music in Schools," n.d.).

The majority of case law on the matter has tended to fall on the side of supporting the use of religiously themed music, as long as it is used for secular purposes and is balanced with music of other religious and secular traditions.

RELIGIOUSLY THEMED DRAMATIC PRODUCTIONS

A similar conversation can be had about the use of religiously themed drama in public schools. While much of the drama that is performed in public schools is secular, there are some commonly used works that are distinctly religious in nature, in one way or another.

One such production is the 1971 off-Broadway musical, *Godspell*. The story of *Godspell* is inspired by the teachings of Jesus, specifically as depicted in the New Testament book of Matthew, but focuses on the lessons presented in the text rather than the miracles Jesus is said to have performed. In 2004, a teacher at Covington High School in New Orleans proposed *Godspell* as a student performance for the coming year but was denied by the school principal on the grounds that several members of the community objected to the show's Christian content (Ware and Glanzer 2005).

Other works that are linked either directly or indirectly to religious characters, events, or themes include *Jesus Christ Superstar, Joseph and the Amazing Technicolor Dreamcoat, Inherit the Wind, Luther, The Crucible, Fiddler on the Roof,* and *Les Miserables*. When teaching or directing such works, public school teachers must be aware of the potential for community objection but, at the same time, must recognize both the secular merit of these works and the fact that they might have much more constitutional leeway than they realize.

The Anti-Defamation League (ADL) addressed this issue in its publication, *Religion in the Public Schools*. The ADL recognized that the

Supreme Court has not specifically ruled on this subject but suggested that religiously themed drama may be appropriate in a public school setting, as long as the content is "primarily secular, objective and educational" and does not "focus on any one religion or religious observance [or] appear to endorse religion over non-religion or one religion over another" ("Teaching about Religious Holidays—'The December Dilemma,'" n.d.).

In short, as with most school subjects that might address religious issues, as long the religious theme is secondary to the secular, objective purpose in discussing the subject, it will likely be considered constitutionally appropriate.

See also: *Abington School District v. Schempp* (1963); First Amendment; Religious Diversity in the United States

Further Reading

"Bauchman, by and through Bauchman v. West High, 900 F. Supp. 254 (D. Utah 1995)." Justia Law. n.d. Accessed July 9, 2020. https://law.justia.com/cases/federal/district-courts/FSupp/900/254/2262359/.

"Florey v. SIOUX FALLS SCH. DIST. 49–5, 464 F. Supp. 911 (D.S.D. 1979)." Justia Law. n.d. Accessed July 9, 2020. https://law.justia.com/cases/federal/district-courts/FSupp/464/911/1520042/.

Gaylor, Annie Laurie. "Religious Music in Public Schools—Freedom from Religion Foundation." Freedom from Religion Foundation. n.d. Accessed July 9, 2020. https://ffrf.org/outreach/item/14027-religious-music-in-public-schools.

Paltrowitz, Adam. "Keep 'Religion' out of Public School Choir." Choral Clarity. November 7, 2016. https://www.choralclarity.com/keep-religion-public-school-choir/.

"Sacred Music in Schools." National Association for Music Education. n.d. Accessed July 9, 2020. https://nafme.org/about/position-statements/sacred-music-in-schools-position-statement/sacred-music-in-schools/.

"School Dist. of Abington Tp. v. Schempp, 374 U.S. 203 (1963)." Justia Law. n.d. Accessed July 9, 2020. https://supreme.justia.com/cases/federal/us/374/203/.

"School District of Abington Township, Pennsylvania v. Schempp." Oyez. n.d. Accessed July 9, 2020. https://www.oyez.org/cases/1962/142.

"Teaching about Religious Holidays—'The December Dilemma.'" n.d. Accessed July 9, 2020. https://www.adl.org/media/2082/download.

Ware, Allen Reeves, and Perry L. Glanzer. "God on Stage? Religious Themes in Public Educational Theatre." *Journal of Church and State* 47, no.3 (2005): 563–81. https://doi.org/10.1093/jcs/47.3.563.

Religious Discrimination in Schools

Discrimination involving religion and religious identity is a considerable problem in American schools today, and incidents have increased since 2015, in some cases dramatically. Religious discrimination in schools ranges from outright acts of bias against students from religious minorities by peers to institutionalized forms of discrimination, such as school policies that alienate students of non-majority faiths. Students representing religious minorities in the United States are frequently subject to bullying by their peers, and even teachers, while microaggressions, stereotyping, and other forms of intimidation or marginalization are common. In worst cases, hatred toward religious minorities manifests as violence.

Religious discrimination, as defined by the U.S. government's Equal Opportunity Employment Commission (EEOC), involves "treating a person . . . unfavorably because of his or her religious beliefs. The law protects not only people who belong to traditional, organized religions, such as Buddhism, Christianity, Hinduism, Islam, and Judaism, but also others who have sincerely held religious, ethical or moral beliefs" (U.S. Equal Opportunity Employment Commission, n.d.). Though the Department of Education does not offer its own definition of religious discrimination, it is addressed in Title IV of the Civil Rights Act of 1964, which "prohibits discrimination based on religion in public primary and secondary schools, as well as public colleges and universities." Title IV concerns are enforced by Civil Rights Division's Educational Opportunities Section, which authorizes the attorney general to bring suit in response to written complaints that a child is being "deprived by a school board of the equal protection of the laws" (Civil Rights Act of 1964 subsection (a)(1)). Title IX of the Education Amendments Act of 1972 also protects students against discrimination in schools. In 2004, Kenneth L. Marcus, from the Department of Education's Office of Civil Rights, published a "dear colleague" letter, asserting that this office "aggressively investigates" allegations of Title VI and Title IX violations such as "race or ethnic harassment against Arab Muslim, Sikh and Jewish students." In 2015, the Civil Rights Division of the U.S. Department of Justice issued a statement on Religious Discrimination in Education, stating, "[S]tudents should not face discrimination or harassment because of their faith background, their beliefs, their distinctive religious dress, or their religious expression" (U.S. Department of Justice 2015). In fall 2016, the Department of Education announced that it would begin collecting data to track religiously motivated discrimination or bullying allegations in schools.

A distinction can be drawn between acts of open and intentional aggression, such as the use of slurs and physical aggression, which are more easily addressed, and less overt forms of discrimination, such as implicit bias and institutional disenfranchisement, which may be less apparent but no less damaging and pervasive. Distinguishing between religious and racial or ethnic discrimination can sometimes be complicated. For example, there have been many cases where South Asian students of Hindu or Sikh background are bullied as if they are Muslim (Costello 2016), itself a symptom of religious illiteracy in our schools. It can also be difficult to determine the motive behind a bias incident if there is no overt verbal abuse.

Acute anti-Semitism has been present in American schools ever since the mid-nineteenth century and increasing Jewish immigration from Europe. Anti-Semitism in schools typically takes the form of vandalism with anti-Semitic messages such as "Kill all Jews" and "No Jews," Nazi/neo-Nazi rhetoric including "Heil Hitler," "white power," the code numbers 14/88 and swastikas, and direct harassment of and assaults on Jewish children (Anti-Defamation League [ADL] 2019: 8). According to a report by the ADL, anti-Semitism overall rose sharply in 2016–2017, especially in K–12 public schools, where the majority of anti-Semitic incidents in the United States occurred that year (ADL 2019: 6). Anti-Semitic incidents in schools doubled two years in a row, jumping from 114 in 2015 to 235 in 2016 to 457 in 2017; the number fell back to 344 in 2018 (ADL 2019). One way the ADL has tried to remedy this is through an online resource titled "Dos and Don'ts in Responding to Anti-Semitism on Campus," which outlines best practices (ADL 2017).

Anti-Muslim bias, or "Islamophobia," has also risen sharply in American schools, becoming a "social fact of school life" for many students, according to researchers Mir and Sarroub (2019: 298). Their systematic study of news media reporting about anti-Muslim harassment in schools between 2015 and 2017 revealed 55 documented cases of "Islamophobia" in the United States reported in major newspapers. The Southern Poverty Law Center (SPLC) conducted a study of 2,000 K–12 teachers, finding that roughly one-third had observed anti-Muslim sentiments growing in schools during the 2016 election cycle (SPLC.org 2016). A survey conducted by the Council on American Islamic Relations (CAIR 2017) found that 55% of Muslim students reported being bullied at schools because of their faith, while almost a third (29%) of students who wore a hijab experienced offensive touching or pulling of their scarves and 45% of high school students reported hearing racist remarks (e.g., terrorist slurs and references to bombs) about Arabs in their classrooms. When 14-year-old Ahmed Mohamed brought a homemade alarm clock to his Texas high school as a science project, he was interrogated by police under suspicion of bringing a bomb and was suspended from school for three days. Muslim teachers, too, are subject to discrimination; for example, a teacher in Gwinnett County, Georgia, received a handwritten note telling her to hang herself with her headscarf (Sharpe 2016).

Hindus as well have been targeted by religious discrimination. A survey of 335 Hindu students conducted by the Hindu American Foundation found that one-third of respondents had been bullied because of their religion, while about half indicated "feelings of awkwardness or social isolation because of their religious identity" (Hindu American Foundation, n.d.). Many of the students surveyed also reported feeling marginalized by their school curriculum that included long debunked claims about Hindu social practices such as the caste system and a poor understanding of the faith contained in textbooks (including a 2006 lawsuit in California), as well as derogatory remarks from teachers. Sikh students also face discrimination in schools. The Sikh Coalition reports that they received more legal intakes related to school bullying in the 2017–2018 school year than in the previous two years combined (Sikh Coalition n.d.).

Grievances of religious discrimination are not exclusive to religious minorities; Christian students who encounter limits on religious expression have also complained that they are being targeted for their faith. When high school students in Massachusetts, for example, were suspended for passing out candy canes with religious messages attached, the Department of Education Civil Rights Division filed a friend-of-the-court brief arguing that the students' First Amendment rights had been violated (Geylikman 2003). In such cases, despite the clear First Amendment implications, Christian students were not the victim of bullying or bias, and the limitations they encountered applied to all students alike.

Acts of religious intolerance have drawn national attention in some cases. In 2015, at Augusta County, Virginia, an incident involving a world geography class caused an uproar when the *Shahada* (Muslim declaration of faith) was used in an Arabic calligraphy lesson. Some in the community called the lesson an indoctrination of faith, and upon receiving numerous threats, schools were forced to close for several days. A Texas schoolteacher who included the donning of Islamic religious apparel as part of a lesson about Islam and the Middle East in 2013 faced national scrutiny when photos of students wearing the clothing went "viral." In the words of Linda Wertheimer (2015b) who documented the incident in *Faith Ed: Teaching about Religion in an Age of Intolerance*, "[R]ight-wing media turned a lesson in tolerance into an excuse for hate." The challenge faced by schools is how to remedy the religious illiteracy that so often leads to discrimination without raising First Amendment concerns.

See also: Religious Pluralism Teaching

Further Reading

Anti-Defamation League. "Audit of Anti-Semitic Incidents: Year in Review 2018." 2019. https://www.adl.org/audit2018.

Anti-Defamation League. "Dos and Don'ts in Responding to Antisemitism on Campus." 2017. https://www.adl.org/resources/tools-and-strategies/dos-and-donts-in-responding-to-anti-semitism-on-campus.

CAIR, n.d. "2017 Civil Rights Report: The Empowerment of Hate." May 2, 2017. https://islamophobia.org/reports/the-empowerment-of-hate/.

Civil Rights Act of 1964 subsection (a)(1). Title VII, Equal Employment Opportunities (1964). https://www.govinfo.gov/content/pkg/COMPS-342/pdf/COMPS-342.pdf

Costello, Maureen. "The Trump Effect: The Impact of the Presidential Campaign on Our Nation's Schools." Southern Poverty Law Center, 2016, 1–16. https://www.splcenter.org/sites/default/files/splc_the_trump_effect.pdf.

Geylikman, Rozanna. "The 'Candy Cane' Case: Implications of the First Amendment in Public Schools." *University of California Irvine Law Forum Journal*, 1 (2003): 16.

Hindu American Foundation. n.d. Accessed June 22, 2020. https://www.hinduamerican.org/.

Joshi, Khyati Y. *White Christian Privilege: The Illusion of Religious Equality in America*. New York: NYU Press, 2020.

Mir, Shabbana, and Loukia Sarroub. "Islamophobia in U.S. Education." In *The Routledge International Handbook of Islamophobia*, edited by I. Zempi and I. Awan, 298–309. Abingdon; New York: Routledge, 2019. https://www.routledge.com/The-Routledge-International-Handbook-of-Islamophobia-1st-Edition/Zempi-Awan/p/book/9780815353751.

Sharpe, J. "Muslim Gwinnett Teacher Told to 'Hang Yourself' with Her Headscarf." 2016. www.ajc.com/news/local/muslim-gwinnett-teacher-told-hang-yourself-with-her-headscarf/XVrOecQFQRbKc7SuggJMtI/.

Sikh Coalition. "Preventing and Addressing School Bullying." n.d. Accessed June 22, 2020. https://www.sikhcoalition.org/our-work/creating-safe-schools/preventing-and-ending-school-bullying/.
U.S. Department of Justice. "Combating Religious Discrimination and Protecting Religious Freedom." 2015. https://www.justice.gov/crt/combating-religious-discrimination-and-protecting-religious-freedom-12.
U.S. Equal Opportunity Employment Commission. "Religious Discrimination." n.d. Accessed July 4, 2019. https://www.eeoc.gov/laws/types/religion.cfm.
Wertheimer, Linda K. "A Burka in a Christian Town: How Fox News and Right-Wing Media Turned a Lesson in Tolerance into an Excuse for Hate." 2015a. https://www.salon.com/2015/08/30/a_burka_in_a_christian_town_how_fox_news_and_right_wing_media_turned_a_lesson_in_tolerance_into_an_excuse_for_hate/.
Wertheimer, Linda K. *Faith Ed: Teaching about Religion in an Age of Intolerance*. First edition. Boston: Beacon Press, 2015b.

Religious Diversity in the United States

The history of religious diversity in America is a story of conflict as well as cooperation. The first religions of America are those of the indigenous peoples, commonly known as American Indians or Native Americans. Indigenous religions follow a wide range of practices often centered around nature and seasonal cycles and invoking animals as symbols used to convey stories and ideas. European settlers arriving in the early 1600s came from a wide range of Protestant and Catholic traditions and would soon begin a process of displacing the Indians, thereby devastating Indian culture and religious traditions. Europeans would also soon bring America's first Muslims as captives in the Atlantic slave trade. A Virginia statute from 1682 refers to slaves of "Mahometan parentage and country," and historical records indicate that the founders owned slaves with Muslim names. According to Diouf (2013), despite countervailing pressures, many Muslim slaves were able to maintain their faith and identity. The non-Muslim Africans brought other religious traditions, some of which are preserved today in syncretistic religions like Santeria and Vodou.

The earliest Jews arrived in 1654, coming from Recife, Brazil, and landing in New Amsterdam where they established the first congregation in North America, Shearith Israel, which still exists today (Angel 2004). Fleeing persecution by the Portuguese of Brazil, they were soon harassed in their adopted home by Dutch governor Peter Stuyvesant. Jewish immigration would continue in cities such as Newport, Philadelphia, and Savannah but remained small, reaching no more than 2,500, or roughly

0.1% of the population, by 1776. The vast majority of America at the time was still Christian. According to professor of religion, Diana Eck (2002), "[T]here were fewer than one hundred Roman Catholic churches in the colonies and only a handful of synagogues, meager numbers compared with the 2000 plus churches controlled by the top four protestant denominations," those being Congregationalists, Presbyterians, Baptists, and Anglicans.

It was not until the mid-nineteenth century that the religious composition of the United States would shift significantly. A wave of immigration from the Ottoman Empire bringing Arab and Turkish Muslims and Sephardic Jews, along with Armenian and Orthodox Christians, began in the mid- nineteenth century and continued until World War I. Sikhs from the Punjab arrived, many settling in California. Though many of these immigrants came seeking economic opportunity with the intent of returning to their homeland, they often ended up settling in the United States permanently (Balgamis and Karpat 2008). One of the largest groups to reach the United States during this time were Catholics from Ireland, mostly as a result of the Great Hunger (Kinealy 1995), and their growing presence and power in American cities would lead to conflict with their Protestant neighbors. Large waves of Chinese immigrants also arrived, beginning in the 1840s, bringing with them Buddhism, Confucianism, Taoism, and other religions, and they too faced severe backlash culminating in the Chinese Exclusion Act of 1882. A massive wave of immigration from southern and eastern Europe from the 1880s through the early 1920s came through Ellis Island, bringing Catholic, Orthodox, Jewish, and Muslim people to America. This wave ground to a halt when the Immigration Act of 1924 established quotas restricting immigration, especially from East Asian countries.

By the early-mid-twentieth century, Arab and Muslim communities began to appear across America, including in Midwest towns such as Ross, North Dakota, site of the first documented mosque and Muslim cemetery, and Dearborn, Michigan, today home to North America's largest Muslim population. In the 1930s, a new wave of Jews fleeing the rise of the Third Reich came, followed by Holocaust survivors during and after World War II. By this time, attitudes toward religious diversity had begun to change. In a landmark testament to this shift, *Protestant-Catholic-Jew: An Essay in American Religious Sociology* (1955), Will Herberg declared religious diversity in America "not merely a historical and political fact . . . [but] the primordial condition of things, an essential aspect of the American Way of Life, and therefore in itself an aspect of religious belief." New ideas about coexistence and cooperation came to be embodied symbolically in an epic tragedy, the sinking of the *Dorchester*, a U.S. Army Transport ship torpedoed by a German U-boat in February 1942. In the words of Diane Moore:

> As the ship went down, four chaplains—two Protestants, one Catholic, and one Jew—assisted the soldiers and sailors into the lifeboats, until they themselves went down with the ship . . . the four chaplains of three faiths worshipping together exemplified the creation of a "Judeo-Christian tradition" that would come to express American ideals guiding the country's wartime mission.

The next significant change to the religious landscape of America came in 1965 with the Immigration and Nationality Act, enacted by Congress during the Johnson administration. Inspired in part by the growing civil rights movement, the act effectively abolished the exclusionary acts of 1882 and 1924 by abandoning the old quotas. By loosening immigration restrictions, it catalyzed the expansion of religious diversity in America, widening the door for Hindus, Muslims, Sikhs, and Jains. Supreme Court Justice Thomas Clark famously called the United States a "nation of Buddhists, Confucianists, and Taoists, as well as Christians" (Prothero 2006).

In the early twenty-first century, virtually every religion on the earth is represented in the United States; still, the vast majority of Americans are Christian. According to Pew Research, the United States ranks as moderately diverse compared with other nations.

Pew and the Public Religion Research Institute both report that for the first time, white Protestants constitute less than 50% of the U.S. population. The share of the public identifying with religions other than Christianity has grown from 4.7% in 2007 to 5.9% in 2014. The fastest growing religious group in the United States today are Muslims. In 2007, Muslims represented 0.4% of respondents to Pew's Religious Landscape Study, climbing to 0.9% by 2014. Since 2003 when the Iraq War began, for example, more than 4,000 Iraqi refugees, mostly Muslim, have settled in the metropolitan Detroit area (Pew Research 2015). The number of Hindus has also grown, from 0.4% in 2007 to 0.7% in 2014. These changes can be attributed to multiple factors, including shifting immigration patterns, changing birth rates, and disaffiliation with organized religions (Cox and Piacenza 2015). Indeed, the biggest shift in the last decade has come from those leaving organized religion altogether. According to a 2021 Pew Research report, the percentage of religiously unaffiliated adults in the U.S. increased from 16% to 29% between 2007 and 2021 (Pew Research 2021). This group, collectively known as religious "nones," is more numerous than either Catholics or mainline Protestants and is second in size only to evangelical Protestants in the United States. Indications are that this trend will continue; as many as one-third of all Millennials are religiously unaffiliated. People also tend to be less siloed in their religious lives; nearly one in five families are from an interreligious home (Pew Research 2016).

Table 1 Religious Affiliations of Americans

Christian		70.6%
	Evangelical Protestant	25.4%
	Mainline Protestant	14.7%
	Historically Black Protestant	6.5%
	Catholic	20.8%
	Mormon	1.6%
	Orthodox Christian	0.5%
	Jehovah's Witness	0.8%
	Other Christian	0.4%
Non-Christian Faiths		5.9%
	Jewish	1.9%
	Muslim	0.9%
	Buddhist	0.7%
	Hindu	0.7%
	Other World Religions	0.3%
	Other Faiths	1.5%
Unaffiliated (religious "nones")		22.8%
	Atheist	3.1%
	Agnostic	4.0%
	Nothing in particular	15.8%
	Don't know	0.6%

Source: Pew Research 2015

It is important to note that in a large country like the United States, religious diversity varies considerably by state/region. Louisiana, for example, is roughly 84% Christian, 2% non-Christians, and 13% unaffiliated, while New York is around 60% Christian, 12% non-Christian, and 27% unaffiliated (Pew Research 2015).

Perceptions and attitudes around religious diversity in America are an important part of this picture, and schools are one place where these attitudes are shaped. As religious diversity began to increase in the early twentieth century, the American "common school" sought to create a uniform, Americanizing experience for all students and essentially using schools to limit the impact of diversity (Glenn 2019; Tyack 1974). As religious diversity in America grows even more rapidly, not all view this as a positive development. A report prepared by the Public Religion Research Institute (PRRI)/Religion News Service (RNS) found that nearly 6 in 10 Americans believe that the United States has a history as a Christian nation but no longer is. Roughly one-third (35%) of Americans maintain that America is and has always been a Christian nation, though that number is down from the 42% who expressed this belief in 2010, and among younger people, only 25% say the United States is a Christian nation (Cox and Jones 2017).

Some of these perceptions may reflect attitudes: an overwhelming proportion of the Americans who say the United States is no longer a Christian nation perceive this is a negative change. Of those expressing their belief that the United States was once but no longer is a Christian nation, 61% view this as a bad thing, and Christians overall are more likely than Americans generally (68% vs. 61%) to say that the loss of American identity as a Christian nation is a negative thing (Cox and Jones 2017).

The Pew Research Center has also found that some groups are viewed more favorably than others. In 2014, 2017 and 2019, U.S. adults were surveyed on their attitudes. According to the survey results, "Both approaches show relatively warm (i.e., positive) public attitudes toward Jews, Catholics and mainline Protestants, and cooler (i.e., more negative) opinions toward Mormons, Muslims and atheists" (Pew Research 2023).

Nonetheless, religious diversity is hailed as a positive development by many Americans. In November 1998, President Bill Clinton said,

"[R]eligious pluralism in our nation is bringing us together in new and powerful ways," while Presidents Bush and Obama both supported interfaith initiatives. Numerous organizations, institutions, and individuals act as champions for religious diversity and pluralism. As Diana Eck, founder of the Harvard Pluralism Project, maintains, Americans "must embrace the religious diversity that comes with our commitment to religious freedom, and as we move into the new millennium we must find ways to make the differences that have divided people the world over the very source of our strength here in the US" (2002: 25).

See also: Bible Riots; Religious Pluralism Teaching; Religious Schools

Further Reading

Angel, Marc, and Shearith Israel. *Remnant of Israel: A Portrait of Americas First Jewish Congregation.* New York: Riverside Book Co., 2004.

Balgamis, A. Deniz, and Kemal H. Karpat (eds.). *Turkish Migration to the United States: From Ottoman Times to the Present.* First edition. Madison: University of Wisconsin Press, 2008.

Cox, Daniel, and Robert P. Jones. "America's Changing Religious Identity." *PRRI* (blog). 2017. https://www.prri.org/research/american-religious-landscape-christian-religiously-unaffiliated/.

Cox, Daniel, and Joanna Piacenza. "Is America a Christian Nation? Majority of Americans Don't Think So." *PRRI* (blog). 2015. https://www.prri.org/spotlight/is-america-a-christian-nation-nearly-half-of-americans-no-longer-think-so/.

Diouf, Sylviane A. *Servants of Allah: African Muslims Enslaved in the Americas.* New York: NYU Press, 2013.

Eck, Diana L. *A New Religious America: How a "Christian Country" Has Become the World's Most Religiously Diverse Nation.* Second edition. San Francisco: HarperSanFrancisco, 2002.

Glenn, Charles L. "Does Catholic Distinctiveness Matter in Catholic Schools?" *The Review of Faith & International Affairs* 17, no. 4 (October 2, 2019): 63–71. https://doi.org/10.1080/15570274.2019.1681757.

Herberg, Will. *Protestant—Catholic—Jew: An Essay in American Religious Sociology.* Garden City, NY: Doubleday, 1955.

Joshi, Khyati Y. *White Christian Privilege: The Illusion of Religious Equality in America.* New York: NYU Press, 2020.

Kinealy, Christine. *This Great Calamity: The Irish Famine 1845–52.* Dublin; Boulder, CO: Roberts Rinehart Pub, 1995 (first pub. in 1994, Dublin: Gill and Macmillan, reprinted with a new Introduction, 2006).

Pariona, Amber. "Religious Demographics of the USA." WorldAtlas. June 26, 2018. worldatlas.com/articles/religious-composition-of-the-united-states.html.

Patel, Eboo. *Sacred Ground: Pluralism, Prejudice, and the Promise of America.* Boston: Beacon Press, 2013.
Pew Research Center. "About Three-in-Ten U.S. Adults Are Now Religiously Unaffiliated." December 14, 2021. https://www.pewresearch.org/religion/2021/12/14/about-three-in-ten-u-s-adults-are-now-religiously-unaffiliated/.
Pew Research Center. "Americans Feel More Positive Than Negative About Jews, Mainline Protestants, Catholics." March 15, 2023. https://www.pewresearch.org/religion/2023/03/15/americans-feel-more-positive-than-negative-about-jews-mainline-protestants-catholics/.
Pew Research Center. "America's Changing Religious Landscape." May 12, 2015. https://www.pewresearch.org/religion/2015/05/12/americas-changing-religious-landscape/.
Pew Research Center. "How Americans Feel about Religious Groups." Pew Research Center's Religion & Public Life Project. July 16, 2014. https://www.pewforum.org/2014/07/16/how-americans-feel-about-religious-groups/.
Pew Research Center. "Nones on the Rise." September 2012. https://www.pewforum.org/2012/10/09/nones-on-the-rise/.
Pew Research Center. "One-in-Five U.S. Adults Were Raised in Interfaith Homes." October 26, 2016. https://www.pewresearch.org/religion/2016/10/26/one-in-five-u-s-adults-were-raised-in-interfaith-homes/.
Prothero, Stephen (ed.). *A Nation of Religions: The Politics of Pluralism in Multireligious America.* New edition. San Francisco: Harper, 2006.
Tyack, David B. *The One Best System: A History of American Urban Education.* Unknown edition. Cambridge, MA: Harvard University Press, 1974.

Religious Pluralism Teaching

Diversity refers to the fact that differences exist, and a school setting typically means a body of students, staff, and faculty comprising people from diverse backgrounds. Pluralism involves an engagement with diversity, connoting appreciation and respect for those differences. Religious pluralism, more specifically, means an environment where people from different religious backgrounds and orientations have open exchanges with and appreciative knowledge about other faith traditions and the ways people practice (or not) (see Patel 2016). It is not the fact of diversity but rather how we approach it.

Religious pluralism can be promoted in the classroom through teaching about world religions as part of the curriculum, but it must be done in accordance with the Establishment Clause. The question of striking a proper balance between the two has been examined in several landmark

Supreme Court decisions, and the Court, over the past half century, has consistently supported the study religion. In *Abington School District v. Schempp*, while ruling against school prayer, Chief Justice Thomas Clark wrote, "It might well be said that one's education is not complete without a study of comparative religion or the history of religion and its relationship to the advancement of civilization." In *Epperson v. Arkansas*, Justice Fortas echoed that view, writing, "the study of religions and of the Bible from a literary and historic viewpoint, presented objectively as part of a secular program of education, need not collide with the First Amendment's prohibition." The latter ruling also stipulated that all religions be treated equal, advancing the idea of a balanced, pluralistic approach.

In the mid-twentieth century, public school curricula still tended to avoid religion, but by the 1980s, views on this began to change. Scholars and educators argued that the "study of religions is not only constitutional but highly desirable: it promotes understanding of peoples whose faith and ethics are different from one's own, and it takes account of the significance of religion in history and culture" (Douglass 2000: 10). The National Council for the Social Studies issued a "Position Statement on Teaching About Religion" in 2014, saying, "Knowledge about religions [is] absolutely necessary for understanding and living in a world of diversity . . . [and] can help promote understanding and alleviate prejudice" (National Council for the Social Studies 2014).

A number of agencies have issued guidelines on teaching religion. In 2000, the U.S. Department of Education distributed to every public school in the nation a series of guides prepared by the Religious Freedom Center, including "A Parent's Guide to Religion in the Public Schools," "A Teacher's Guide to Religion in the Public Schools," and "Public Schools & Religious Communities" (Religious Freedom Center, n.d.). A coalition of major religious and educational organizations issued "Religion in the Public School Curriculum: Questions and Answers," stating, "the study about religion is essential to understanding both the nation and the world . . . knowledge of the roles of religion in the past and present promotes cross-cultural understanding essential to democracy and world peace" (1990: 310). The Association for Supervision and Curriculum Development (ASCD) published "Religion in the Public School Curriculum," calling for inclusion of religion in the curriculum (Zakariya 1987), and ASCD and the First Amendment Center jointly published "Taking Religion Seriously across the Curriculum" (Nord and Haynes 1998). The National Education Association also offers guidance in a document titled "Religion and Public Schools: Promoting Mutual Respect and Understanding" (National Education Association, n.d.).

A number of courageous highs schools have pioneered programs aiming to promote religious pluralism. In 1992, largely in response to tensions around the rapidly growing immigrant Muslim population, Cobb High School in southeastern Michigan formed a Committee on Cultural Understanding, with the goal of encouraging understanding and acceptance of all cultures. The school administration coordinated with the Yemeni community members to accommodate academic, religious, social, and cultural norms of the newcomers. Cobb, as well as another local school with a predominantly Lebanese American population, also hired a community liaison (Sarroub 2005). In Modesto, California, also in response to tensions around diversity, the school launched a novel World Religions course for 9th-grade students. One objective was to improve students' mutual respect for other religions through knowledge about different faiths and an understanding of the First Amendment and religious freedom in America. The course avoided an emphasis on disagreements between religions and the exoticization of unique rituals and practices. One of the key components of the curriculum was Modesto's focus on encouraging students to engage with members of other faiths respectfully by modeling civil discussion about religion (Lester and Roberts 2011). Ultimately, an assessment of the course's impact suggested that students who took the course demonstrated "increases in passive tolerance, their willingness to refrain from discriminatory behavior, and active respect, the willingness to take action to counter discrimination" (Lester and Roberts 2011: 264; see also Fraser 2016; Wertheimer 2015).

Calls for promoting religious pluralism have also come from higher education. Stephen Prothero (2006) of Boston University has found that Americans are generally uninformed about other religions and calls for a fundamental religious literacy that every American ought to have. Eboo Patel, founder of the Interfaith Youth Core, points out that achieving religious pluralism means going beyond teaching religion as a series of rituals, customs, and doctrines. According to Patel, we are not "dealing with abstract systems in textbooks, but actual people interacting in real-world situations" (2016: 113). The American Academy of Religion has adopted Guidelines for Teaching about Religion in K–12 Public Schools prepared by a team from Harvard Divinity School led by Professor Diane Moore. Harvard's Religious Literacy Project offers a model for teaching about religion in American K–12 schools. It begins by defining religious literacy as "the ability to discern and analyze the fundamental intersections of religion and social/political/cultural life through multiple lenses" (Harvard.edu, n.d.). Four key principles are sketched out as follows:

1. recognize the validity of normative theological assertions without equating them with universal truths about the tradition itself;
2. religions are internally diverse as opposed to uniform;
3. religions evolve and change over time as opposed to being ahistorical and static;
4. religious influences are embedded in all dimensions of culture as opposed to the assumption that religions function in discrete, isolated, "private" contexts. (Harvard.edu, n.d.)

Drew University in New Jersey, in partnership with the Interfaith Youth Core, developed a program with Madison High School to help students engage with religious pluralism. Members of the school's Diversity Club and students affiliated with Drew's Center on Religion, Culture and Conflict designed and implemented a schoolwide survey on attitudes toward religious diversity and used the data to develop a series of workshops.

In practice, the line between what constitutes appropriate teaching about religion and preaching is not always clear, and there is significant disagreement on this matter. In 1988, the California State Board of Education adopted a curriculum that highlights religion in World and U.S. History classes, teaching "the basic ideas of the major religions and the ethical traditions of each time and place" (2001: 7). But some have criticized the curriculum, charging that the 7th-grade world history unit on Islam indoctrinates students in the tenets of the faith by compelling students to participate in worship activities." California's "3 Rs Project" (rights, responsibility, and respect), a program based largely on the First Amendment Center's *Finding Common Ground* (Haynes and Thomas 2007), encourages teaching religion but advises against re-enacting religious practices in public schools (http://ca3rsproject.org/).

When a world geography teacher at Riverheads High School in Augusta County, Virginia, included a lesson on Arabic calligraphy as part of a unit on Islam in 2015, again there was controversy. Students were asked to copy in Arabic the *Shahada*, the Islamic statement of faith, as a way to teach appreciation for the artistic complexity of calligraphy. Translated into English, the *Shahada* reads, "There is no God but Allah, and Mohammed is the messenger of Allah." Outraged parents and community members saw the lesson as a form of Islamic indoctrination, and the school faced a fierce backlash, including threats, causing it to close briefly. In other cases, opponents object to the way their own religion is taught in schools, believing that the "academic approach (as opposed to the devotional approach) contradicts their theological convictions" and that this is better left to parents and the faith community (Moore 2007: 6).

See also: Abington School District v. Schempp (1963); Religious Discrimination in Schools; Religious Diversity in the United States

Further Reading

Berglund, Jenny. "Islamic Religious Education in Europe and the United States." 2015. https://www.brookings.edu/research/islamic-religious-education-in-europe-and-the-united-states/.

Bigelow, M. *Mogadishu on the Mississippi: Language, Racialized Identity, and Education in a New Land.* Malden, MA: Wiley-Blackwell, 2010.

The California Three Rs Project http://ca3rsproject.org/.

Douglass, Susan L. *Teaching about Religion in National and State Social Studies Standards. Executive Summary.* Fountain Valley, CA: Council on Islamic Education, 2000. https://eric.ed.gov/?id=ED456076.

Evans, John H. "Religious Pluralism in Modern America: A Sociological Overview." In *Gods in America*, edited by C. Cohen and R. Numbers, 42–55. Oxford: Oxford University Press, 2013.

Fraser, James W. *Between Church and State: Religion and Public Education in a Multicultural America.* Second edition. Baltimore, MD: Johns Hopkins University Press, 2016.

Harvard.edu. "What Is Religious Literacy?" n.d. Accessed June 23, 2020. https://rpl.hds.harvard.edu/what-we-do/our-approach/what-religious-literacy

Haynes, Charles. *Finding Common Ground: A First Amendment Guide to Religion & Public Education.* Nashville, TN: Freedom Forum First Amendment Center 1994.

Haynes, Charles C., and Oliver Thomas. *Finding Common Ground: A First Amendment Guide to Religion and Public Schools.* Nashville, TN: First Amendment Center, 2007.

History-Social Science Framework for California Public Schools K-12. 2001. Published by the California Department of Education https://www.cde.ca.gov/ci//cr/cf/documents/histsocsciframe.pdf

Lester, Emile, and Patrick S. Roberts. "Learning about World Religions in Modesto, California: The Promise of Teaching Tolerance in Public Schools."

Politics and Religion 4, no. 2 (2011): 264–88. https://doi.org/10.1017/S1755048311000174.

Moore, Diane L. *Overcoming Religious Illiteracy: A Cultural Studies Approach to the Study of Religion in Secondary Education.* New York: Palgrave Macmillan, 2007.

National Council for the Social Studies. "The Study of Religion in the Social Studies Curriculum." socialstudies.org. 2014. https://www.socialstudies.org/positions/study_about_religions.

National Education Association. "Religion and Public Schools: Promoting Mutual Respect and Understanding." n.d. https://www.nea.org/professional-excellence/student-engagement/tools-tips/teaching-about-religion.

Nord, Warren, and Charles Haynes. *Taking Religion Seriously across the Curriculum.* First edition. Alexandria, VA; Nashville, TN: Association for Supervision & Curriculum Development, 1998.

Patel, Eboo. *Interfaith Leadership: A Primer.* Boston: Beacon Press, 2016.

Pew Forum. "Teaching about Religion in Public Schools: Where Do We Go from Here?" May 20, 2003. https://www.pewforum.org/2003/05/20/teaching-about-religion-in-public-schools-where-do-we-go-from-here/.

Prothero, Stephen (ed.). *A Nation of Religions: The Politics of Pluralism in Multireligious America.* New edition. San Francisco: Harper, 2006.

"Religion in the Public School Curriculum: Questions and Answers." *Journal of Law and Religion* 8, no. 1/2 (1990): 309–12.

Religious Freedom Center. https://www.freedomforum.org/.

Sarroub, Loukia K. *All American Yemeni Girls: Being Muslim in a Public School.* Philadelphia: University of Pennsylvania Press, 2005.

Wertheimer, Linda K. *Faith Ed: Teaching about Religion in an Age of Intolerance.* First edition. Boston: Beacon Press, 2015.

Zakariya, Sally Banks. *Religion in the Curriculum: A Report from the ASCD Panel on Religion in the Curriculum.* Association for Supervision and Curriculum Development, 125 N, 1987. https://eric.ed.gov/?id=ED288776.

Religious Schools

Religious schools are private elementary, middle, or high schools affiliated with a religious organization. The term "parochial school," from parish, refers specifically to Catholic schools, the most common form of religious schools in America. However, there are also Jewish, Islamic, Hindu, Sikh, and other religious schools. Most religious schools in the United States follow a curriculum that includes both religious education and secular subject matter (e.g., social studies, science, math). Like any private school in the United States, religious schools are not eligible for direct public funding.

Since their inception, religious schools have involved questions about the role that schools play in indoctrinating children into American culture and values. Many Americans celebrate the establishment of religious schools as fulfilling the promise of religious pluralism in America and recognize ways that religious schools can contribute positively to society by preparing students to be "good liberal citizens" (Dagovitz 2004: 165). Others see religious schools as sectarian, or even un-American. Religious schools often find themselves navigating between the progressivism of many public schools and the lure of materialism, immorality, and hedonism in American culture (Cooper, Mulvey and Maloney 2010). Religious and public schools compete for students and the resources needed to serve them, particularly in recent years with the expansions of voucher programs.

The earliest religious schools in what would become the United States were Dutch schools associated with the Dutch Reform Church. The first Quaker school in America was founded in 1682. With the rise of Protestant-dominated public school systems in the mid-nineteenth century, Catholic schools became an increasingly common alternative for Catholics that felt marginalized (Herberg 1955). Catholic leadership had been struggling with anti-Catholic bias prevalent in schools at the time when Archbishop of New York John Hughes sought to challenge the schools' use of the King James Bible. With public schools leaning toward Protestant interests (Fessenden 2011), Hughes and other leaders sought to establish a separate Catholic school system.

In the late nineteenth century, over 5 million Catholics immigrated to the United States. The dramatic increase in the number of Catholics sometimes led to a conflation of "Catholic" and "foreign," eliciting a Protestant "nativist" response that turned violent at times. For many Catholic Americans, parish schools were viewed as the only way the Catholic Church could survive in the United States (Ronan 2010; Sweeney 1965). Concerned that Catholic children would become alienated from their heritage, Pope Pius IX urged American Catholics to increase both the number and the quality of parochial schools. To staff the rapidly expanding Catholic schools, Catholic sisters immigrated to the United States—by 1900, there were more than 40,000—and setting a precedent whereby private schools, religious or not, do not require the same standards of certification for teachers as public schools (Walch 1996).

Jewish Americans also faced a quandary regarding how to embrace the "Americanization" that public schools offered while maintaining their religious and cultural heritage. The first Jewish Day School in America was established in 1731 in affiliation with Shearith Israel, the Spanish Portuguese Synagogue of New York. Ashkenazi schools began to merge in the mid-nineteenth century. Recognizing the benefits of socialization offered in public schools, American Jews would ultimately come to embrace them (Joselit 2018); some were concerned that religious schools could negatively impact their political and social status in the United States. Not wanting to abandon religious education altogether, Jews created a hybrid model whereby children supplemented their secular public school education with part-time Hebrew schools (Ingall 2010; Jacobs and Eisenstein 1906). At the beginning of the twentieth century, as a wave of Yiddish-speaking immigrants from eastern Europe arrived, Orthodox Jews attempted to recreate the Old World model of Torah study, launching the first Yeshiva in Brooklyn. Jewish day schools proliferated, with 23 schools in the greater New York area alone by 1939 (Joselit 2018). By the mid-twentieth century, Jewish day schools with non-Orthodox affiliations (e.g., Solomon Schechter Schools) were created with the goal of teaching Jewish and American content and values side-by-side. By the late 1990s, there were nearly 670 Jewish day schools in the United States. The most recent (2013–2014) census of Jewish schools lists 861 (Schick 2014).

There are somewhere around 250 private Islamic schools in the United States today (Berglund 2016; Niche, n.d.), and in 2011, the Islamic School League of America estimated that there were 40,000 students enrolled in Islamic schools (ISLA, n.d.). The majority of Islamic schools are K–6, though there are also Islamic high schools. Many of these schools combine a secular educational program with classes in Arabic and Islamic religious education. Muslim families sometimes turn to Islamic schools because of harassment in public schools, while those Islamic schools, in turn, have faced scrutiny and backlash. In 2007, for example, an online petition calling for a total ban on Islamic schools circulated, claiming "such institutions are imposing religion and backward traditions on children" (Glenn 2016), and specific schools such as the Khalil Gibran International Academy in Brooklyn have been targeted.

Hindu schools, such as the Bal Vihar schools, serve Hindu children, though many families follow the "Sunday school" model. The first charter school affiliated with the Sikh community was established in Sacramento, California, in 2011, though as a charter school, it is open to all local residents. Ultimately, all these schools are no different from other faith schools in their goal of providing space in which children can learn mainstream subjects in the context of their faith and culture (Merry and Driessen 2009; Thobani 2010).

There are also religious schools for Protestant Christians, typically Evangelicals, who feel that public schools promote values that contradict their own. Amid a textbook controversy in West Virginia in the 1970s, Connie Marshner urged families to abandon the public school system altogether and register their children in Christian schools (see "Secularism and Secular Humanism"). In Texas, Marshner worked with Mel and Norma Gabler to help grow the burgeoning Christian school movement.

Throughout the history of education in America, there have also been efforts to thwart the expansion of religious schools. Some states added provisions to their constitutions specifically blocking support for religious schools (Issel 1979). In 1875, President Ulysses S. Grant called for a constitutional amendment mandating free public schools while banning the use of public funding for religious or "sectarian" schools. Public schools, Grant argued, should be "unmixed with atheistic, pagan or sectarian teaching" (Hesseltine 1935). When Senator James G. Blaine of Maine proposed such an amendment to the Constitution in 1874, it failed to pass Congress. But so-called Blaine Amendments, blocking the funding of religious schools, were added to 34 state constitutions in the ensuing years (Green 1992). In some cases, resistance to religious schools is linked with anti-immigrant sentiment. In 1891, for instance, the National Council of Education made efforts to prevent "non-American" influence (Tyack and Hansot 1982). As immigration increased, so did the pressure on public schools to "Americanize" immigrant children (Glenn 2019: 59). In other cases, religious schools have been inhibited by laws requiring English only as the language for teaching major subjects in all schools, but often these laws have not held up. Wisconsin's Bennett Law was passed in 1889 but was repealed two years later. Similarly, Nebraska's Siman Act, restricting foreign-language education, was passed in 1919 but ruled a violation of the Fourteenth Amendment's Due Process Clause by the Supreme Court in *Meyer v. Nebraska* in 1923 (U.S. Supreme Court 262 U.S. 390). In 1922, Oregon went even further in passing the Compulsory Education Act (aka the Oregon School Law), requiring all students to attend public schools. The question came before the Supreme Court in 1925 in *Pierce v. Society of Sisters*, with the Court declaring the act unconstitutional. The decision, considered by supporters as "the Magna Carta of the parochial school system" (Davis 2009), expanded coverage of the Fourteenth Amendment's Due Process Clause to recognize personal civil liberties (i.e., school choice) and has been cited as a precedent in more than 100 Supreme Court cases.

By the mid-1960s, Catholic school enrollment began to see a sharp decline. According to the National Catholic Educational Association, there had been 5.2 million students attending nearly 13,000 elementary and secondary Catholic schools, but by 2016, there were fewer than 2 million students enrolled in less than 7,000 schools (United States Conference of Catholic Bishops, n.d.). This shift can be attributed to several factors. Changing demographics, particularly a decrease in Catholic immigration from Europe, have played a role. Though Catholics continue to emigrate from Latin America, Hispanics account for just 4% of students attending Catholic schools. Increases in the cost of living have forced more families to opt for free public school education. Religious leaders, such as New York archbishop Timothy Dolan, have pointed to a rising disconnect between the schools and the communities, undermining the original community engagement goals of the Catholic school system (Dolan 2010).

According to National Center for Education Statistics, in 2015, roughly 6 million students were enrolled in private schools, with 36% attending Catholic schools and 39% in other religiously affiliated schools. As voucher programs expand, this could change in the future (National Center for Education Statistics 2020).

Recently, the Supreme Court has ruled in favor of religious freedom when it comes to school choice. In *Espinoza v. Montana Dept of Revenue*, the Court decided that states may not deny financial benefits to parents who opt to send their children to accredited private schools on the basis of their being religious. States, according to the ruling, are not required to subsidize private schools, but if they do, they must treat public and private schools equally. In fact, the Supreme Court has consistently ruled in favor of religious freedom generally, and often by a lopsided majority, indicating that this is not as political or partisan a question as it is sometimes construed. Ultimately, the *Espinoza* ruling represents a reversal of the Blaine Amendments, viewed by many as antiquated anti-Catholic laws that serve to discriminate against religion generally.

See also: Bible Riots; School Vouchers; Secularism and Secular Humanism

Further Reading

Berglund, Jenny. "Islamic Religious Education in Muslim Schools: A Translation of Islam to the Swedish School System." In *Religious Education in a Global-Local World*, edited by Jenny Berglund, Yafa Shanneik, and Brian Bocking,

109–21. *Boundaries of Religious Freedom: Regulating Religion in Diverse Societies.* Cham: Springer International Publishing, 2016. https://doi.org/10.1007/978-3-319-32289-6_7.

Cooper, Bruce S., Janet D. Mulvey, and Arthur T. Maloney. *Blurring the Lines: Charter, Public, Private and Religious Schools Come Together.* IAP, 2010.

Dagovitz, Alan. "When Choice Does Not Matter: Political Liberalism, Religion and the Faith School Debate." *Journal of Philosophy of Education* 38, no. 2 (2004): 165–80. https://doi.org/10.1111/j.0309-8249.2004.00373.x.

Davis, Derek. "Aid to Parochial Schools." The First Amendment Encyclopedia. 2009. https://www.mtsu.edu/first-amendment/article/902/aid-to-parochial-schools.

Dolan, Timothy M. "The Catholic Schools We Need." *America Magazine*, 13T00:00:00–0400. 2010. https://www.americamagazine.org/issue/747/article/catholic-schools-we-need.

Espinoza v. Montana Dept of Revenue 591 U.S. ___ (2020). n.d. https://www.law.cornell.edu/supremecourt/text/18-1195.

Fessenden, Tracy. *Culture and Redemption: Religion, the Secular, and American Literature.* Princeton, NJ: Princeton University Press, 2011.

Glenn, Charles L. *The American Model of State and School: An Historical Inquiry.* New York: Continuum, 2012.

Glenn, Charles L. "Does Catholic Distinctiveness Matter in Catholic Schools?" *The Review of Faith & International Affairs* 17, no. 4 (October 2, 2019): 63–71. https://doi.org/10.1080/15570274.2019.1681757.

Glenn, Charles L. "Muslims in the Melting Pot | Charles L. Glenn." *First Things*. 2016. https://www.firstthings.com/article/2016/04/muslims-in-the-melting-pot.

Green, Steven K. "The Blaine Amendment Reconsidered." *The American Journal of Legal History* 36, no. 1 (1992): 38–69. https://doi.org/10.2307/845452.

Herberg, Will. *Protestant—Catholic—Jew: An Essay in American Religious Sociology.* Garden City, NY: Doubleday, 1955.

Hesseltine, William B. *Ulysses S. Grant, Politician.* New York: Dodd, Mead & Company, 1935.

Ingall, Carol K. *The Women Who Reconstructed American Jewish Education, 1910–1965.* Lebanon, NH: Brandeis University Press, 2010.

Issel, William. "Americanization, Acculturation and Social Control: School Reform Ideology in Industrial Pennsylvania, 1880–1910." *Journal of Social History* 12, no. 4 (1979): 569–590.

ISLA. "Islamic Schools League of America." n.d. Accessed June 24, 2020. https://theisla.org/.

Jacobs, Joseph, and Judah David Eisenstein. *JewishEncyclopedia.com*. 1906.

Joselit, Jenna Weissman. "A History of Jewish Day Schools." *Tablet*. 2018. http://education.jed.macam.ac.il/article/3647.

Merry, Michael S., and Geert Driessen. "Islamic Schools in North America and the Netherlands: Inhibiting or Enhancing Democratic Dispositions?"

Alternative Education for the 21st Century: Philosophies, Approaches, Visions (2009): 101–122.

National Center for Education Statistics. "The Condition of Education—Preprimary, Elementary, and Secondary Education—Elementary and Secondary Enrollment—Private School Enrollment—Indicator." May 2020. https://nces.ed.gov/programs/coe/indicator/cgc?tid=4.

Niche. "Niche: Explore Schools, Companies, and Neighborhoods." n.d. Accessed June 24, 2020. https://www.niche.com/.

Ronan, Marian. "Rewriting the History of Catholic Schools in America." *Religion Dispatches*. December 9, 2010. https://religiondispatches.org/rewriting-the-history-of-catholic-schools-in-america/.

Schick, Marvin. "A Census of Jewish Day Schools in the United States 2013–2014." Avi Chai Foundation. 2014. https://avichai.org/wp-content/uploads/2014/10/Census-2013-14.pdf.

Sweeney, David Francis. *The Life of John Lancaster Spalding : First Bishop of Peoria, 1840–1916*. First edition. New York: Herder & Herder, 1965.

Thobani, Shiraz. *Islam in the School Curriculum: Symbolic Pedagogy and Cultural Claims*. A&C Black, 2010.

Tyack, David, and Elizabeth Hansot. *Learning Together: A History of Coeducation in American Public Schools*. Revised edition. New York: Russell Sage Foundation, 1992.

Walch, Timothy. *Parish School: American Catholic Parochial Education from Colonial Times to the Present*. A Crossroad Herder Book. New York: Crossroad, 1996.

United States Conference of Catholic Bishops. "Catholic School Fact Sheet." n.d. https://www.usccb.org/beliefs-and-teachings/how-we-teach/catholic-education/upload/Catholic-Schools-FACT-Sheet-2016.pdf.

U.S. Supreme Court 262 U.S. 390 *Meyer v. Nebraska*. 1923. https://www.law.cornell.edu/supremecourt/text/262/390

Religious Symbols

Conflicts around religious symbols on school property have arisen in schools across the nation. Such controversies involve questions related to the First Amendment "dilemma," which prohibits the state from "respecting the establishment of a religion," while guaranteeing free exercise. Symbols that are typically the object of controversy include models of the Ten Commandments, images of Jesus, and nativity scenes. The central questions at the heart of these matters are: What is the school's intent in displaying these symbols? Does the display in question bear the "imprimatur" of the school? Is the state promoting religion or a particular religion by displaying symbols of a certain faith?

Much like the debate over Bible studies in public school, the question of context is central to religious symbol conflicts; for example: is the symbol intended to convey devotional meaning, or does it serve some other educational purpose? This was a central question in the Supreme Court case *Stone v. Graham*, when Kentucky parents challenged a state law that required public schools to display the Ten Commandments in classrooms. In a 5–4 decision, the Court ruled that the Kentucky law violated the Establishment Clause by failing the first part of the "Lemon Test" since the posting of the Ten Commandments "had no secular legislative purpose" and was "plainly religious in nature." The Ten Commandments, in the Court's view, are not limited to secular matters (e.g., injunctions against murder and stealing) but clearly go into matters of worship and devotion of God and religious observance (e.g., keep the Sabbath, thou shalt love the Lord, thy God). In *County of Allegheny v. Greater Pittsburgh ACLU*, the Supreme Court examined: Does the object have the effect of endorsing religion? Would viewers reasonably understand the purpose of the display to be religious? In another case, involving a print of Jesus, the Court decided that the image did have "the effect of endorsing religion in general and Christianity in particular," since it was not part of a larger display, nor was it incorporated into a class, lecture, or other educational context. In *McCreary County v. ACLU of KY*, the school argued that the Ten Commandments represent the "foundations of American law," but in the Court's view, an observer could reasonably conclude that the government was endorsing religion.

There are instances, however, where religious symbols can serve a vital educational purpose. In *Stone v. Graham*, Justice Rehnquist wrote a dissenting opinion arguing that the Establishment Clause does not require the prohibition of all activities that may have a religious significance or origin. He pointed to precedents set in cases such as *Abington School District v. Schempp*, whereby the Court acknowledged that "[t]he history of man is inseparable from the history of religion." Justice Rehnquist also quoted Justice Jackson's opinion in *McCollum v. Board of Education*, 333 U.S. 203, 235–6 (1948):

> [F]or good or for ill, nearly everything in our culture worth transmitting, everything which gives meaning to life, is saturated with religious

influences, derived from paganism, Judaism, Christianity—both Catholic and Protestant—and other faiths accepted by a large part of the world's peoples. One can hardly respect the system of education that would leave the student wholly ignorant of the currents of religious thought that move the world society for a part in which he is being prepared. (47)

Such controversies frequently involve questions about whether the display qualifies as school-sponsored material. In *Stone v. Graham*, the school district argued that since the displays were paid for with private donations, the state was not involved. By this logic, however, the school could display anything it wanted so long as it was paid for with private money. It is also very difficult to separate expenditures: were the people who collected and handled the donations as part of their job paid with taxpayer dollars? When such questions arise, courts often apply what is known as the "Imprimatur Test," which examines the extent to which an activity carries the imprint of the school or whether it can reasonably disclaim activities occurring on school property. In cases such as *Bannon* and *Hazelwood* (see later), courts looked at whether the expression in question (i.e., religious symbols) occurs in the context of curricular activities or noncurricular activities.

The 2004 case *Bannon v. School District of Palm Beach* involved students who participated in a program to paint murals near the main office and hallway of the school. When some of those students contributed religious messages and symbols, the school ordered them removed. The appellees argued that the murals did not constitute school-sponsored activity on four counts: (1) the school did not require students to participate, (2) no grade or credit was involved, (3) the activity occurred outside of regular school hours, and (4) students were required to pay a small fee to participate. The 11th Circuit Court of Appeals upheld the school's decision ordering the removal of the religious content. The Court invoked the 1988 case *Hazelwood School District v. Kuhlmeier*, which concerns school-sponsored expression, maintaining that the "prominent locations" of the murals left "no question students, parents, and other members of the public might reasonably believe [the] murals bear the imprimatur of the school" (*Bannon v. School District of Palm Beach*: 1214).

Religious symbol controversies also involve issues of diversity and inclusion. It is often argued that the symbols in question represent heritage shared by all students and do not favor one religion over others. In *Stone v. Graham*, for example, the school argued that the Ten Commandments are for all, not just for Christians. This ignores the millions of people of other faiths—Hindus, Sikhs, Buddhists, Jains—in the United States who do not count the Ten Commandments in their religious heritage. This question was also addressed in *Washegesic v. Bloomingdale Public Schools* (33 F. 3d 679; 6th Cir. 1994), when students asked that a portrait of Jesus be removed from the school. The school argued that the image was not religious because Jesus has meaning to people of other faiths and that Jesus is recognized as a historical figure and moral leader. The 6th Circuit Court disagreed, stating that "any reasonable observer would find that the picture of Jesus transmits a religious message." The court also rejected the argument that the image constitutes no more than "mere exposure," pointing to its prominent display, and thus imprimatur, calling it a "portrait of the leading figure of the Christian religion" (*Washegesic v. Bloomingdale* 1994).

A guideline for teachers prepared by Teaching Tolerance.org (Wicht 2014) offers suggestions on how to frame the presentation of religious material within parameters that conform with the Establishment Clause. Religious symbols are permissible if used as instructional aids in a context where they are referenced during class to assist students in understanding a particular religious tradition. The Ten Commandments, for example, could be shown in a classroom if used temporarily in a lesson on the Bible as a literary source in a comparative literature class. A Muslim prayer rug may be presented to illustrate the Muslim practice of Salah (prayer), or a display in a history class on the Crusades that depicts people holding crosses (Wicht 2014). The Tanenbaum Center and the American Academy of Religion have also produced useful guidelines for teaching religion in the classroom (for more on this subject see "Bible Study").

See also: *Abbington School District v. Schempp* (1963); Religion and School Dress Code

Further Reading

ALLEGHENY COUNTY v. GREATER PITTSBURGH ACLU No. 87–2050 (1989). U.S. Supreme Court. Argued: February 22, 1989. Decided: July 3, 1989. n.d. https://caselaw.findlaw.com/us-supreme-court/492/573.html.

Bannon v. School District of Palm Beach, 387 F.3d 1208 (11th Cir. 2004). No. 03–13011. Decided: October 12, 2004. n.d. https://caselaw.findlaw.com/us-11th-circuit/1302084.html.

County of Allegheny v. American Civil Liberties Union, Greater Pittsburgh Chapter, 1989 No. 87-2050 https://www.law.cornell.edu/supremecourt/text/492/573.

Hazelwood School District v. Kuhlmeier, 484 U.S. 260, 108 S.Ct. 562, 98 L.Ed.2d 592 No. 86–836 (1988). U.S. Supreme Court. Argued October 13, 1987. Decided January 13, 1988. n.d. https://supreme.justia.com/cases/federal/us/484/260/.

Kim, W. et al. U.S. District Court for the District of New Jersey. "Brief of the United States as Amicus Curiae in Support of the Plaintiffs' Motion for Summary Judgment." U.S. Department of Justice, Civil Rights Division, Educational Opportunities Section. Amicus Brief filed in the District of New Jersey. n.d. https://www.justice.gov/sites/default/files/crt/legacy/2010/12/14/frenchtown.brief.pdf.

McCollum v. Board of Education, 333 U.S. 203 (1948). Illinois ex rel. McCollum v. Board of Education of School District. No. 71, Champaign County, Illinois. No. 90 Argued December 8, 1947. Decided March 8, 1948. n.d. https://supreme.justia.com/cases/federal/us/333/203/.

McCreary County v. American Civil Liberties Union of KY. June 27, 2005. https://www.law.cornell.edu/supct/html/03-1693.ZO.html.

Sydell Stone et al. v. James B. Graham, Superintendent of Public Instruction of Kentucky. No. 80-321. Nov. 17, 1980. https://www.law.cornell.edu/supremecourt/text/449/39.

Washegesic v. Bloomingdale Public Schools, 33 F. 3d 679 (6th Cir. 1994). Dott WASHEGESIC, as next friend of Eric Pensinger; Eric Pensinger, with Dott Washegesic as next friend of, Plaintiffs-Appellees, v. BLOOMINGDALE PUBLIC SCHOOLS, a Michigan Corporation; Bloomingdale Public School Board, Defendants-Appellants. No. 93–1248. U.S. Court of Appeals, 6th Circuit. Argued June 6, 1994. Decided September 6, 1994. n.d. https://openjurist.org/33/f3d/679/washegesic-v-bloomingdale-public-schools.

Wicht, S. "You CAN Teach about Religion in Public School!" Teaching Tolerance.org. 2014.

Religious Texts as Literature and Research Sources

In the landmark U.S. Supreme Court case, *Abington School District v. Schempp* (1963), the Court ruled that public schools may not sponsor or lead readings from the Bible. Doing so, the Court opinion read, violates the First Amendment's Establishment Clause, by giving the impression (intentionally or not) that the school, as a government agency, is advocating for a particular religion ("School Dist. of Abington Tp. v. Schempp, 374 U.S. 203 (1963)," n.d.) (see *"Abington School District v. Schempp* (1963)").

The Court's ruling does not, however, outright prohibit the use of religious text in a classroom, as long as the purpose for referring to the text is "non-devotional." Writing for the majority, Justice Thomas C. Clark explained that the ruling "does not foreclose teaching about the Holy Scriptures or about the differences between religious sects in classes in literature or history" ("School Dist. of Abington Tp. v. Schempp, 374 U.S. 203 (1963)," n.d.). He went on to suggest that many subjects in the social sciences and humanities would be "impossible to teach meaningfully" without mentioning religion, an opinion still held by many people today (see "Bible Instruction, Teaching in Schools" and "Comparative Religion and World Religion, Teaching in Schools").

The question that educators must then contend with is: when is it appropriate to use religious texts, such as the Bible, as class resources, and when is it not?

RELIGIOUS TEXTS AS LITERATURE

One circumstance in which use of a religious text as a resource would most likely be considered constitutionally protected and appropriate would be when examining the text for its literary merits. The Bible, for instance, is considered by many literary critics to be an important work of literature in large part because of the influence it has had on Western culture. Northrop Frye, professor and author of literary theory and criticism, once wrote that the Bible "is a book that has had a continuously fertilizing influence on English literature from Anglo-Saxon writers to poets [of the modern age]" (quoted in Wachlin 1997).

In a 1997 study, five common approaches to studying Bible literature were identified: evaluating the Bible as literature (i.e., examining its literary merits); studying the Bible in relation to other works of literature (e.g., looking for extensive use of biblical themes and allusions); combining the study of the Bible with other works of literature (e.g., by genre or theme); examining the context of the Bible (e.g., the culture in which it was produced); and studying the Bible to better understand other works of literature (e.g., examining often-quoted passages and stories to inform one's understanding of English and American literature (Wachlin 1997). All these methods, as presented, would most likely qualify as secular study of a religious text and would therefore probably be supported by legal statute.

A significant challenge in the endeavor to teach the Bible as literature, though, is that many teachers do not have adequate training or background to address the Bible in this way. This problem was noted by scholars in the years soon after the *Abington v. Schempp* ruling, when Thayer Warshaw, an English teacher, wrote that even if a teacher attempted to examine the Bible "in the same open and many-sided manner that he would any other literature," the teacher would have to discuss the Bible's religious content or themes. Doing so, Warshaw argued, would "undoubtedly" leave an opening for "possible religious indoctrination, conscious or not" (Warshaw 1971). To address this issue, Warshaw co-founded the Indiana University Summer Institute on Teaching the Bible in Secondary Education, along with Indiana University professor James Ackerman (Biondo and Fiala 2013). Together, Warshaw and Ackerman developed instructional programs that would teach educators how to teach the Bible in a more appropriately academic way and produced and published supporting materials, including a student textbook, *The Bible As/In Literature*, which is currently in its second edition and is still in use in Bible instruction programs today.

RELIGIOUS TEXTS AS RESEARCH RESOURCES

Another circumstance in which a religious text might be used in the classroom in a constitutionally protected way is as a source for research. This use comes with some added complications, though, because some students, and possibly even teachers, might not recognize when and how the text works as an authoritative source for a particular argument or might present information from the text in a way that is not universally recognized in academic circles.

Using the Bible, again, as an example, there is considerable debate among self-identified Christians as to whether the Bible is to be read more literally, more figuratively, or both. (This is not taking into account people who identify with another religion or no religion, who might view the Bible as having no authoritative weight at all.) The creation story outlined in the opening chapters of Genesis, for example, indicates that God created the first human, Adam, from dust and that Eve, the first woman, was created from Adam's rib. This story could be taken quite literally, treating each detail as a historical account of the beginning of humanity, or it could be read more as an allegorical creation myth, with the details being used to describe the relationship between humanity and its creator (see "Creationism"). In the context of an academic research paper, using the Bible as a source to describe the factual origins of creation would be problematic, as many academics and scholars would dispute the historicity of the account.

That said, the Bible might be a meaningful and an appropriate research source, depending on the assignment. Furthermore, if a student opted to use the Bible, or any religious text, in this way, he or she would almost certainly be protected by the First Amendment. The American Center for Law and Justice (ACLJ), a Christian religious liberty advocacy group, addressed such a scenario, in which a 7th-grade student claimed that her teacher refused to let her use the Bible as a source for a writing project on Roman history. Attorneys for the ACLJ advised the student to "bring reliable sources to the teacher evidencing that the Bible, although a religious book, also has historical significance" (Heil 2012). In this case, the teacher relented, and no litigation was needed; however, the case reveals how easily such a disagreement or misunderstanding could escalate to a legal challenge.

One way to ensure that a religious text is being used appropriately as a research source is if it is paired with another source that addresses the same content or issues in a more academically objective way. For instance, in the case of an assignment about Roman history, the Bible could be used to illustrate how characters in the Bible perceived their era, or "as a starting point for further research on issues such as Roman occupation, Hebrew political history and historical figures in the Bible" (Thompson, n.d.); the writing, however, should also include sources that offer a less subjective viewpoint.

See also: *Abington School District v. Schempp* (1963); Bible Instruction, Teaching in Schools; Bible Study; Creationism; First Amendment; Student-Initiated Prayer, Clubs

Further Reading

Biondo, Vincent, and Andrew Fiala. *Civility, Religious Pluralism and Education.* New York: Routledge, 2013.

Heil, CeCe. "Student Can Use Bible as Reference." American Center for Law and Justice. June 12, 2012. https://aclj.org/school-prayer/student-allowed-use-bible-school.

"School Dist. of Abington Tp. v. Schempp, 374 U.S. 203 (1963)." Justia Law. n.d. Accessed July 9, 2020. https://supreme.justia.com/cases/federal/us/374/203/.

"School District of Abington Township, Pennsylvania v. Schempp." Oyez. n.d. Accessed July 9, 2020. https://www.oyez.org/cases/1962/142.

Thompson, Van. "Can the Bible Be Cited as a Research Reference?" Pen and the Pad. n.d. Accessed July 9, 2020. https://penandthepad.com/can-bible-cited-research-reference-22379.html.

Wachlin, Marie Goughnour. "The Place of Bible Literature in Public High School English Classes." *Research in the Teaching of English* 31, no. 1 (1997): 7–50. Accessed August 23, 2020. http://www.jstor.org/stable/40171263.

Warshaw, Thayer S. "Teaching English Teachers to Teach the Bible." *The Phi Delta Kappan* 52, no. 9 (1971): 539–40. Accessed August 23, 2020. http://www.jstor.org/stable/20373002.

Robertson, M. G. "Pat"

In the American evangelical Christian movement, there are few figures as well known as Marion Gordon "Pat" Robertson. A vocal advocate for conservative causes, Robertson was at the forefront of social and political movements for half a century.

Robertson was the son of former U.S. senator Willis Robertson (1887–1971). He was born on March 22, 1930, in Lexington, Virginia, to the senator, and his wife, Gladys Churchill née Willis. Named after one of his father's cousins, Robertson picked up the nickname "Pat" from his older brother Willis Robertson Jr.'s habit of patting his cheeks when he was a baby. As he grew older, Robertson continued to use the nickname "Pat," because he felt that his given name, Marion, "sounded a touch effeminate" and "M. Gordon" sounded pretentious (Robertson, n.d.).

In the fall of 1941, in the wake of Japan's attack on Pearl Harbor and the formal entry of the United States in World War II, Robertson was enrolled in McDonogh School, a military preparatory school outside of Baltimore, Maryland. He attended McCallie Prep School in Chattanooga, Tennessee, for his last two years of high school, where students had "dorm prayer meetings, chapel meetings, compulsory church attendance, [and] Sabbath observance" (Robertson, n.d.). After high school, he enrolled at Washington & Lee University, where he graduated magna cum laude before joining the marine corps. In 1950, Robertson enrolled at the University of London for a survey course in the British arts, and in 1952, he enrolled at Yale University Law School. He graduated from the law school in 1955.

Failing to find personal satisfaction or success in a career in law, Robertson eventually found purpose and direction in the field of Christian ministry. He'd been considering a career in the ministry, when he had a dinner meeting with Dutch missionary Cornelius Vanderbreggen. During the meeting, Robertson confessed his faith in Jesus Christ and, from that point forward, felt that God had "turned on a light within" him (Robertson, n.d.). Robertson went on to enroll in the Biblical Seminary in New York, and in 1959, he graduated with a master of divinity degree.

In the 1970s, the United States underwent a cultural revolution as members of a new religious Right movement began to make waves in the world of politics and push for a return to what they believed was a more morally righteous and decent society. Many religious leaders in this movement believed that American society was in a state of moral decay, evidenced by such Supreme Court decisions as *Engel v. Vitale* (1962), which outlawed prayer in school, and *Roe v. Wade* (1973), which prohibited states from making laws that unduly restricted access to abortion. They believed that they were enduring "calculated attacks on their religious freedom and their own detached kingdoms of God" (Harrell 1987). For Robertson's part, he was an ally in this movement but maintained a distance from some of its more prominent leaders, focusing his attention on the Christian Broadcasting Network (CBN), a television network and production company founded by Robertson in 1960.

Robertson was instrumental in the founding of several powerful conservative organizations, in addition to CBN, including the Freedom Council, the National Legal Foundation, the American Center for Law and Justice (ACLJ), and the Christian Coalition, a U.S. Christian advocacy group. He also established Regent University (originally Christian Broadcasting Network University) in Virginia Beach, Virginia, where he has served as chancellor since its founding in 1977 (Harrell 1987).

Like his allies in such conservative religious groups as the Moral Majority, Robertson worried about the state of public education in the United States. Recognizing an increase in "secularization of the public school system" (Harrell 1987), Robertson advocated in the 1980s for Christians to educate their children in schools where they would learn biblical principles and lifestyles; he took public stands in favor of legislation to require that Creationism be taught alongside the theory of evolution, and he spoke in support of a constitutional amendment allowing for the reestablishment of prayer in public school.

Over the years, Robertson has made several controversial comments on the subject of prayer in school, such as comparing U.S. policy on the matter to those of Nazi Germany and the Soviet Union and suggesting that the U.S. Supreme Court's 1962 ruling on prayer in school was analogous to "gang rape," claiming that the decision was a "rape of our nation's religious heritage, our national morality, of time-honored customs and institutions" (Boston 1996).

Robertson and others also have claimed that the absence of prayer in school, and the overall distancing from religious education in general, has led to or coincided with rises in teenage pregnancies, abortion, drug and alcohol use, depression and suicide, and violent crime (Robertson 1993).

Toward the end of the twentieth century, Robertson noted that one of the most promising signs of a "turning tide" toward more inclusion of religion in public schools was an increase in students engaging in more overt religious activities in school, such as praying before sporting events, distributing religious newspapers, and publicly speaking against the removal of religious words and images from school facilities (Robertson 1993).

"[S]tudents are beginning to make prayer a civil rights issue," Robertson wrote. "If this becomes the big civil rights cry—if the students of the 1990s say that to preserve their rights as Americans they must be allowed to pray—we're looking at something that could mobilize the world" (Robertson 1993). Robertson died in June 2023 at the age of 93.

See also: *Abington School District v. Schempp* (1963); Creationism; Evolution, Teaching; First Amendment; Intelligent Design; School Vouchers; Secularism and Secular Humanism; Student-Initiated Prayer, Clubs

Further Reading

American Center for Law and Justice. n.d. https://aclj.org/.
Boston, Rob. *The Most Dangerous Man in America? Pat Robertson and the Rise of the Christian Coalition.* Amherst, NY: Prometheus Books, 1996.
The Christian Broadcasting Network. n.d. http://www1.cbn.com/.
"Engel v. Vitale, 370 U.S. 421 (1962)." Justia. n.d. Accessed April 9, 2019. https://supreme.justia.com/cases/federal/us/370/421/.

Harrell, David Edwin. *Pat Robertson: A Personal, Religious, and Political Portrait*. San Francisco: Harper & Row, 1987.
Marley, David John. *Pat Robertson: An American Life*. Lanham, MD: Rowman & Littlefield, 2007.
Regent University. n.d. https://www.regent.edu/.
"Robertson, Absalom Willis (1887–1971)." Biographical Directory of the U.S. Congress. n.d. http://bioguide.congress.gov/scripts/biodisplay.pl?index=r000317.
Robertson, Pat. *Answers to 200 of Life's Most Probing Questions*. CBN Partners edition, revised edition. Nashville, TN: T. Nelson, 1985.
Robertson, Pat. "Pat Robertson: Biography." The Official Site of Pat Robertson. n.d. http://www.patrobertson.com/Biography/index.asp.
Robertson, Pat. *The Turning Tide: The Fall of Liberalism and the Rise of Common Sense*. Dallas, TX: World, 1993.
"Roe v. Wade, 410 U.S. 113 (1973)." Justia. n.d. Accessed April 9, 2019. https://supreme.justia.com/cases/federal/us/410/113/.

S

School Calendar, Religious Holiday Observances

SCHOOL CALENDAR ORIGINS

The typical calendar for a public school in the United States generally follows a 10-month schedule, running from approximately the beginning of September to the middle of June. These school calendars usually average about 180 instructional or contact days, with small breaks throughout the year, and a summer recess that runs primarily during the months of July and August (Pedersen 2012). The 10-month calendar has historically been seen as a "vestige" of the calendar used in America's more agrarian past, in which the summer months would have been essential to working farms, though other reasons for having a month or more of summer recess include increased student absenteeism during these months due to heat, epidemics, and family vacations (Pedersen 2012).

Within those months of instruction fall many religious holidays, from across the theistic spectrum. The challenge this poses for schools is that while they are usually bound by law to provide a minimum number of instructional days, they also must be cognizant of the fact that at one point or another, many of their students and faculty will encounter conflicts between their academic obligations and their observance of religious holidays.

To address these potential conflicts, many schools schedule their breaks to coincide with major religious holidays, and according to First Amendment scholar Charles Haynes and educator Oliver Thomas, they are free to do so as a "matter of administrative convenience" (Haynes and Thomas 2007). If a school were to remain open on a major religious holiday, such as Christmas, it would almost certainly see excessive absenteeism, as many families would opt to keep their children home. That said, a public school may *not* close *in observance* of a religious holiday, for to do so would amount to an endorsement of a particular faith, an act prohibited by the First Amendment (see "Religious Symbols").

RECOGNIZING RELIGIOUS HOLIDAYS

The question then becomes, when developing an academic year calendar, around which religious holidays, if any, should a district schedule its breaks and recesses, so as not only to minimize student absenteeism but also to avoid inadvertently promoting one faith over another?

"The most common religious holiday for which students in public schools are released from attendance is Christmas" (Blankenship-Knox and Geier 2018). Often referred to as "Winter Recess" or "Holiday Recess," these breaks usually fall between Christmas and New Year's Day. Despite the implicit association with a Christian holiday, this recess is largely recognized by the American public as being "both a secular and non-secular holiday" (Blankenship-Knox and Geier 2018). A 2019 Gallup poll found that Christmas is "celebrated by the majority of non-Christian Americans—who may celebrate the holiday more secularly than their Christian counterparts" and that even "19% of Catholics and 13% of Protestants also claim their celebrations are 'not too religious'" (Hrynowski 2019).

In contrast to the nearly universally celebrated Christmas stand holidays such as Good Friday, which is the Friday just preceding Easter Sunday, which is, itself, the holiest day of the year for Christians. Good Friday as a school holiday was the subject of legal scrutiny in the case of *Metzl v. Leininger* (1994). In this case, Chicago public school teacher Andrea Metzl brought suit against school officials, alleging that the Illinois School Code violated the Establishment Clause of the U.S. Constitution and Article I, Section 3 of the Constitution of the state of Illinois by designating Good Friday as a state-mandated school holiday ("Metzl v. Leininger, 850 F. Supp. 740 (N.D. Ill. 1994)," n.d.). The designation dated back to 1941, and although "no legislative history exists explaining the legislature's purpose" in making such a designation ("Metzl v. Leininger, 850 F. Supp. 740 (N.D. Ill. 1994)," n.d.), the decision was lauded in 1942 by Illinois governor Dwight Green, who issued the proclamation "direct[ing] attention to this significant day, Good Friday," "commend[ing] the secret rites and ceremonies of the occasion to the thoughtful consideration of churchgoers and believers throughout our State" ("Metzl v. Leininger, 850 F. Supp. 740 (N.D. Ill. 1994)," n.d.).

The Court found in that case that the state's "designation of Good Friday as a legal school holiday was primarily motivated by a desire to endorse the Christian faith and conveys the impermissible message that Christianity is a favored religion within the state of Illinois" ("Metzl v. Leininger, 850 F. Supp. 740 (N.D. Ill. 1994)," n.d.) and declared the challenged portion of the school code to be unconstitutional.

As the examples of Christmas- and Good Friday–linked school holidays indicate, school districts in the United States generally are given leeway to designate widely recognized religious holidays as school holidays but only when doing so is in the interest of maintaining a school calendar that allows for the most students to attend the most school days and when the observance is framed in secular terms.

INCLUSIVE CALENDARS

One challenge to forming a fully inclusive school calendar, though, is when the population of a state or school district is particularly diverse. In 2015, New York City mayor Bill de Blasio announced that, starting the following school year, students would get days off to observe two Islamic holidays, citing Islam as "one of the fastest growing" faiths in city (Blankenship-Knox and Geier 2018). Muslims make up about 9% of the population in New York City ("MAP-NYC-Report-Web-3.Pdf," n.d.). New York City schools also close for the Jewish holidays of Rosh Hashanah and Yom Kippur and for the Lunar New Year, which is largely observed in Chinese and Korean cultures. Jews account for about 13% of the population in the city (Berger 2012), while the ethnic Chinese and ethnic Korean populations account for about 7% and about 1%, respectively ("American FactFinder: Selected Population Profile in the United States: 2014 . . .," n.d.a; "American FactFinder: Selected Population Profile in the United States: 2017 . . .," n.d.b; Asian American Federation 2019).

Despite the largely inclusive nature of the New York City school calendar, notably, its list of official holidays does not include Diwali, the festival of lights celebrated by Hindus, Sikhs, Jains, and some Buddhists (Blankenship-Knox and Geier 2018). People of South Asian descent make up about 2.7% of the population of New York City ("American FactFinder: Selected Population Profile in the United States: 2014 . . .," n.d.a; "American FactFinder: Selected Population Profile in the United States: 2017 . . .," n.d.b). A resolution to recognize Diwali as a school holiday was introduced before the New York City Council, but as of 2019, the resolution is "in limbo" with only five sponsors, well short of the 26 votes it would need to be approved by the council (Touré 2019). Even if such a resolution were to garner enough support from the council, the mayor pledged in 2015 to not add any other school holidays "anytime in the foreseeable future," citing the challenge of creating "a balance in the calendar and protect[ing]" the required 180 instructional days (Barkan 2015).

THE FIRST AMENDMENT AND RELIGIOUS ACCOMMODATIONS

In the event that a school district does not observe a particular religious holiday, students and faculty are still largely protected, should they choose to stay home from school. Haynes and Thomas recommend that school districts "encourage all students and staff members to appreciate and be tolerant of each other's religious views," adding that "students and staff members should be excused from participating in practices which are contrary to their religious beliefs unless there are clear issues of overriding concern that would prevent it" (Haynes and Thomas 2007). Most states, they indicate, have laws that permit for a certain number of excused absences for religious holidays, adding that "[w]here no statutory exemption exists, the First Amendment's Free Exercise clause would seem to require a reasonable number of excused absences for such religious observance" (Haynes and Thomas 2007).

For school staff and faculty who wish to take personal leave to observe a religious holiday, the protections are slightly more complicated. While "Title VII of the Civil Rights Act of 1964 requires school boards to make 'reasonable accommodation' of their employees' religious needs, . . . [school boards] are not required to accept the accommodation proposed by the employee" (Haynes and Thomas 2007). This interpretation of the Civil Rights Act was challenged in the case of *Levinsky v. the Scarborough School Department*, in which a teacher alleged that her employer discriminated against her "because of her religion (she happened to be Jewish) when she was required to use personal days to take time off from work for religious observances" (Pringle 2002). The complainant argued that Christian employees effectively receive more personal days to use for personal business because they were "not required to work on major Christian holy days because schools are closed" (Pringle 2002).

In this, and other similar cases, the courts found that reasonable accommodations had been offered. In an earlier case, *Pinsker v. Joint District No. 28-J of Adams and Arapahoe Counties*, the Court stated that a reasonable accommodation "need not spare the employee all costs" and that while the teacher was required to take unpaid leave, "his job was not jeopardized nor was his observation of religious holidays jeopardized" (Pringle 2002).

See also: First Amendment; Religion in Performances; Religious Discrimination in Schools; Religious Diversity in the United States; Religious Symbols

Further Reading

"American FactFinder: Selected Population Profile in the United States: 2014 American Community Survey 1-Year Estimates." U.S. Census Bureau. n.d.a. Accessed July 9, 2020. http://factfinder.census.gov/bkmk/table/1.0/en/ACS/14_1YR/S0201/1600000US3651000/popgroup~013.

"American FactFinder: Selected Population Profile in the United States: 2017 American Community Survey 1-Year Estimates." U.S. Census Bureau. n.d.b. Accessed July 9, 2020. https://factfinder.census.gov/bkmk/table/1.0/en/ACS/17_1YR/S0201/1600000US3651000/popgroup~016.

Asian American Federation, Profile of New York City's Korean Americans. 2019. https://www.aafederation.org/wp-content/uploads/2020/12/2019kr.pdf.

Barkan, Ross. "Bill de Blasio: Don't Expect Any New School Holidays after Lunar New Year." *Observer*, June 23, 2015. https://observer.com/2015/06/bill-de-blasio-dont-expect-any-new-school-holidays-after-lunar-new-year/.

Berger, Joseph. "Aided by Orthodox, City's Jewish Population Is Growing Again." *New York Times*, June 11, 2012, sec. New York. https://www.nytimes.com/2012/06/12/nyregion/new-yorks-jewish-population-is-growing-again.html.

Blankenship-Knox, Ann E., and Brett A. Geier. "Taking a Day Off to Pray: Closing Schools for Religious Observance in Increasingly Diverse Schools." *Brigham Young University Education and Law Journal* 2 (2018): 1–51.

Haynes, Charles C., and Oliver Thomas. *Finding Common Ground: A First Amendment Guide to Religion and Public Schools*. Nashville, TN: First Amendment Center, 2007.

Hrynowski, Zach. "More Americans Celebrating a Secular Christmas." Gallup.Com. December 20, 2019. https://news.gallup.com/poll/272378/americans-celebrating-secular-christmas.aspx.

"MAP-NYC-Report-Web-3.Pdf." n.d. Accessed July 9, 2020. https://www.ispu.org/wp-content/uploads/2018/07/MAP-NYC-Report-Web-3.pdf.

"Metzl v. Leininger, 850 F. Supp. 740 (N.D. Ill. 1994)." Justia Law. n.d. Accessed July 9, 2020. https://law.justia.com/cases/federal/district-courts/FSupp/850/740/2132263/.

Pedersen, James M. "The History of School and Summer Vacation." *Journal of Inquiry & Action in Education* 5, no.1 (2012): 54–62.

Pringle, Harry R. "Personal Leave Days and Religious Discrimination." *Drummond, Woodsum & MacMahon: School Law Advisory*. 2002.

Touré, Madina. "Advocates Renew Pressure to Recognize Diwali as a School Holiday." *Politico*. October 31, 2019. https://politi.co/2psbkM8.

School Vouchers

School voucher programs often conflict with the First Amendment and Establishment Clause when they involve the redirection of public funds toward private religious schools. In recent years, school voucher programs have rapidly expanded, and the practice of using public funds to pay for tuition at religious schools is increasingly common. While some view this as simply offering families a choice, others object to this as a violation of the Establishment Clause.

Vouchers are taxpayer-funded tuition subsidies provided by the government to parents who choose to send their children to private schools rather than their assigned public schools (Cierniak, Billick, and Ruddy 2015: 1). Voucher systems in the United States have their roots in the late nineteenth century when small towns that did not have schools of their own were forced to send children elsewhere. By the mid-twentieth century, Milton Friedman (1955) introduced the idea that school choice, and thus competition, would lead to improvements in the public education system. In recent decades, it has become a common practice in many states to offer vouchers where schools are unable to provide adequate services, as with special needs services, and increasingly, to offer alternatives to underperforming schools.

Though the vast majority of American students attend public schools, some states have larger voucher programs than others, in which case the subsidies are often used toward religious school tuition. Indiana, where roughly 90% of vouchers go toward Catholic schools, provides a good example. Nearly one-third of the schools in Indiana (317 of 969 schools) participated in the state's Choice Scholarship Program in 2014–2015. Of those 317 schools, virtually all ($n = 306$) are religious schools, roughly half of which are Catholic schools ($n = 173$) (Catt 2014).

Intended or not, voucher programs have had the effect of redirecting government funds from public schools to religious institutions. This trend coincides with what had been declining enrollments in Roman Catholic schools; by the 2013–2014 school year, more than 50% of the school choice vouchers nationwide were going to Catholic schools. The impact on churches affiliated with the religious schools has varied. In Milwaukee, there has been a significant increase in private school vouchers, much of it going toward roughly 6,500 Catholic schools in the city, and the program is expanding as Catholic schools statewide begin to accept vouchers. One study found that while subsidies for parishes participating in the voucher program provided a much-needed infusion of funds, in many cases, it has come with a decrease in donations and nonschool activities in the affiliated churches (Hungerman, Rinz, and Frymark 2018).

FIRST AMENDMENT OBJECTIONS

Opponents of the use of vouchers for religious school tuition object on several grounds; foremost, this practice violates the First Amendment's Establishment Clause by "respecting the establishment of religion." Many of the concerns relate to curricular content taught in the schools accepting vouchers. In some cases, such as Indiana, states are prohibited from regulating the curriculum of these schools, meaning that taxpayer dollars may be funding curricula that include religious content such as Bible stories, Creationism, and pseudoscience. It is important to note that while the vast majority of voucher recipients are Christian schools, other religiously affiliated schools also have access to these programs. For example, one of the largest recipients of voucher funding in Indiana is MTI (Madrasa Tul-Ilm), an Islamic School, where 90% of students use vouchers to cover tuition.

Though not specifically about vouchers, the 1983 case, *Mueller v. Allen*, set a precedent for future cases concerning "private choice" and the constitutionality of programs where public funds are steered toward religious institutions (Cierniak, Billick, and Ruddy 2015). In *Mueller v. Allen*, the Supreme Court examined a challenge to a Minnesota law that allowed taxpayers to deduct expenses incurred in providing tuition, textbooks, and transportation for their children's elementary or secondary school education, including parochial schools, from their state income tax. Applying the Lemon Test, the Court ruled that the law did not have "the primary effect of advancing the sectarian aims of the non-public schools," nor did it "excessively entangle" the state with religion. Justice Rehnquist stressed that deductions were available to all parents and thus did not "confer any imprimatur of state approval" on religious schools (*Mueller v. Allen* 1983). In 2002, the Supreme Court directly addressed the voucher question in *Zelman v. Simmons Harris*, a case involving Cleveland's voucher program, where 96% of participating students used vouchers to attend religious schools (https://www.law.cornell.edu/supct/html/00-1751.ZS.html). The Court held that such programs are not unconstitutional because their primary objective of offering educational choice to financially disadvantage children was secular in nature. As in *Mueller*, the Court pointed to the fact that funding goes directly to parents who then could elect to spend the money at any school, religious or not, thus avoiding any direct entanglement for the state.

Similar cases have arisen at the state level. In 2011, Indiana public school teachers joined by local clergy sued the state, arguing that the voucher program violated provisions in the state constitution prohibiting the use of tax dollars to support religion, especially when vital funding needed by local public school systems was being diverted to the religious schools. The Indiana Supreme Court, however, held that this was not the case since voucher dollars went to the parents and not directly to the schools.

ASSESSMENT

Supporters of voucher programs often claim that it affords children the opportunity to receive a better education. In fact, there are three main arguments for vouchers: (1) exit option for children who want to attend a better school; (2) competition can improve the whole public system; and (3) differentiation, allowing for the option to attend a school better suited to a family's desire for religious or other form of specialized education. As to the question of "better" schools, research has shown little to no evidence that students perform better in voucher-driven schools; in fact, results are often worse. Researchers at Notre Dame University examined data from the first three years of Indiana's program (Waddington and Berens 2018), finding that math scores of students who switched from public to voucher schools actually declined compared with those remaining in public schools. Indiana's public school students also scored higher on English exams, while voucher school student scores stayed flat. Students at several Christian schools with larger numbers of voucher students had among the lowest standardized test scores in the state (Indiana Department of Education 2019). This same trend is seen elsewhere as independent studies of highly touted voucher programs in cities such as Milwaukee, Cleveland, and Washington D.C. also found no evidence that voucher students outperformed children in public schools (Center for Tax and Budget Accountability [CTBA] 2015; Rouse and Barrow 2009). Rouse and Barrow (2009) have argued that the ostensible competitive pressure has not led to improvements in public schools, largely because public schools lack resources to respond to competition from private schools subsidized by vouchers. Diane Ravitch, a vocal critic of public schools, is equally dubious, stating ". . . fifteen years after the [Milwaukee voucher] program's expansion to include religious schools, there was no evidence of dramatic improvement for the neediest students or the public schools they left behind" (Ravitch 2016: 132).

It is also unclear whether voucher programs are having the intended outcome of providing alternatives for students from failing urban schools. Indiana's program, started in 2011 under Republican governor Mitch Daniels, was initially conceived as a means to offer educational alternatives for poor, minority children stuck in underperforming public schools and was capped at 7,500 vouchers. In 2013, then governor Mike Pence expanded the program dramatically, increasing the minimum income for eligibility and allowing students already enrolled in private schools to accept the tuition subsidies (Indiana Department of Education 2019). Indiana's Department of Education reported that following these changes, more than 60% of students using vouchers are white, and a rising number come from affluent suburban neighborhoods (Indiana Department of Education n.d.; Broughman and Swaim 2013). Moreover, according to the bipartisan think tank, the CTBA, the rapid rise in the percentage of Indiana's white children receiving vouchers in relation to the next largest racial group (44% points) means the program will contribute to an increase in racial stratification within the state's K–12 public schools (CTBA 2015). Ultimately, it is not even clear whether the program translates to real choice when over half of the voucher students never attended public school in the first place. Outside of test scores, surveys show that parents who can opt for private schools are more satisfied, and choice parents display greater satisfaction than public school parents (Rhinesmith 2017), suggesting that vouchers may succeed in terms of offering differentiation.

Finally, it is noteworthy that privately funded school voucher programs and scholarship tax credit programs, such as NJ Seeds (https://seeds access.org/), are expanding even faster than direct publicly funded voucher programs.

See also: Religion and Pseudoscience

Further Reading

Broughman, Stephen P., and Nancy L. Swaim. *Characteristics of Private Schools in the United States: Results from the 2011–12 Private School Universe Survey. First Look. National Center for Education Statistics. NCES 2013–316.* Jessup, MD: National Center for Education Statistics, 2013. https://eric.ed.gov/?id=ED544030.

Catt, Andrew D. *Exploring Indiana's Private Education Sector. Friedman Foundation for Educational Choice.* School Survey Series. Indianapolis: Friedman Foundation for Educational Choice, 2014. https://eric.ed.gov/?id=ED560671.

Center for Tax and Budget Accountability. "CTBA Releases Analysis of Indiana School Choice Scholarship Program." April 16, 2015. https://www.ctbaonline.org/press-room/ctba-releases-analysis-indiana-school-choice-scholarship-program.

Cierniak, Katherine, Rebecca Billick, and Anne-Maree Ruddy. "The Indiana Choice Scholarship Program: Legal Challenges, Program Expansion, and Participation. Informing Policy and Improving Practice. Policy Brief." Center for Evaluation and Education Policy. 2015.

Friedman, Milton, and Robert Solo (eds.). "The Role of Government in Education." In *Economics and the Public Interest: Collected Works of Milton Friedman*, 123–44. New Brunswick, NJ: Rutgers University Press, 1955. https://miltonfriedman.hoover.org/collections.

Hungerman, Daniel M., Kevin Rinz, and Jay Frymark. "Beyond the Classroom: The Implications of School Vouchers for Church Finances." *The Review of Economics and Statistics* 101, no. 4 (November 2, 2018): 588–601. https://doi.org/10.1162/rest_a_00782.

Indiana Department of Education. "Find School and Corporation Data Reports | IDOE." 2019. https://www.doe.in.gov/accountability/find-school-and-corporation-data-reports.

Indiana Department of Education. "Indiana Choice Scholarship Program | IDOE." n.d. Accessed June 23, 2020. https://www.doe.in.gov/choice.

Mueller v. Allen, 463 U.S. 388 (1983). n.d. https://supreme.justia.com/cases/federal/us/463/388/.

NJ Seeds. https://seedsaccess.org/.

Ravitch, Diane. *The Death and Life of the Great American School System: How Testing and Choice are Undermining Education.* Basic Books, 2016.

Rhinesmith, Evan. "A Review of the Research on Parent Satisfaction in Private School Choice Programs." *Journal of School Choice* 11, no. 4 (2017): 585–603. https://doi.org/10.1080/15582159.2017.1395639.

Rouse, Cecilia Elena, and Lisa Barrow. "School Vouchers and Student Achievement: Recent Evidence and Remaining Questions." *Annual Review of Economics* 1, no. 1 (2009): 17–42.

Waddington, R. Joseph, and Mark Berends. "Impact of the Indiana Choice Scholarship Program: Achievement Effects for Students in Upper Elementary and Middle School." *Journal of Policy Analysis and Management* 37, no. 4 (2018): 783–808. https://doi.org/10.1002/pam.22086.

Zelman, Superintendent of Public Instruction of Ohio, et al v. Simmons-Harris, et al (Syllabus), 536 U.S. 639 (U.S. Supreme Court 2002). https://www.law.cornell.edu/supct/html/00-1751.ZS.html

Scopes Trial

The State of Tennessee v. John Thomas Scopes (1925) court case is one of the most famous trials in U.S. history. Also known as the Scopes Trial, or Scopes Monkey Trial, the case centered on the question of whether evolution should be taught in public schools. The trial involved several of the most well-known figures of the day and made headlines around the country, bringing the question of religion in school to the forefront of the American consciousness.

Events leading up to the Scopes trial began in March 1925 when Tennessee's legislature passed the Butler Act, prohibiting the teaching of any material that contradicted the biblical account of creation, especially the theory of evolution that religious fundamentalists regarded as heresy. The American Civil Liberties Union (ACLU), founded just five years earlier, wanted to challenge the law and offered to defend anyone who faced legal action for teaching evolution. At the behest of prominent residents of

Dayton, Tennessee, John Scopes, a 24-year-old science teacher and football coach, agreed to test the Butler Act by teaching evolution in his classroom.

The case swiftly attracted national attention as two of the most famous attorneys in America stepped forward to argue the case. Renowned labor lawyer Clarence Darrow defended Scopes along with ACLU general counsel, Arthur Garfield Hays. On the other side, former secretary of state and three-time U.S presidential candidate William Jennings Bryan represented the state of Tennessee. Bryan was a devout Christian who espoused a literal interpretation of the Bible, while Darrow was an avowed agnostic. The defense's strategy was to demonstrate that the Tennessee law established the Bible, a religious document, as the standard of truth in a public institution, thus violating the First Amendment's Establishment Clause. The sharply opposing views of the two men, along with equally polarizing coverage of the case by figures like the journalist and social critic, H. L. Mencken, seemed to put religion itself on trial.

The trial was held in July 1925 at the Rhea County Courthouse, with State Circuit judge John T. Raulston presiding. Dubbed the "trial of the century," the case was covered by hundreds of journalists from across the United States. It was noted for the heated, dramatic arguments, as well as the heat of the sweltering Tennessee summer, especially inside the courthouse.

Though larger questions about modernity and traditional values loomed large in the trial, Judge Raulston attempted to keep the focus on the narrow question of whether Scopes had violated the Butler Law. Raulston viewed broader questions about the validity of evolution, academic freedom, and tensions between science and religion as immaterial to this basic question and, thus, ultimately blocked testimony from the expert scientific witnesses that Darrow had lined up in an attempt to prove that evolution was true. Darrow, forced to shifted strategies, attempted instead to disprove the Bible by exposing flaws in a literal reading of the scripture. In a dramatic move, Darrow put Bryan himself on the stand as an expert witness on the Bible, raising questions about whether the Bible should be taken literally. Bryan would be forced to concede that not every word of the Bible could be taken literally. Still, Judge Raulston insisted on keeping the trial focused on the limited question of whether Scopes has violated the Butler Act.

The trial came to an abrupt end on July 21, 1925, when the defense decided to make no plea, and Scopes was found guilty in a verdict that took less than nine minutes to reach. Scopes was fined $100, but the case would go to the State Supreme Court, and, ultimately, the fine was thrown out on a technicality. Strangely, Bryan would die just days after the conclusion of the trial at the age of 85.

Nationally, the trial had become a symbol for the struggle between progressive secular values and traditional fundamentalism, but the reality was much more complex. Bryan, for example, a longtime leader of the Democratic Party, not only rejected the theory of natural selection because of its religious implications but also, as a humanist, objected to the way it was being co-opted to justify social Darwinism and what he declared to be "the merciless law by which the strong crowd out and kill off the weak." In *Trying Biology*, Adam Shapiro (2013) considers the role that money, politics, and the textbook industry played in the time before, during, and since the trial.

As it were, in the years following the *Scopes* trial, multiple states overturned laws prohibiting the teaching of evolution. By 1967, the case would appear again in the Supreme Court, with the Court ruling that Tennessee's Butler Law prohibiting the teaching of evolution was unconstitutional on grounds it assumed Christianity as the established religion of the state. Even Judge Raulston, himself a devout Christian, revisited his views of fundamentalism and education in the ensuing years. According to his obituary in the *New York Times*, the former judge "questioned the power of the Legislature to make laws abridging the right to teach science when such science did not damage the morals of the students" (*New York Times*, n.d.).

The case has also been commemorated in popular culture. The story was depicted in the 1955 play *Inherit the Wind*, which, in turn, was made into a film starring the leading actor Spencer Tracy, though Larsen's book *Summer for the Gods* (1997) argues that the book and the film do not give an accurate picture of the trial and the times. The trial is also mentioned in a number of popular songs. In 1977, the Rhea County Courthouse, originally built in 1891, was designated a National Historic Landmark by the National Park Service, and in 1979, a $1 million restoration of the courthouse and Scopes Trial Museum project was completed.

See also: Creationism; Evolution, Teaching; Intelligent Design

Further Reading

Ginger, Ray. *Six Days Or Forever? Tennessee V. John Thomas Scopes*. New York: Oxford University Press, 1974.

Horvath, Anthony (Ed.) *The Transcript of the Scopes Monkey Trial: Complete and Unabridged.* By William Jennings Bryan and Clarence Darrow. Greenwood, WI: Suzeteo Enterprises, 2018.

Larson, Edward J. *Summer for the Gods: The Scopes Trial and America's Continuing Debate over Science and Religion.* New York: Basic Books, 1997.

New York Times. "JOHN T. RAULSTON, JURIST, 87, DEAD." Obituary. n.d. https://www.nytimes.com/1956/07/12/archives/john-t-raulston-jurist-87-dead-presiding-judge-at-scopes-monkey.html.

Shapiro, Adam R. *Trying Biology: The Scopes Trial, Textbooks, and the Antievolution Movement in American Schools.* Chicago: University of Chicago Press, 2013.

Secularism and Secular Humanism

WHAT IS "SECULARISM"?

The term "secular," in its strictly denotative sense, means of or relating to the worldly, or having no basis in religion or spirituality. Etymologically, it derives from the Late Latin *saecularis*, "pertaining to a generation or age" ("Secular | Origin and Meaning of Secular," n.d.), implying a connection to a physical and temporal "here and now." In the context of the debate over religion in American institutions, however, the word has taken on a more controversial meaning, in that, depending on what side of the debate one falls, it has come to represent either the core of American values or the antithesis.

"Secularism," as a term, was coined by British writer George Holyoake in 1851, in his book, *English Secularism: A Confession of Belief.* In the publisher's preface, Paul Carus defines "secularism" as being a belief that "espouses the cause of the world versus theology; of the secular and temporal versus the sacred and ecclesiastical" (Holyoake 1896). Secularism, Carus continues, "claims that religion out never be anything but a private affair" and that "it denies the right of any kind of church to be associated with the public life of a nation" (Holyoake 1896).

This notion of separation of private religious affairs from public life might not have been known as "secularism" prior to Holyoake's writing, but it was certainly central to many of the foundational documents and philosophies of the United States in the century prior.

The Declaration of Independence (1776), for instance, speaks of a government that derives its "just powers from the consent of the governed" ("Declaration of Independence: A Transcription" 2015) as opposed to from any god or gods (Cline 2018). The Constitution (1787) and the Bill of Rights (1789) are even more distinctly secular, with the only references to religion being in the First Amendment, which reads, "Congress shall make no law respecting an establishment of religion, or prohibiting the free exercise thereof" and in Article VI, Section 3, which reads, "[N]o religious test shall ever be required as a qualification to any office or public trust under the United States" ("The Constitution of the United States: A Transcription" 2015).

WHAT IS "SECULAR HUMANISM"?

Secular humanism is a related but distinctly different concept, which focuses on humanity's role and responsibility in leading an ethical and productive existence. The Center for Inquiry, a secular humanist advocacy group, describes it as "a nonreligious worldview rooted in science, philosophical naturalism, and humanist ethics" that uses "compassion, critical thinking, and human experience to find solutions to human problems" rather than turning to "faith, doctrine, or mysticism" ("What Is Secular Humanism" 2018).

Despite the close association between secularism and humanism, not all humanism is secular. In fact, humanism as a philosophy has some very strong traditional ties to religion. The first Humanist Manifesto, a document written in 1933 that outlined the beliefs and positions of humanism, was written primarily by Raymond Bragg, a Unitarian minister, and included the signatures of 13 Unitarian ministers and a Jewish rabbi (Cline 2019b). The affirmations expressed in the Manifesto do not dismiss religion but rather propose a new form of religion, grounded in the natural world and the human experience within it, which rejects "supernatural or cosmic guarantees of human values" ("Humanist Manifesto I," n.d.). Religion, according to the Manifesto, "consists of those actions, purposes, and experiences which are humanly significant," including "labor, art, science, philosophy, love, friendship, [and] recreation" ("Humanist Manifesto I," n.d.).

The final aim of humanism, at least according to the first Manifesto, is to "affirm life rather than deny it," "seek to elicit the possibilities of life, not flee from them," and "endeavor to establish the conditions of a satisfactory life for all, not merely for the few" ("Humanist Manifesto I," n.d.).

The Manifesto was followed by two others, one in 1973 and one in 2003, both of which restated and expanded upon the beliefs expressed in the first document.

Secular humanism is largely similar in philosophy with the key distinction that it denies connection to anything spiritual or religious. A religious humanist and a secular humanist might, for instance, hold nearly identical views of humanity and its place in the world but disagree on whether to characterize that worldview as "religious" (Cline 2019a).

SECULARISM AND SECULAR HUMANISM IN MODERN AMERICA

The ideals described in documents such as the first Humanist Manifesto, as well as the two that followed, often were those that many, if not most, Americans would support, at least in theory. The second Manifesto, for example, calls for a "full range of civil liberties in all societies," including freedom of speech and the press, fair judicial process, and religious liberty ("Humanist Manifesto II," n.d.). The third Manifesto, the most recent, calls for the resolution of conflict without violence and treating all people with dignity and speaks of the importance of all people participating in the democratic process ("Humanism and Its Aspirations: Humanist Manifesto III, a Successor to the Humanist Manifesto of 1933," n.d.).

Yet secular humanism has often come under fire from conservative and religious figures and organizations in America, who view secularism as more than an innocuous social philosophy. From their perspective, secularism is a willful rejection of religion, faith, and morality. Some evangelical Christians, for example, such as Pat Robertson and Jerry Falwell, and associated organizations, such as the Moral Majority, include overcoming the influence of secularism as part of their spiritual mission.

The most vocal evangelical leaders of the past few decades have taken direct aim at secularism as being not only detrimental to the fabric of American society but also inviting the disapproval of God, himself.

Famously, in the days following the terrorist attacks of September 11, 2001, Falwell appeared on Robertson's religious television program, *The 700 Club*, and said, "I really believe that the pagans, and the abortionists, and the feminists, and the gays and the lesbians who are actively trying to make that an alternative lifestyle, the ACLU, People For the American Way—all of them who have tried to secularize America—I point the finger in their face and say 'you helped this happen'" (Goodstein 2001).

Falwell walked back his statement the day after his appearance, laying blame for the attacks squarely on the perpetrators who hijacked the airplanes, but held fast to his position that organizations that had "attempted to secularize America, [had] removed our nation from its relationship with Christ on which it was founded," which "created an environment which possibly has caused God to lift the veil of protection" from America ("Falwell Apologizes to Gays, Feminists, Lesbians" 2001).

SECULARISM AND SECULAR HUMANISM IN PUBLIC SCHOOLS

Many in the conservative and religious community, particularly evangelical Christians, have expressed concern over the past several decades that secularism or secular humanism is the pernicious byproduct of Supreme Court rulings that they claim have taken religion out of public schools (see "*Abington School District v. Schempp* (1963)").

In a 1987 article in *Crisis Magazine*, a publication focused on "authentic Catholic perspectives," Jesuit priest and scholar Virgil C. Blum wrote that when Supreme Court "forbade the teaching of the traditional religions" in public schools, it effectively established secularism as a new religion, which, according to Blum, suppressed not only "the teaching of religion but also of religiously-grounded moral values" and, by extension, taught "that those values are false, or at least irrelevant to man's affairs" (Blum 1987).

While public schools are, indeed, charged with presenting all information to students in a secular way (such as teaching the Bible as literature, or studying the Five Pillars of Islam in a course on comparative religion), they are not permitted to teach secularism or secular humanism as a preferred system of belief or as being inherently better than another system of belief, as doing so would violate the Establishment Clause of the First Amendment.

The Secular Coalition for America, an advocacy organization that represents "atheists, humanists, agnostics, and other nonthesists," does not suggest that secularism should be taught as a system of belief but that curriculum should be "evidence-based and religiously neutral" ("Education," n.d.).

As for whether a school can or should teach moral values, the Center for Inquiry has indicated that morality, far from being anathema to secularism, serves an important role in humanity's existence, as it "helps to provide security to members of the community, create stability, ameliorate harmful conditions, foster trust, and facilitate cooperation in achieving shared or complementary goals" (Lindsay 2010). For the secular humanist, though, morality is more appropriately discovered through and defined by critical reasoning than by turning to a particular religious doctrine.

See also: Americans United for Separation of Church and State; Falwell, Jerry; First Amendment; Freedom from Religion Foundation; *Lemon v. Kurtzman* Supreme Court Decision; Robertson, M. G. "Pat"

Further Reading

Blum, Virgil C. "Secularism in Public Schools." *Crisis Magazine*. March 1, 1987. http://www.crisismagazine.com/1987/secularism-in-public-schools.

Cline, Austin. "Declaration of Independence and the Christianity Myth." Learn Religions. July 30, 2018. https://www.learnreligions.com/declaration-of-independence-and-christianity-myth-249684.

Cline, Austin. "Religious vs. Secular Humanism: What's the Difference?" Learn Religions. April 26, 2019. https://www.learnreligions.com/religious-vs-secular-humanism-248117.

Cline, Austin. "What Is Religious Humanism?" Learn Religions. March 16, 2019. https://www.learnreligions.com/what-is-religious-humanism-248118.

Cline, Austin. "What Is Secular Humanism?" Learn Religions. March 8, 2017. https://www.learnreligions.com/what-is-secular-humanism-248120.

"The Constitution of the United States: A Transcription." National Archives. November 4, 2015. https://www.archives.gov/founding-docs/constitution-transcript.

"Declaration of Independence: A Transcription." National Archives. November 1, 2015. https://www.archives.gov/founding-docs/declaration-transcript.

"Education." Secular Coalition for America. n.d. Accessed August 23, 2020. https://secular.org/key-issue/education/.

"Falwell Apologizes to Gays, Feminists, Lesbians." CNN.Com. September 14, 2001. https://www.cnn.com/2001/US/09/14/Falwell.apology/index.html.

Goodstein, Laurie. "After the Attacks: Finding Fault; Falwell's Finger-Pointing Inappropriate, Bush Says." *New York Times*, September 15, 2001, sec. A.

Holyoake, George Jacob. *English Secularism: A Confession of Belief*. Brighton, England: The Open Court Publishing Co., 1896. https://www.gutenberg.org/files/38104/38104-h/38104-h.htm.

"Humanism and Its Aspirations: Humanist Manifesto III, a Successor to the Humanist Manifesto of 1933." American Humanist Association. n.d. Accessed August 23, 2020. https://americanhumanist.org/what-is-humanism/manifesto3/.
"Humanist Manifesto I." American Humanist Association. n.d. Accessed August 23, 2020. https://americanhumanist.org/what-is-humanism/manifesto1/.
"Humanist Manifesto II." American Humanist Association. n.d. Accessed August 23, 2020. https://americanhumanist.org/what-is-humanism/manifesto2/.
Lindsay, Ronald A. "What Is the Purpose of Morality?" Center for Inquiry. June 19, 2010. https://centerforinquiry.org/blog/what_is_the_purpose_of_morality/.
"Secular | Origin and Meaning of Secular." *Online Etymology Dictionary*. n.d. Accessed July 9, 2020. https://www.etymonline.com/word/secular.
"What Is Secular Humanism." Center for Inquiry. May 22, 2018. https://centerforinquiry.org/definitions/what-is-secular-humanism/.

Student-Initiated Prayer, Clubs

The U.S. Supreme Court has ruled in multiple cases that public schools may not require or lead students in any activity that gives the impression of endorsing or criticizing a particular religion, whether implicitly or explicitly (see "*Abington School District v. Schempp* (1963)"; "*Edwards v. Aguillard* (1987)"). These rulings have effectively outlawed practices that were once common in schools, such as mandatory prayer at the beginning of a school day and the reading of Bible passages in class.

Some people have taken these rulings to mean that religious expression has no place in a public school setting at all, but in fact, students still have considerable leeway to practice their religion under protection of the First Amendment's Free Exercise Clause.

WHAT DOES THE LAW SAY ABOUT STUDENT-INITIATED RELIGIOUS PRACTICE?

The text of the First Amendment states that, among other limitations on its power, "Congress shall make no law . . . prohibiting the free exercise" of a person's religion. It is this explicit statement, often referred to at the Free Exercise Clause, that prevents school staff, faculty, or administrators from interfering with most student expressions of faith ("The Constitution of the United States: A Transcription" 2015). In general, the only reason that a school might legally have for stopping a student from expressing his or her faith is if that expression is disruptive to classroom instruction or activities, or if the student attempts to force others to participate in a religious practice ("ACLU Defense of Religious Practice and Expression in Public Schools," n.d.).

Despite these protections, from time to time, school officials still attempt to prohibit or limit student expressions of faith, usually in the interest of maintaining what they understand as a required "separation of church and state," a phrase that is not found in the language of the Constitution. For example, a teacher might stop a student from saying a blessing before lunch, attempt to disband a group of students meeting to pray or study scripture between classes, or prohibit a student from wearing religious garments. In each of these cases, the student's right to free exercise would supersede school policy, and protect the students in the expression of their religious faith.

Groups such as the American Center for Law and Justice (ACLJ), a Christian legal advocacy organization, and the American Civil Liberties Union (ACLU) often work on behalf of students and parents who believe that a student's rights have been violated to inform schools of their constitutional responsibility and to urge them to take appropriate remedial action. Such intervention can help the school and the family of the students affected from entering costly and time-consuming litigation.

ORGANIZED PRAYER ON SCHOOL GROUNDS

One of the ways in which students can express their religious faith while still remaining within the limits of constitutional protection is through organized prayer meetings. These meetings may be held on school grounds, and possibly even during school hours, but are usually subject to very specific rules and guidelines. An example of this sort of organized prayer meeting is "See You at the Pole," an annual event in which students gather at their school flagpole before the beginning of school to pray as a group for "their friends, families, teachers, school, and nation" ("See You at the Pole" 2020).

"See You at the Pole" began in 1990 as a grassroots movement involving only 10 students and has evolved into a nationwide event involving millions of students. A feature that is crucial to its success as a constitutionally protected event is that it is entirely student led. The official website for the event emphasizes this point, indicating that "adult volunteers and parents should not lead" the gatherings ("See You at the Pole" 2020). Such adult involvement, while possibly well intended, would derail the event by giving the appearance that it is endorsed by the school, which would be in violation of another element of the First Amendment, the Establishment Clause. The Establishment Clause, as it has been historically understood, prohibits the government from making any law "respecting an establishment of religion" ("The Constitution of the United States: A Transcription" 2015). If teachers, as representatives of a government entity (i.e., a public school), lead an organized prayer event, or if adults not associated with the school lead the event on school grounds, the event could be challenged as unconstitutional.

RELIGIOUS CLUBS

Another way in which students can participate in organized religious expression on school grounds is through membership in an extracurricular club. Clubs dedicated to a particular religion, or that involve prayer, study of a religious text, or other form of religious faith expression, are protected under a federal law known as the "Equal Access Act." Under the law, any public secondary school that permits use of its facilities for *any* student-led and student-run, and non-curriculum-related, group, must open its facilities to *all* such groups, even if the group is religious in nature ("Student-Initiated Religious Clubs" 2017) (see "Equal Access Act (Title 20)"). While these clubs may meet during the school day, their activities must take place during noninstructional time, such as during a lunch period, and may not be "contrary to the educational mission of the school" or pose any danger to anyone's health and safety ("Student-Initiated Religious Clubs" 2017).

But as with events such as "See You at the Pole," to remain under constitutional protection, religiously oriented clubs must be truly student-led organizations. What this means is that while a member of the school staff or faculty should be present at club meetings to monitor or supervise students, that adult employee may not participate in or lead the meeting activities (see "Equal Access Act (Title 20)"). Furthermore, no "outsider," such as a clergy member, may initiate or run club meetings. In some cases, an outsider may be invited to attend religious club meetings but only if such invitations are consistent with the school's policy on outside visitors. In other words, if a school would not permit visitors for other club meetings, it can prohibit visitors for religious club meetings as well ("Student-Initiated Religious Clubs" 2017).

DISTRIBUTION OF RELIGIOUS MATERIALS BY STUDENTS

Some students may feel compelled by their religious faith to distribute religious literature, such as pamphlets or Bibles, and to some extent, this action can be interpreted as an act of protected speech.

The Supreme Court case *Tinker v. Des Moines Independent Community School District* (1969) held that student speech is not only limited to what students literally say but also includes their actions. In the case of *Tinker*, students were suspended for wearing black armbands in protest of the Vietnam War. Writing for the majority, Justice Abe Fortas wrote that the students' wearing of armbands was "closely akin to 'pure speech'" and that students do not "shed their constitutional rights to freedom of speech or expression at the schoolhouse gate" ("Tinker v. Des Moines Independent Community School District, 393 U.S. 503 (1969)" n.d.). This opinion would almost certainly apply to the distribution of religious literature.

Yet there are some circumstances in which the distribution of religious material might not be constitutionally protected speech. In the case of *Tinker*, the school argued that suspending the students was necessary because their wearing of the black armbands would result in disruption of school discipline and instruction. The Court did not agree with this assessment in that situation; however, had the school been able to demonstrate that the armbands caused a disruption, the Court might well have ruled differently.

If students distribute religious literature in a manner that does not pose any disruption of instruction, or that does not infringe upon the rights of other students, the courts would generally uphold their right to do so. But should students distribute materials in an inappropriate way, such as during instructional time, or in a way that made other students feel pressured or coerced into accepting the literature, a school would be within its rights to limit or restrict such distribution ("Can Students Distribute Religious Literature in a Public School?" n.d.).

Despite rulings such as *Tinker*, schools may legally prohibit students from distributing religious materials by implementing a total ban on all nonschool or third-party materials. Under such a ban, though, the school would need to consistently apply the rule to all materials from third-party sources, whether religious or secular. Any indication that such a ban was not being universally applied could open the school to legal challenges.

See also: *Abington School District v. Schempp* (1963); Equal Access Act (Title 20); First Amendment; Prayer in School; Religion and School Dress Code; Virginia Statute for Religious Freedom

Further Reading

"ACLU Defense of Religious Practice and Expression in Public Schools." American Civil Liberties Union. n.d. Accessed July 9, 2020. https://www.aclu.org/aclu-defense-religious-practice-and-expression-public-schools.

"Can Students Distribute Religious Literature in a Public School? | Freedom Forum Institute." Freedom Forum Institute. n.d. Accessed July 9, 2020. https://www.freedomforuminstitute.org/about/faq/can-students-distribute-religious-literature-in-a-public-school/.

"The Constitution of the United States: A Transcription." National Archives. November 4, 2015. https://www.archives.gov/founding-docs/constitution-transcript.

"See You at the Pole 2020." See You at the Pole. n.d. Accessed July 9, 2020. https://syatp.com/.

"Student-Initiated Religious Clubs." Anti-Defamation League. March 3, 2017. Accessed July 9, 2020. https://www.adl.org/education/resources/tools-and-strategies/religion-in-public-schools/clubs.

"Tinker v. Des Moines Independent Community School District, 393 U.S. 503 (1969)." Justia Law. n.d. Accessed July 9, 2020. https://supreme.justia.com/cases/federal/us/393/503/.

Theistic Spectrum

The Spectrum of Theistic Belief, or Theistic Spectrum, is a term used to describe the wide range of views and beliefs about the existence of God, spanning from belief in God who created the universe, and is active in its everyday doings to the insistence that there is absolutely nothing supernatural in the world.

In simplest terms, theism is a belief in a higher or divine being, usually construed as God or gods. Theism often involves a belief that God is responsive and active in the world. In common language, theists are usually referred to as believers or people of faith. Atheism is the belief that God does not exist, or, more generally, the proposition that there are no gods (Draper 2017). Definitions of atheism, however, can vary. Philosopher Antony Flew (1972) defined "atheism" as a psychological state of not believing in the existence of God (or gods). In his conception, "an atheist becomes not someone who positively asserts the non-existence of God; not someone who positively asserts the non-existence of God; but someone who is simply not a theist." Flew suggested the terms "positive theism" for doctrine of nonexistence and "negative atheism" for the person who is not a theist (1972: 30). Flew also advanced the concept known as "presumption of atheism," where the onus of proof must lie with the theist (1972: 30). More recently, Jeanine Diller (2016) has drawn a distinction between local atheism, which denies the existence of one sort of God, and global atheism, which is the proposition that there are no gods of any sort. Near to the atheist on the spectrum is the "agnostic," a term first coined by Thomas Huxley (1889), who argued that since neither theistic beliefs nor atheistic beliefs can be supported by evidence, it is best to withhold judgment on whether or not there is a God. In other words, agnostics tend to view the existence of God as unknowable. "Deism," then, is a term used to describe the belief that there is a supernatural being who created the universe and its laws but who neither interacts nor intervenes. Deism was an important intellectual movement of the seventeenth and eighteenth centuries, closely associated with the founding fathers of the United States. And although few people today would claim deists as their religious affiliation, there are followers of all formal religions who likely fall in this region of the spectrum. Another tradition on this end of the theistic spectrum is secular humanism, which has played a pivotal role with regard to the question of religion in schools.

In recent years, several schemes of level of belief, or theistic spectra, have been proposed. Diller and Kasher (2013) outline nine conceptual models of God: (1) atheism; (2) agnosticism; (3) deism; (4) theism or monotheism; (5) pantheism; (6) polytheism; (7) henotheism; (8) panentheism, plus the author's own proposal; and (9) eschatological panentheism. There are also naturalist forms of theism (e.g., Bishop 2007; Buckareff and Nagasawa 2016; Diller and Kasher 2013; Ellis 2014).

A study conducted by researchers at the University of Tennessee at Chattanooga explored the varied ways that nonbelievers self-identify and devised a typology of six different categories of nonbelief: Academic or Intellectual Atheists, Activist Atheist/Agnostics, Seeker Agnostics, Antitheists, Nontheists, and the Ritual Atheist/Agnostics (Silverman 2015). The latter is fairly novel as a category but may, in fact, describe the position of many people who find value and meaning in traditional, ritual, and ceremonial activities, even if they are unsure about the existence of God. Similarly, Activist describes people who engage in the pursuit of social justice, inspired in many cases by their religious heritage, even without faith. Perhaps the most extreme of these categories are the Antitheists who actively attempt to convince people that religion is harmful or negative (Silverman 2015). This may be closer to the view of philosopher Thomas Nagel, who famously quipped in *The Last Word*, "It isn't just that I don't believe in God and, naturally, hope that I'm right in my belief. It's that I hope there is no God!" (2001: 130–31).

In a current, popular approach to the question, Richard Dawkins treats the existence of God as "a scientific hypothesis like any other." Dawkins' *The God Delusion* (2006) outlines a "spectrum of probabilities" between two extremes of opposite certainty, with seven basic "milestones":

1. Strong theist. 100% probability of God
2. De facto theist. Very high probability but short of 100%

3. Leaning toward theism. Higher than 50% but not very high
4. Completely impartial
5. Leaning toward atheism. Lower than 50% but not very low
6. De facto atheist. Very low probability but short of zero
7. Strong atheist. "I know there is no God"

Dawkins, along with other popular authors—Daniel Dennett, Sam Harris, and Christopher Hitchens—comprise a movement sometimes called the "New Atheism." According to the *Stanford Encyclopedia of Philosophy*, this group has not advanced any "distinctive philosophical position or phenomenon" but rather deems it a "popular label for a movement—whose work is uniformly critical of religion" (Taliaferro 2019).

Several relatively new terms, though not necessarily recognized as part of a formal theistic spectrum, warrant mention nonetheless because of their significant contribution to understanding where people may position themselves on the spectrum. "Nones" is a broad term that stems from an increasingly common response to the question: what religion do you follow ("none")? It is frequently lumped together with atheists and agnostics (see, e.g., Alper 2018), though this may be misleading since many so-called nones are neither atheistic nor agnostic but simply reject organized religion (Alper 2018). "Spiritual but not religious" (SBNR) is built on the idea that organized religions, while focused on traditional teachings, ritual/ceremonial practice, and formalized leadership structures, may fail to encompass a true inner spiritualism. The term was made popular by Sven Erlandson (2000) in his book *Spiritual but Not Religious* and reflects a growing disenchantment among young people with organized religion. According to a 2017 Pew survey, the number of people identifying as SBNR has jumped from 19% in 2012 to 27% in 2017 (Lipka and Gecewicz 2017). Data for students under 18 is difficult to obtain, though a 2014 Pew Research religious Landscape Survey of younger millennials (ages 18–25) revealed that fewer younger Americans say they believe in God and/or follow a formal religion. Of this group, only 26% told Pew Research that they believe in God with any certainty, while 26% said they do not believe, and the remainder were uncertain (Pew Research 2014). Finally, the term "faithiest" was popularized by Chris Stedman in his book by that name, to describe atheists who want to engage with people of faith (the term's roots are derogatory, as in an atheist deemed not critical enough of the religious). Indeed, the book's subtitle, "How an Atheist Found Common Ground with the Religious," reflects the author's call for nonbelievers to move beyond defining themselves in opposition to religion, both in practice and in belief (Stedman 2013).

Despite the growing popularity of these various nonreligious orientations, in schools, atheist/nonbeliever groups have had a hard time organizing student groups and gaining formal recognition. It is typically student groups with specific religious affiliations that vie for club funding and permission to organize activities at school.

See also: Secularism and Secular Humanism

Further Reading

Alper, Becka A. "Why America's "Nones" Don't Identify with a Religion Alper." Pew Research Center. 2018.

Bishop, John. "How a Modest Fideism May Constrain Theistic Commitments: Exploring an Alternative to Classical Theism." *Philosophia* 35, no. 3 (December 1, 2007): 387–402. https://doi.org/10.1007/s11406-007-9071-y.

Buckareff, Andrei, and Yujin Nagasawa. *Alternative Concepts of God: Essays on the Metaphysics of the Divine*. Oxford; New York: Oxford University Press, 2016.

Dawkins, Richard. *The God Delusion*. Boston; New York: Houghton Mifflin Co., 2006.

Diller, Jeanine. "Global and Local Atheisms." *International Journal for Philosophy of Religion* 79, no. 1 (February 1, 2016): 7–18. https://doi.org/10.1007/s11153-015-9550-1.

Diller, Jeanine, and Asa Kasher. *Models of God and Alternative Ultimate Realities*. New York: Springer Science & Business Media, 2013.

Draper, Paul. "Atheism and Agnosticism." *The Stanford Encyclopedia of Philosophy*. Fall 2017 edition. Edited by Edward N. Zalta. https://plato.stanford.edu/archives/fall2017/entries/atheism-agnosticism/.

Ellis, Fiona. "Why I'm Not an Atheist." *Philosophers' Magazine* 64 (2014): 33–40. https://doi.org/10.5840/tpm20146410.

Erlandson, Sven E. *Spiritual but Not Religious: A Call to Religious Revolution in America*. Bloomington, IN: iUniverse, 2000.

Flew, Antony. "The Presumption of Atheism." *Canadian Journal of Philosophy* 2, no. 1 (1972): 29–46.

Huxley, Thomas Henry. "Agnosticism." 1889. https://mathcs.clarku.edu/huxley/CE5/Agn-X.html.

Lipka, Michael, and Claire Gecewicz. "More Americans Now Say They're Spiritual but Not Religious." Pew Research Center. 2017. https://www.pewresearch.org/fact-tank/2017/09/06/more-americans-now-say-theyre-spiritual-but-not-religious/.

Nagel, Thomas. *The Last Word*. Oxford; New York: Oxford University Press, 2001.
Pew Research Center. "Religion in America: U.S. Religious Data, Demographics and Statistics." *Pew Research Center's Religion & Public Life Project* (blog). 2014. https://www.pewforum.org/religious-landscape-study/.
Silverman, David. *Fighting God: An Atheist Manifesto for a Religious World*. New York: Macmillan, 2015.
Stedman, Chris. *Faitheist: How an Atheist Found Common Ground with the Religious*. Boston: Beacon Press, 2013.
Taliaferro, Charles, and Harriet A. Harris and Christopher J. Insole (eds.). "The God's Eye Point of View: A Divine Ethic." In *Faith and Philosophical Analysis: The Impact of Philosophy on the Philosophy of Religion*, 85–99. London: Routledge, 2019. https://doi.org/10.4324/9781315255521-6.

V

Virginia Statute for Religious Freedom

The law commonly known as the Virginia Statute for Religious Freedom was first proposed as Virginia State Bill No. 82, "A Bill for Establishing Religious Freedom," by Thomas Jefferson. The Virginia Statute for Religious Freedom, a landmark in the history of religion freedom, evolved in the broader context of a fledgling union holding together independent states, each finding their own way. The Virginia Statute played a vital role not just in the state of Virginia but in shaping the religious clauses of the First Amendment to the U.S. Constitution. The Statute also had the effect of disestablishing the Church of England as the official state church of Virginia, a status held since the colony was first settled in 1607.

The Bill for Establishing for Religious Freedom, an early version of the Virginia Statute, was formally introduced into the Virginia State Assembly by Jefferson in 1779. During the years between its proposal and its passage on January 16, 1786, questions about religious liberty were frequently debated. In 1776, the first General Assembly of Virginia appointed a Committee of Revisors, including Jefferson, George Wythe, and Edmund Pendleton, to review the existing laws and revise where necessary. Jefferson, influenced by the Enlightenment ideas of Locke and driven by a strong belief in freedom of conscience, proposed the Statute in an effort to guarantee religious liberty for "the Jew, the Gentile, the Christian, the Mahometan, the Hindoo, and [the] infidel of every denomination" (Virginia Statute for Religious Freedom). Forced religion, argued Jefferson, begets hypocrisy since it could induce one to publicly declare beliefs they did not sincerely hold. He also thought it unjust to force someone to give money to religious institutions they did not follow, including schools. "Forcing him to support this or that teacher of his own religious persuasion" says the Statute, "is depriving him of the comfortable liberty of giving his contributions to the particular pastor whose morals he would make his pattern, and whose powers he feels most persuasive to righteousness" (Virginia Statute). The Statute reads:

> Be it enacted by General Assembly that no man shall be compelled to frequent or support any religious worship, place, or ministry whatsoever, nor shall be enforced, restrained, molested, or burthened in his body or goods, nor shall otherwise suffer, on account of his religious opinions or belief; but that all men shall be free to profess, and by argument to maintain, their opinions in matters of religion, and that the same shall in no wise diminish, enlarge, or affect their civil capacities.

Meanwhile, the Virginia Declaration of Rights, which also contained important language about religious liberty, was adopted in 1776. Its primary author, George Mason, called for "Toleration in the Exercise of Religion," while Madison proposed a small but significant change of phrasing, striking *Toleration* and substituting "all men are equally entitled to the free exercise of religion, according to the dictates of conscience." Virginia's Declaration of Rights, which would heavily influence other state constitutions, passed by a unanimous vote. When Jefferson proposed the Virginia Statute for Religious Freedom, it too had strong support, especially among religious dissenters such as Presbyterians and Baptists who had endured infringement on their own religious freedom.

The Virginia Statute also had opponents, most famously, the patriot and revolutionary Patrick Henry. In 1784, Henry introduced into the Virginia General Assembly "A Bill Establishing a Provision for Teachers of the Christian Religion," compelling all Virginians to "pay a moderate tax or contribution annually for the support of the Christian religion, or of some Christian church," including the salary of religious teachers in Christian schools. While all Christian denominations would be eligible for the funds, non-Christians would not. Henry's bill had the support of many influential Virginians who believed that religion serves as the guardian of morals and wanted to keep Christianity in the schools.

James Madison led opposition to Henry's general assessment tax and, in 1785, wrote his *Memorial and Remonstrance against Religious Assessments*. In this document, Madison advanced the argument for religious liberty, asserting that religion "must be left to the conviction and conscience of every man." As such, religious liberty constituted an inalienable right, akin to other rights the American Revolution had fought for. The document also argued against any form of government support for religion, including for religious instruction. The *Memorial and Remonstrance* was a powerful statement that helped defeat Henry's bill and also helped lay the groundwork for the passage of the Virginia Statute for Religious Freedom the following year.

Jefferson had been the primary author and initial driving force behind the bill. However, his duties as the Unites States' first minister to France carried him abroad during the final legislative process. Madison took over the process and saw the bill through its passage in 1786.

Following passage of the Statute, Madison wrote to Jefferson, sharing the good news and describing the process. "The table was loaded with petitions and remonstrances from all parts against the interposition of the Legislature in matters of Religion. A general convention of the Presbyterian church prayed expressly that the bill in the Revisal might be passed into a law, as the best safeguard short of a constitutional one, for their religious rights" (Madison 1786). With passage of the bill, Madison informed his friend, they had "extinguished forever the ambitious hope of making laws for the human mind." That people must follow "the evidence contemplated by their own minds" and "cannot follow the dictates of other men." Decades later, Madison was concerned about encroachment by the state in religious affairs and referred to the Virginia Statute for Religious Freedom as "a true standard of Religious liberty: its principle the great barrier agst. usurpations on the rights of conscience. As long as it is respected & no longer, these will be safe" (Madison 1820).

While serving as president, Jefferson argued even more forcefully for keeping government out of religious affairs and, in an 1802 letter to the Danbury Baptist Association of Connecticut, invoked the now famous phrase: "a wall of separation between Church and State." According to Denise Spellberg, author of *Thomas Jefferson's Qur'an*, the impact of the Virginia Religious Freedom Act was that "the right to one's chosen Faith was to be understood ever after as a natural endowment" (2015: 120). Nearly 80 years later, the Supreme Court took its first case testing the Establishment Clause in *Reynolds v. the United States* (1879). The Court unanimously agreed that the Virginia Statute served as a definition for the very concept of religious freedom (see Ragosta 2013). "Our civil rights," urges the Statute, "have no dependence on our religious opinions . . . and . . . no man shall be compelled to frequent or support any religious worship place or ministry whatsoever . . . all men shall be free to profess and by argument to maintain, their opinion in matters of religion."

Of the many accomplishments of America's third president, the Virginia Statute for Religious Freedom was among those of which Jefferson was most proud. Upon passage of the Statute, he had the text translated into French and Italian so as to be distributed throughout Europe. Jefferson also requested that any memorial erected in his honor list the Statute alongside the Declaration of Independence and the founding of the University of Virginia.

See also: First Amendment; Religious Diversity in the United States

Further Reading

"A Bill Establishing a Provision for Teachers of the Christian Religion." n.d. https://classroom.monticello.org/media-item/a-bill-establishing-a-provision-for-teachers-of-the-christian-religion/.

"A Bill for Establishing Religious Freedom." President Thomas Jefferson, Founders Online, National Archives (June 18, 1779): 545–7. See also Hening, William W. *The Statutes at Large*. Vol. 12. Richmond, VA: George Cochran, 1823, 84–86. https://founders.archives.gov/documents/Jefferson/01-02-02-0132-0004-0082.

"Catalogue of Bills Prepared by the Committee of Revisors." President Thomas Jefferson, Founders Online, National Archives (June 1–5, 1779): 329–35.

Fleet, Elizabeth (ed.). "Madison's 'Detached Memoranda.'" *William and Mary Quarterly* 3 (1946): 534–68.

"Jefferson and Wythe to Benjamin Harrison." *PTJ* 2 (June 18, 1779): 301–4 (transcription available at Founders Online).

Madison, James. "Detached Memoranda." ca. January 31, 1820. *The Papers of James Madison*, Retirement Series, edited by David B. Mattern, J. C. A. Stagg, Mary Parke Johnson, and Anne Mandeville Colony. Charlottesville: University of Virginia Press, 2009, 1: 611. Transcription available at Founders Online.

"Madison to Jefferson." *PTJ* 9 (January 22, 1786): 194–203. Transcription available at Founders Online. The Statute passed the Virginia Senate on January 16, 1786, a date now celebrated as Religious Freedom Day. The Statute was signed into law on January 19, 1786.

Peterson, Merrill D., and Robert C. Vaughan. *The Virginia Statute for Religious Freedom: Its Evolution and Consequences in American History*. Cambridge, England: Cambridge University Press, 1988.

Pfeffer, Leo. "Madison's 'Detached Memoranda': Then and Now." In *The Virginia Statute for Religious Freedom: Its Evolution and Consequences in American*

History, edited by Merrill D. Peterson and Robert C. Vaughan, 283–312. Cambridge, England: Cambridge University Press, 1988.

Ragosta, John A. *Religious Freedom: Jefferson's Legacy, America's Creed*. Charlottesville: University of Virginia Press, 2013.

Ragosta, John A. Virginia Statute for Religious Freedom. 2018. https://www.monticello.org/site/research-and-collections/virginia-statute-religious-freedom#footnote6_y3bawag.

Reynolds v. United States, 98 U.S. 143, 163 (1879). See generally Ragosta, John A. *Religious Freedom: Jefferson's Legacy, America's Creed*. Charlottesville: University of Virginia Press, 2013, 101–31 (and materials cited therein).

Spellberg, Denise. *Thomas Jefferson's Qur'an: Islam and Founders*. New York: Alfred A. Knopf, 2013.

Thomas Jefferson Foundation. Monticello Podcasts. "Jefferson's Words: On Religion." n.d.

Annotated Bibliography

Cary, Eve, Alan H. Levine, and Janet R. Price. *ACLU Handbook: The Rights of Students.* **Revised edition. New York: Puffin Books, 1997.**
This text provides a summary and description of the rights that students should expect as participants in American public school systems. Among the rights addressed are the right to free public education, rights that pertain to personal appearance, corporal punishment, sex discrimination, and First Amendment rights. The text is structured as a series of questions and answers (e.g., "Do school officials have the right to conduct religious exercises in school?" and "Can student groups meet on school property during instructional time for religious purposes?"). Authors Eve Cary and Alan H. Levine both served as staff attorneys for the New York Civil Liberties Union and have established records as successful litigators on matters of civil rights, equal opportunity, and constitutional challenges. Author Janet Price is a former director of the Manhattan Borough President's Task Force on Education and Decentralization and a former managing editor for Advocates for Children of New York, an organization that provides advocacy for public school students in New York City.

Colby, Kimberlee W. *A Guide to the Equal Access Act.* **Revised edition. Annandale, VA: Center for Law and Religious Freedom, 1993.**
In this text, author Kimberlee Colby provides an outline and summary of the Equal Access Act, discussing in detail who and what the act does and does not protect. Colby provides a history of the law's passage and subsequent court challenges, including discussion of earlier cases pertaining to equal access, the passage of the law in 1984, and the landmark Supreme Court decision that upheld the act in 1990. The text includes a series of questions and answers about the act (e.g., "What is a 'limited open forum'?" and "May a religious student group engage in fund-raising?"). Colby is a graduate of the University of Illinois and Harvard Law School,

assisted in the congressional passage of the Equal Access Act, and has represented religious groups in several appellate cases, including before the U.S. Supreme Court. She is the author of this and several other works published by the Christian Legal Society's Center for Law and Religious Freedom.

Dawkins, Richard. *The God Delusion.* **Boston: Mariner Books, 2008.**
The God Delusion is one of the more well-known publications by evolutionary biologist and author Richard Dawkins. In this text, Dawkins posits that there is almost certainly no supernatural creator or "God." As a self-described atheist, Dawkins has publicly argued against Creationism and, in this text, suggests that "[i]n parts of the United States, science is under attack from a well-organized, politically well-connected and, above all, well-financed opposition" that puts the teaching of evolution in "the front line trench" (91). Dawkins has served as the Charles Simonyi Professor of the Public Understanding of Science at Oxford University and is a Fellow of the Royal Society and of the Royal Society of Literature.

Douglass, Susan L. *Teaching about Religion in National and State Social Studies Standards.* **Executive Summary. Fountain Valley, CA: Council on Islamic Education, 2000. https://eric.ed.gov/?id=ED456076.**
This report offers an overview of the current national and state standards for teaching about religion, based on a complete study of seven national curriculum documents and the academic standards documents and curriculum frameworks developed and adopted by most of the 50 states. References to religion in each document are identified, and the placement, quantity, and characteristics of content on religion are analyzed. The authors find that religion holds "a secure place in state and national standards," yet their study also indicates "limitations and gaps in integrating discussion of the human religious experience in the nation's social studies standards" and questions whether the topic is being pursued with much seriousness or depth.

Falwell, Jerry. *Falwell: An Autobiography.* **Lynchburg, VA: Liberty House, 1997.**
In this autobiography, Rev. Jerry Falwell recounts his life history, from his family's origins in rural Virginia to his rise to prominence as the founder of Liberty University and the Moral Majority. He identifies and describes

several perceived threats to American society, including the prevalence and availability of abortions, the increase of drug and alcohol abuse in schools, and the decline of the "traditional American family." In his chapter on the Moral Majority, Falwell makes clear his positions on religion in schools, indicating that children should "be able to pray in their schools" but that the prayers should be "voluntary [and] nonsectarian" and that no public officials should mandate prayer, nor should a child be intimidated for not participating.

Falwell, Jerry. *Listen, America!* Toronto: Bantam Books, 1981.
In *Listen, America!*, Rev. Jerry Falwell addresses several key issues that he suggests are "corrupting America" and calls upon "moral Americans" to "band together to save [their] beloved nation." The text is presented in three parts, with the first discussing the importance of liberty, the second addressing the issue of morality, and the third laying out a "Biblical plan of action" and highlighting the imperative nature of this plan. In Part II, "Morality–The Deciding Factor," Falwell directly addresses problems that he sees in the American educational system, including the removal of the Bible and prayer from public schools; an increased emphasis on secularism and secular humanism in public schools, colleges, and universities; and the proliferation of instructional materials and texts that promote immoral attitudes and behaviors and undermine American values. The effect of these problems, according to Falwell, is an increase in sexual promiscuity on school campuses, as well as more violence and criminal activity among students.

Fraser, James W. *Between Church and State: Religion and Public Education in a Multicultural America*. Second edition. Baltimore, MD: Johns Hopkins University Press, 2016.
Professor of religion and Pastor James Fraser examines the ways in which a democratic society that is increasingly diverse should deal with questions about religion in the public schools. Fraser explores a series of controversies in the United States concerning the place of religion in the schools, including school prayer, the teaching of evolution/Creationism, the representation of sexuality in the classroom, and whether or not it is the school's responsibility to teach morals. The author reminds the reader that disagreements over the proper relationship between religion and public education go back to our nation's foundations. Fraser grapples with the

question of how issues of faith, which are private, can be reconciled with the public nature of schooling and argues that we should strive to be a multicultural society that respects religious pluralism and is religiously informed.

Greenawalt, Kent. *Does God Belong in Public Schools?* **Princeton, NJ: Princeton University Press, 2005.**
In this text, constitutional and legal scholar Kent Greenawalt discusses American educational policies as they pertain to the religious liberties of students and parents. Greenawalt opens with a series of scenarios that illustrate the challenges that come with providing a comprehensive public education that may conflict with the values and beliefs of some members of a school community (e.g., a speaker at a high school graduation plans to urge the audience to "turn their lives over to Jesus," and parents ask for the removal of school texts that they feel "deeply offend their religious convictions"). The scenarios he depicts in this introduction are not, he suggests, simply matters of sound educational decisions but rather of constitutional interpretation, which he goes on to explore throughout the rest of the text. Chapters include "A Brief History of American Public School and Religion," "Moments of Silence," "Teaching and Religion in the Public School," and "Morals, Civics, and Comparative Religion." Greenawalt concludes this text with a section on student rights, particularly religious liberty and free speech.

Harvard Divinity School - Religion and Public Life (RLP). "Resources for Educators." n.d. https://rpl.hds.harvard.edu/programs/religious-literacy-education/resources-educators.
Harvard's Religion and Public Life, Resources for Educators provides a model for teaching about religion in American public schools (K–12). This works aims to promote religious literacy, defined as "the ability to discern and analyze the fundamental intersections of religion and social/political/cultural life through multiple lenses" (Harvard.edu), by educating youth via the public school system. The RLP offers, through an open access website, scholarly resources in the general study of religion as well as in specific religious traditions. Collected resources as well as original materials are designed primarily for use of public school teachers and their students. Resources include material on historical and contemporary events involving religious issues in America, as well as current research on this subject.

Haynes, Charles C. *A Teacher's Guide to Religion in the Public Schools.* **N.p.: First Amendment Center; Holt, Rinehart and Winston, 2004.**

A Teacher's Guide to Religion in the Public Schools is presented as a primer for educators on how to navigate the complexities of teaching in a way that is consistent with the First Amendment's provisions protecting religious liberty. The text is presented as a series of questions and answers, which aim to clarify what role religion does and does not play in the public school setting (e.g., "Is it constitutional to teach about religion?" and "How do I respond if students ask about my religious beliefs?") Author Charles C. Haynes is vice president of the Freedom Forum Institute/Religious Freedom Center and a senior scholar at the First Amendment Center. He is the author or coauthor of several books on First Amendment rights and education. The Freedom Forum Institute is an organization founded in 1991 to raise awareness of First Amendment freedoms.

Jones, Jeffrey Owen. *The Pledge: A History of the Pledge of Allegiance.* **New York: Thomas Dunne Books, 2010.**

Published posthumously, this text by Jeffrey Owen Jones provides an in-depth look at the history and significance of the Pledge of Allegiance. Opening with an overview of the origin of the Pledge, Jones recounts the story of how Francis Bellamy penned the first draft in 1892, how the Pledge evolved and took hold as a uniquely American statement of patriotism, and the controversies that have surrounded the Pledge since its inception. In Chapter 9, "A Victory for Jehovah," Jones describes the first Supreme Court case over the Pledge, *Minersville School District v. Gobitis* (1940), which ruled that schools could require students to recite the Pledge, and the subsequent case, *West Virginia State Board of Education v. Barnett* (1943), which overturned the *Gobitis* decision.

Kniker, Charles R. *Teaching about Religion in the Public Schools.* **Bloomington, IN: Phi Delta Kappa Educational Foundation, 1985.**

Author Charles R. Kniker, a professor of secondary education at Iowa State University, wrote this text against the backdrop of the 1984 U.S. presidential election. During that time, the United States saw a surge in religious fervor in the political sphere, with popular figures such as Rev. Jerry Falwell and his Moral Majority influencing the Republican Party to adopt a more conservative platform and focus on "returning" religion to public schools. As Kniker points out, though, religion was never outlawed in schools. Dispelling this misconception, among others, is the central purpose of this text. This publication provides historical context, a summary of the situation as it stood in the 1980s, and an acknowledgment of the challenges that come with teaching about religion in public schools. Kniker discusses these challenges and suggests resources that educators might use to more effectively navigate this complex situation.

Lester, Emile, and Patrick S. Roberts. "Learning about World Religions in Modesto, California: The Promise of Teaching Tolerance in Public Schools." *Politics and Religion* **4, no. 2 (2011): 264–88. https://doi.org/10.1017/S1755048311000174.**
In response to rising tensions around religious diversity, one school in Modesto, California, created a novel World Religions course for 9th-grade students. The course aimed to improve students' mutual respect for other religions by expanding knowledge about different faiths as well as the First Amendment and religious freedom in America. One of the key components of the curriculum was Modesto's focus on encouraging respectful engagement with members of other faiths by modeling civil discussion about religion while de-emphasizing disagreements between religions and the exoticization of unique rituals and practices. Ultimately, an assessment of the course's impact suggested that students who took the course demonstrated "increases in passive tolerance, their willingness to refrain from discriminatory behavior, and active respect, the willingness to take action to counter discrimination."

McMillan, Richard C. *Religion in the Public Schools: An Introduction.* **Macon, GA: Mercer, 1984.**
In this text, author Richard C. McMillan provides an in-depth review of the relationship between the U.S. Constitution and its laws and the American public school system. His central thesis is that the United States is a "pluralistic society dedicated to religious freedom," and our public schools can and should provide education *about* religion, though it is beyond the purview of public schools to sponsor or require any acts of religious devotion. The text is divided into different sections, including an overview of the First Amendment, an introduction to the religion-government relationship and further discussion of the religion-public education relationship, and a collection of summaries of relevant Supreme Court cases (e.g., *Engel*

v. *Vitale*, School District of Abington Township, Pennsylvania v. *Schempp*, and *Wisconsin v. Yoder*).

Mooney, Carla, and Lena Chandhok. *Comparative Religion: Investigate the World through Religious Tradition.* **White River Junction, VT: Nomad Press, 2015.**
This publication, by Carla Mooney and Lena Chandhok, presents an introduction to and overview of world religions in a format that is accessible to young teens. The book opens with a timeline, indicating key events in the history of world religions (e.g., the life of Abraham and Moses, the writing of the four Vedas of Hindu, the crucifixion of Jesus, the first revelation to the prophet Muhammad, and the spread of Buddhism to China). Each chapter of the book includes text, colorful illustrations, maps, and diagrams to help explain the origins, core beliefs, and practices of five major world religions. The final chapter addresses pivotal moments of historical religious conflict, commonalities among faiths, and the importance of religious acceptance in a pluralistic society.

Moore, Diane L. *Overcoming Religious Illiteracy: A Cultural Studies Approach to the Study of Religion in Secondary Education.* **New York: Palgrave Macmillan, 2007.**
Director of Harvard's Program in Religion and Secondary Education, Diane Moore, discusses the lack of knowledge among most Americans' regarding the world's religions and even our own religious history. The author offers ways to remedy this, making a powerful argument for the inclusion of teaching about religion in public schools. The book provides suggestions for pedagogy and content, including a specific case study on how to teach about Islam. The final chapter titled "Incorporating the Study of Religion Throughout the Curriculum: American History, Economics, Biology and Literature" offers recommendations for how to incorporate religion into the curriculum.

Patel, Eboo. *Interfaith Leadership: A Primer.* **Boston: Beacon Press, 2016.**
Eboo Patel, founder of Interfaith America (form. Interfaith Youth Core), discusses the rewards and challenges of religious diversity in America. Patel asserts that achieving religious pluralism means going beyond teaching religion as a series of rituals, customs, and doctrines. The author

implores the reader to move past our thinking about religion as abstract systems in textbooks and to look instead to the stories of actual people interacting in real-world situations, including college campuses and public schools. Patel provides a number of such stories, about religious pluralism in the United States, in this work.

Prothero, Stephen (ed.). *A Nation of Religions: The Politics of Pluralism in Multireligious America.* **New edition. San Francisco: Harper, 2006.**
Based on evidence suggesting that many Americans are generally uninformed about other religions, Professor of religion Stephen Prothero calls for a fundamental level of religious literacy that every American ought to have. This book includes a collection of essays from a wide range of voices about religious diversity in America. *A Nation of Religions* takes a close look at the ways in which faith communities that are relatively new to the United States are influencing our nation's values, rites, and institutions.

Robertson, Pat. *Answers to 200 of Life's Most Probing Questions.* **N.p.: Thomas Nelson, 2008.**
Pat Robertson, founder of the Christian Broadcasting Network, Regent University, and the American Center for Law and Justice, presents this text as an attempt to answer the sorts of questions that people might ask God, if they had the opportunity. Robertson provides answers derived from the Bible to 200 such questions as, "Why is there suffering in the world?" "Does the Bible teach evolution?" and "What is the one true church?" These questions are presented in chapters and sections, grouping together questions on similar themes. In the section on "Christians and Government," Robertson speaks to the issue of what rights the state has over Christians and their children, offering pointed criticism of sex education in public schools, as well as the attempt to "indoctrinate young children into the teachings of humanism." Humanist values, he argues, threaten to "wean children away from Biblical Christianity."

Scott, Eugenie C. *Evolution vs. Creationism: An Introduction.* **Second edition. Berkeley: University of California Press, 2009.**
In *Evolution vs. Creationism*, anthropologist Eugenie Scott offers a comprehensive view of the controversy surrounding the teaching of evolution and Creationism/Intelligent Design in public schools. The author presents the scientific evidence for evolution as well as discussion of the legal and

educational basis for teaching evolution in our schools. Taking a balanced approach, Scott provides an overview of various religious perspectives while also taking a critical look at the history of how America has dealt with questions about the place of religion and science in the classroom. The book also includes an assemblage of primary source documents relevant to these issues.

Trafzer, Clifford E. *Boarding School Blues: Revisiting American Indian Educational Experiences.* **Lincoln: University of Nebraska Press, 2006.**
In this text, Clifford E. Trafzer, a Distinguished Professor of history and Rupert Costo Chair at the University of California, Riverside, presents a collection of essays by several authors that explore the experiences of American Indians in U.S. government–created boarding schools. While ostensibly designed to provide education to indigenous peoples in North America, these boarding schools have come to be recognized by many scholars as a system designed to, as Trafzer puts it, "destroy their cultural identity." Within the essays, the contributors to this volume describe the experience at these boarding schools as "assimilation" and an effort to "replace all that [American Indian children] had known," including family customs and religious traditions.

Vaughan, Joel D. *The Rise and Fall of the Christian Coalition: The Inside Story.* **Eugene, OR: Resource Publications, 2009.**
Author Joel Vaughan, chief of staff for Focus on the Family and executive sponsor of its Diversity & Inclusion Council, writes this text not as a "tell all" or "exposé" of controversial central Christian Coalition figures, such as Pat Robertson, but rather, as he puts it, as an "accurate history of the organization that can be useful to other non-profit groups" and a means through which readers can perceive what it was like to be part of the organization throughout the years. The text describes the growth of the Christian Coalition from its founding in 1989 to its decline in prominence in the early 2000s; the organization's involvement in national, state, and local politics during its heyday; and the lasting impact its influence might have on the American cultural and political landscape in the years ahead. Among the political issues addressed in the text are several that pertain to American public schools, including instructional materials that may be considered part of a "pro-homosexual" curriculum, voluntary prayer at school functions, and school choice (i.e., the ability of parents to receive a voucher or tax credit to take their children out of public schools if they choose).

Walker, Samuel. *In Defense of American Liberties: A History of the ACLU.* **N.p.: New York, 1990.**
Samuel Walker, Professor Emeritus of criminal justice at the University of Nebraska at Omaha, presents in this text a history of the American Civil Liberties Union (ACLU), from its origins in the 1910s, to the late twentieth century. The text is divided into several sections, each of which addresses an era during the twentieth century during which the ACLU was particularly active, saw a period of growth, or faced significant challenges (e.g., "Lean Years, 1920–1932," "American Inquisition: The Cold War," and "The Rights Revolution, 1964–1974"). Key issues involving religious liberties and public schools covered within the text include children refusing to say the Pledge of Allegiance on religious grounds, the constitutionality of compulsory school prayer, and the use of public school facilities for religious purposes.

Wertheimer, Linda K. *Faith Ed: Teaching about Religion in an Age of Intolerance.* **First edition. Boston: Beacon Press, 2015.**
In *Faith Ed*, Wertheimer takes a close look at questions about the teaching of religion in public schools by examining specific cases involving schools/school districts around the country. The author recounts her visits to communities where there have been controversies surrounding the teaching of religion, including questions about what age is appropriate for certain content and what are the limits of experiential learning involving religion. Wertheimer interviews students, teachers, parents, and clergy from a range of faith backgrounds to gain firsthand perspectives on these questions.

Index

Bold page numbers indicate the location of main entries. Page numbers followed by *t* indicate tables.

Abington School District v. Schempp, xvi, xx, xxx, **1–4**, 27, 36, 50, 86, 117, 135, 161, 176, 187, 190, 217
Accommodations, **4–8**
   dietary, 5–6
   holiday, 202
Agnostic/Agnosticism, xxiv, 172*t*, 223–224
American Academy of Religion, 28, 37, 38, 39
American Association of School Administrators, 37
American Center for Law and Justice, 94, 193, 195, 218
American Civil Liberties Union, 1, **9–10**, 15, 20, 29, 62, 76, 121, 122, 131, 147, 209, 215, 218
American Council on Education, **10–13**
American Federation of Teachers, 37
American Indian Religious Freedom Act, xxx, 101
American Jewish Congress, 37

Americans United for Separation of Church and State, **13–16**, 29, 77
Anti-Defamation League, 51, 163, 166
Arkansas, 43
Atheist/Atheism, xxiv, 48, 94, 172*t*, 223–225

Bannon v. School District of Palm Beach, xxxi, 188
Baptist Joint Committee on Public Affairs, 37
Bellamy, Francis, 130
Bible
   curriculum, 29
   instruction/teaching in schools, 17–23, 92
   King James, 23, 181
   reading in schools, 1, 86
   as subject of study in school, xx, 27–31
Bible instruction, teaching in schools, **17–23**, 92
Bible Riots, xxix, **23–27**

Bible study, xx, **27–31**
Bill of Rights, xv, xvi, xvii, xx, xxix, 148
Black, Hugo, Supreme Court Justice, 2, 7, 14, 66, 111
Blaine Amendments, 183, 184
Board of Education v. Allen, 86
Brennan, William, Supreme Court Justice, 2–3, 57, 59
Bryan, William Jennings, 71, 209–210
Buddhist/Buddhism, xxiii, 165, 170, 171, 172*t*, 189
Bush, George W., 75, 151

California, 170, 178
   3 Rs Project, 178
   Modesto, CA, xviii, 177
   and sex education, 153
Carson v. Makin, xxi, xxxi
Catholic/Catholicism, xxiii, xxiv, 181
   in America, 23, 169, 171–172, 172*t*, 181, 184
   anti-Catholic nativism, 23, 181, 184
   Catholic schools, 23–26, 66, 109, 180, 184
   Douay Bible, 24
Chatham, NJ, xviii, 52
Christian Broadcasting Network, 195
Christian Coalition of America, **33–35**, 152, 195, 243
Christian Legal Society, 37
Christianity/Christians
   advocacy for religion in schools, 18, 19, 20, 29, 37, 54, 111, 120, 128, 134, 167, 189, 195, 230
   Christian schools, 83, 173, 205, 207
   as predominant religion in United States, xviii, xix, xxiii, xxv, 19, 20, 29, 33, 87, 102, 120, 170, 171, 172*t*, 173, 200–201, 202–203, 211
Church of England, xx
Church of Jesus Christ of Latter-day Saints, 37
Circuit Court, Ninth, xxi
Civil Rights Division, Department of Justice, 146, 165
Clark, Thomas, Supreme Court Justice, 2, 3, 19, 27, 117, 118, 171
Clinton, William Jefferson, President, 6, 173–174
   Memorandum on Religious Expression in Public Schools, 6
Clubs
   gay-straight alliance clubs, 62–63
   religious clubs, 60, 61, 62, 63, 123, 219
   secular clubs, 60, 62, 123
Communism, xxx, 130
   Communist Revolution, 9
Comparative religion and world religion, teaching in schools, **35–42**
Confucianism, 170–171
Constitution, U.S., xv, xvii, xxix, 84
   Article VI, xvii, 85
   Bill of Rights, 84
Constitutional Convention, xvii
COVID-19 pandemic, xxvi

Creationism, xvii, 9, **42–46**, 52, 57–59, 71, 94, 105, 106–107, 134, 142–143

Darrow, Clarence, 9, 209–211
Darwin, Charles, xix, 42, 44, 68
  Darwinian theory, 68–79, 105
  The Descent of Man, and Selection in Relation to Sex, 69
  Galapagos Islands, 69
  human evolution, 70
  On the Origin of Species by Means of Natural Selection, 42, 68–70
Dawkins, Richard, 19, **47–50**, 224
Deism, 223–224
Department of Education, United States, 54, 78, 176
  Office of Civil Rights, 165–166, 167
Department of Justice, Civil Rights Division, 146, 165
Devotional/Doctrinal Curriculum, **50–56**
Dobson, James, 88, 89, 152
Drew University, 178
Dutch, 169
  Reform Church, 181
  schools, 181

Edwards v. Aguillard, xxvi–xxvii, 44, **57–59**, 71
Engel v. Vitale, 2, 27, 85, 117, 135, 195
Epperson v. Arkansas, 43, 176
Equal Access Act (Title 20), xxxi, **60–65**
Espinoza v. Montana Department of Revenue, xx–xxi, xxxi, 184

Establishment Clause, xiii, xv, xvii, xix, xxii–xxiii, xxv, xxvii, 4, 7, 20, 36, 48, 84–85, 109, 175, 219
  and Bible study, 27
  and evolution, 43, 57, 104–105
  non-preferentialism, 66–67, 87
  and religious symbols, 187
Evangelical, 29, 172*t*
Everson v. Board of Education of the Township of Ewing, xvii, xx, xxix, 14, **65–68**, 86
Evolution, teaching, xix, 57, **68–73**, 94
  natural selection, 68

Faith-Based Initiative, **75–80**
Falwell, Jerry, 29, **80–84**, 113, 152
Fellowship of Christian Athletes, 54
Feminism and feminists, 91, 214
First Amendment, xiv, xv, xvi, xvii, xviii, xxii, xxix, **84–88**, 109, 146
  Establishment Clause, 18
  Free Exercise Clause, 36, 85, 109
  Free Speech Clause, 151
  Imprimatur Test, xx, 187, 188
  Reynolds v. United States, 85
  "strict scrutiny," 148
First Amendment Center, xix, xxii, 4, 7
Florida, 28
Focus on the Family, **88–90**
Fourteenth Amendment, xx, xxiv, 2, 109, 146, 183
Fraser, James, xxvii, xxviii, 237
Free Exercise Clause, 36, 48

Freedom from Religion
 Foundation, **91–97**, 161
Fundamentalism, 49, 209, 211

Gaylor, Annie, 91, 92, 161, 162
Genesis, Book of, 28, 43,
 142–143
Georgia, 167
The God Delusion, 47, 224, 236
Gorsuch, Neil, Supreme Court,
 xxii, xxv
Gould, Stephen J., 44

Harvard University
 Religion and Public Life
  (RLP), "Resources for
  Educators," 238
 Religious Literacy Project,
  177–178
*Hearn and United States v.
 Muskogee PSD*, 146–147
Heritage Foundation, 100,
 150, 152
Hindu/Hinduism, xxiii, 165, 166,
 167, 171, 172*t*, 189
 Hindu schools, 180, 182
Holiday observances, school
 calendar, 199–204
Holocaust education, xxv
Hughes, John, Archbishop,
 25, 181
Humanism, secular, xix, 212, 224
 spiritual but not religious,
  xxiv, 225
Humanist Manifesto, xxix

Immigration Act of 1965, xxx
Indiana, 28

Indigenous Americans/Native
 Americans, 169
 boarding schools,
  102–103, 243
 faiths, 87, 99–104
Indigenous faiths, 87, **99–104**
Intelligent Design, **104–108**
 *Kitzmiller v. Dover School
  District*, 10, 72, 106–107
 Of Pandas and People, 72, 107
 "Wedge Strategy," 105
Irish Americans, 24–25, 170
Islam/Muslim, xviii, 165, 166,
 169, 170, 171, 172*t*, 177
 Council on Islamic Arab
  Relations (CAIR), 147,
  166–167
 hijab, 147
 Islamophobia, 166
 Muslim schools, 180, 181
 Muslim students, 5
 Ramadan, 5
 teaching Islam in schools, 29,
  167–168, 178–179, 189

Jackson, Robert H., Supreme
 Court Justice, xx, 66, 187
Jain, 171, 172*t*, 189, 201
Jefferson, Thomas, 87, 111
 letter to Danbury Baptist
  Association, xxii, 66,
  84, 231
 Virginia Statute for Religious
  Freedom, 229–230, 231, 232
Jehovah's Witnesses, 5, 172*t*
Jewish/Judaism, xxiii, 165, 169,
 170, 172*t*
 anti-Semistism, 166, 171

Menora v. Illinois High School Association, 147
  schools, 180, 181–182

Kansas, xxvi
Kennedy v. Bremerton School District, xxi–xxii, xxv, xxvi, 53, 137–138
Kentucky, xxvi, 28, 187

Lear, Norman, 127
Lee v. Weisman, xx, 111, 136
Lemon v. Kurtzman Supreme Court decision, xxx, 3, **109–112**
  Lemon Test, 3, 57, 109–111, 187
Liberty University, 80, 82, 83, 236
Louisiana, 57–59, 71, 106
Lynch v. Donnelly, xxii, xxiii

Madison, James, 66, 87, 230–231
  Memorial and Remonstrance against Religious Assessments, 66, 84, 230–231
Maine, xxi
Marshall, Thurgood, Supreme Court Justice, 57, 111
Maryland, xxiii, 2
McCollum v. Board of Education, 7, 92, 187
McLean v. Arkansas Board of Education, 9, 43
Michigan, xxvi, 6, 170, 171, 177
Minersville School District v. Gobitis, 130–131
Minnesota, 71

Missouri, 28
Moore, Diane L., 39, 171, 177, 241
Moral Majority, xxxi, 9, 80, **113–115**, 117, 134
Morality, 2, 18, 20, 27, 44, 53, 61, 62, 70, 82, 88, 110, 123, 150, 151, 165, 181, 189, 195, 211, 214, 215, 216, 230, 237, 238
Mormon, 41, 133, 172t, 173

National Association of Christian Educators and Citizens for Excellence in Education, 19
National Association of Evangelicals, 37, 76, 87
National Center for Education Statistics (NCES), xxv
National Conference of Christians and Jews, 37
National Council on Bible Curriculum in Public Schools (NCBCPS), 29–30
National Council on Education, xxiv
National Council on Religion in Public Education, xxx, **117–120**
National Education Association (NEA), 4–5, 6, 7, 176–177
Native American Rights Fund, 101
Nativism, 23–26
Nebraska, 61, 137, 183
New Jersey, xxv, 65, 152
New York, xxvi, 7
New York Times, xxvi
No Child Left Behind, 5, 6, 77

"Nones" religious, xxiv, 225
Nontraditional religious identities, **120–125**
  Rastafarianism, 122–123
  Satanism, 123–124
  Wicca and Paganism, 120–122, 214
North Dakota, 28–29, 170

Obama, Barack, 79, 151, 174
O'Connor, Sandra Day, Supreme Court Justice, xvii–xviii, 5, 148
Odessa, Texas, 20

Palmer Raids, 9
Parent Teacher Association (PTA), xiii, 4, 7
Parents Bill of Rights, xxv-xxvi
Patel, Eboo, 177, 241
Pennsylvania, 1–4, 86, 109–110
  Philadelphia, 23–26
People for the American Way, **127–129**, 215
Pew Research Center, xxiii, xxviii, 41, 99, 120, 121, 171–172, 173, 225
Phenix, Philip H., 37, 38
Pledge of Allegiance, xxx, 51, **129–133**
Prayer
  defining, 133–134
  in school, xx, 34, 85, 114, 133–139
  at school functions, 93
Prayer in school, xx, 34, 85, 114, **133–139**
Protestant/Protestantism, xxiii, 14, 15, 16, 23–25, 100, 133, 169, 171–172, 172*t*, 181
  Evangelical, xxiii, 21, 29, 33, 37, 77, 80, 83, 113, 117, 133, 134, 172*t*, 183, 194, 214
  Protestant-Catholic tensions, 23–26
Protestants and Other Americans United for Separation of Church and State. *See* Americans United for Separation of Church and State
Prothero, Stephen, 177, 242
Pseudoscience. *See* Religion and pseudoscience

Qur'an, 29

Reagan, Ronald, 60, 113–114, 151
Regent University, 195
Religion and pseudoscience, 107, **141–145**
Religion and school dress code, **146–150**
  hairstyles, 122, 156–157
Religion and sexual education, teaching in schools, vxii, **150–155**
  abstinence-only education, 150–151, 152
Religion and sports competition, **156–160**
Religion in performances, **160–164**
Religious discrimination in schools, **165–169**
Religious diversity in the United States, **169–175**
Religious Freedom Clause, xiii, xv, xxii, xxvii

Religious Freedom Restoration Act (RFRA), 6, 147, 148
Religious pluralism, teaching, **175–181**
Religious schools, **180–186**. *See also* Catholic/Catholicism, Catholic schools; Christianity/Christians, Christian schools
Religious symbols, **186–190**
Religious texts as literature and research sources, **190–194**
Reynolds v. the United States, 85, 231
Rhode Island, xxii, 109–110
Riverheads High School, xviii
Roberts, John, Supreme Court Justice, xxi
Robertson, M. G. "Pat," 33, 152, **194–197**
Roe v. Wade, xxvi, 82, 91, 195
Russia, 9

Santa Fe Independent School District v. Doe, 93
School
 charter, 15, 78, 182
 parochial, 14, 18, 23, 26, 66, 86, 111, 159, 180, 181, 183, 206
 secular, 18
School calendar, religious holiday observances, **199–204**
School vouchers, 15, 34, 181, 184, **204–209**
Scopes Trial, xix, xxix, 9, 42, 70–71, **209–212**
Scott, Eugenie, 71, 106, 144, 242–243

Secular Coalition for America, 215
Secular Humanism. *See* Secularism and Secular Humanism
Secularism and Secular Humanism, 82, **212–217**
Separation of Church and State, xiii, xv, xvi. xvii, xix, xxii–iii, 13–14, 66, 86, 231
Sikh/Sikhism, 6, 165, 166, 167, 170, 171, 180, 182, 189
Soviet Union, xxx, 71, 113, 130, 196
Standardized curriculum, xxv
Stewart, Potter, Supreme Court Justice, 2–3
Stone v. Graham, 28, 92, 187, 188–189
Student-initiated prayer, clubs, 60, 61, 62, **217–221**
Supreme Court of the United States, xix, xx, xxiv, xxv, xxvii, 7, 11, 14, 18, 19, 27, 30, 36, 38, 43, 44, 50, 53, 57, 60–62, 65–67, 85, 102, 109–111, 113, 114, 117, 127–128, 131–132, 134–135, 137–138, 146–148, 161, 164, 171, 176, 183, 184, 187, 190, 195, 196, 206, 211, 215, 217, 220

Teaching Tolerance, 189, 240
Ten Commandments, 48, 54, 186, 187, 189
Tennessee, 152, 209–210
 Butler Law, 71, 209–210, 224
Texas, 147, 181
 and sex education, 153
Theistic Spectrum, **223–227**

Thomas More Law Center, 52
Tinker v. Des Moines Independent Community School District, 146, 220
Trinity Lutheran Church of Columbia v. Comer, xx, xxxi
Trump, Donald, 11–12, 79, 151

United States Congress, xxiii
United States Constitution. *See* Constitution, U.S.
Utah, 62, 106

Virginia, 28, 178
Virginia Statute for Religious Freedom, xxix, 84, **229–233**

Wallace v. Jaffree, 135
Warren, Earl, Supreme Court Chief Justice, 2
Washegesic v. Bloomingdale, xix, xx, 189
West Virginia, 28, 183
Widmar v. Vincent, 61

About the Authors

Jonathan M. Golden, PhD, is Director of the Center on Religion, Culture and Conflict at Drew University, where he is Associate Professor of Teaching in the Theological School, teaching classes in Conflict Resolution, Civic Engagment, Comparative Religion and Anthropology.

Joseph J. McCallister is a teacher of English and language arts at Northern Valley Regional High School in Demarest, New Jersey, and is a doctoral candidate at Drew University.